HUMOR

Theory • History • Applications

About the Author

Frank MacHovec is a clinical psychologist who has authored more than 50 books and journal articles, on a variety of subjects involving the mind. His work has been cited in the books and articles of others and he has been quoted in *Psychology Today, Newsweek, USA Today, Brain-Mind Bulletin* and on the nationwide Gannett News Network. He has presented his original research at state, regional, national and international professional conferences. He is listed in *Who's Who Among Human Services Professionals* and in *Who's Who in the South and Southwest*. He has a B.A. degree in General Studies, an M.A. in educational and counseling psychology and a Ph.D. degree in clinical psychology with clinical internships in Alaska and Idaho.

Dr. MacHovec has served as psychologist or chief psychologist in clinics and hospitals in Manitoba and Alberta, Canada, Washington, D.C. and in Virginia. In 1982 he was awarded a national Certificate of Recognition by the Division of Psychologists in Public Service of the American Psychological Association. He has taught graduate, undergraduate and non-credit courses in psychology and human relations and has held numerous appointive and elective offices in professional organizations in Canada and the United States.

In 1984 he founded the Center for the Study of the Self, a private research institute to study subjects outside of or not in the mainstream of scientific publications. "Anything the mind can perceive," Dr. MacHovec maintains, "is an appropriate subject for research." The Center is dedicated to an "open search for truth regardless of its source." The present volume is a result of this philosophy, embracing all sources, art and science, popular and scientific literature, worldwide, from earliest records to the present. The Center has been productive since its 1984 beginning, with books on hypnosis complications, expert witness testimony, and a second grade reader series on personal and street safety.

His interest in humor arises from his own sense of humor and his active participation in parades, fairs and childrens' hospitals as the clown "Uncle Dunkle," with the Acca Temple Shriners in Richmond. He has presented workshops for mental health workers, teachers and training specialists on applying humor to their work.

HUMOR

Theory • History • Applications

By

FRANK J. MacHOVEC, Ph.D.

AN AUTHORS GUILD BACKINPRINT.COM EDITION

iUniverse, Inc.
Bloomington

HUMOR
Theory, History, Applications

AN AUTHORS GUILD BACKINPRINT.COM EDITION

Published by iUniverse, Inc.

For information address:
iUniverse
1663 Liberty Drive
Bloomington, IN 47403
www.iuniverse.com
1-800-Authors (1-800-288-4677)

Originally published by Charles C Thomas • Publisher

ISBN: 978-1-4759-6004-4 (sc)

Printed in the United States of America

iUniverse rev. date: 11/29/2012

Mirth is like a flash of lightning
That breaks through a gloom of clouds
And glitters for a moment;
Cheerfulness keeps up
A kind of daylight in the mind
And fills it with
A steady and perpetual serenity

Joseph Addison (1672-1719)
The Spectator, No. 381
May 17, 1712

*To fun times
and funny people:
The world is
in desperate need
of both!*

ACKNOWLEDGMENT

TO ALL THOSE who told me so many jokes, too many to include but all well-intentioned; to my wife, Evelyn, for her proofreading "above and beyond the call," and to Darien Fisher, Librarian Extraordinaire, who "bird dogged" me to many valuable references.

FOREWORD

IT IS customary in scientific books and journals to cite the need for more information in the field under study. This is true for humor, its definition and applications. It is ironic that we are daily exposed to humor, and the world's literature abounds with examples, yet humor eludes precise definition. I suggest this is because it is a complex of interacting variables and therefore does not lend itself to simple analysis The joke teller as a personality and his or her joke telling technique, each listener's personality and receptivity, time, place and the antagonist, protagonist and situation of the joke are important variables. Major and minor premises of the joke are manifest and direct or latent, indirect, and these, too, are involved in the psychodynamics of humor.

Humor is not unique in this respect. In point of fact, all behavior is complex, multicausational, involving direct and subtle variables any one of which can tip the balance and lead careful researchers off in different, seemingly contradictory directions. Plato's derision theory and Aristotle's theory of disappointment or frustrated expectation are not opposite but composite, facets of the same phenomenon. Humor can coldly cut or warmly bind together. It can be cerebral and/or visceral. Advocates can champion any one of these aspects, but humor embraces all of them. Buddha taught this as the nature of truth.

The quest for a single, universal definition of humor is reminiscent of the search for personality and intelligence, neither of which have definitions accepted by all. In physics, definitions elude us for gravity, electricity and the basic components of the atom. In psychotherapy, there is no system of practice effective for all those in need despite a hundred years of theory and practice, increased sophistication in diagnosis and a variety of professions, diligently searching. What helps best is quite similar to what is perceived by an individual as funny. It is unique and subjective.

Step off a balcony and you will fall down, not up, even though the force of gravity that ensures your rapid descent is not understood. Turn

the lights out and electricity, whatever that is, stops flowing. Psychologists can reliably test how "bright" you are without an agreed definition
of intelligence. Psychotherapy helps you discover who you really are
without knowing what personality itself is. Hear or see something funny
and laugh. But why? Like all these other subjects, no one has as yet for-
mulated a definition of humor that everyone accepts, neither the humorists themselves nor the scientists or writers who have observed
humor for more than 2000 years. That in and of itself suggests the complexity of the subject as well as the subjectivity of the observer who
laughs at or passively misses what's funny.

All this is enough to deter if not frighten away many from further
study. It was so for me for many years. But as Aristotle observed "man
by nature must know." We, by nature, have a great need to know what
everything around us is and means to us. The mind stops at or stumbles
over what it does not understand and examines it more and more. "We
will never cease from exploring," T.S. Eliot wrote, "and the end result
will be to arrive at the same place and know it for the first time." This
book is a further exploration of an area of the mind still not thoroughly
known, one more step toward "knowing that place for the first time."

Modesty forbids me from claiming to have solved the great riddle of
definition. Much of this book reflects what we already know. That has
served as the foundation for what I have added, namely humor's complexity and variety and its polarity and valence. And from my preoccupation with humor came a study across time, language, and culture, the
arts and sciences, in an open search for truth regardless of its source. For
complex subjects, such a Taoist free, open search is the best approach.
From this a commonality or "what's funny" emerged, a universal which
permeates all humor, a common denominator. It requires a playful, receptive mood and it is the joyous, simple, pure, childlike quality psychoanalysts identify as regression. All humor has this "common denominator."

This book explores theories, descriptions and examples of humor
from earliest historical sources to the present. Initially, the intent was to
help others develop their own sense of humor and to apply it in the
workplace, classroom, in government, everywhere. The world is sad
enough. There is great need for more humor. It is better to smile or
laugh than to despair and weep. Toward these goals, the varieties of humor are described and indexed for quick reference. This can be a "joke
book" as well as a serious reflection on the nature of humor—it, yours
and mine. It is hoped it will also be a ready reference for speeches and

lesson plans, to enrich everyday conversations, and for personal amusement on rainy days.

Above all, this book attempts to be practical and useful, a helping hand to bring more humor to the world, but also theoretical in moving closer to defining humor. These two goals are in conflict! To be practical it must be clear and simple. To be theoretical it must touch on all that has come before, in philosophy which preceded psychology, in literature and the behavioral sciences. This theoretical aspect is enormous, crossing language, culture worldwide in scope and in depth rooted in antiquity.

You will not find everything in it funny. I haven't found all the contents of any book on humor funny to me, even what are described as jokes. That in and of itself proves the subjectivity of humor much of which is truly in the eyes, ears and mind and times of the beholder. One secret of developing humor is to use what's funny to the broadest cross-section of people. This is what makes great comics and what sustains their popularity. It is also a test of the true nature of humor. If we can understand the dynamics of jokes which have remained funny across generations we can know more about the what and why of being funny.

It's equally certain that professional researchers will quibble over the content of this book. That's good science. While gathering notes from Max Eastman's 1922 book on humor, I was struck by the fact that it was written and published before I was born. I reflected that someone will extract from this book long after I'm gone. Whether it's a positive or negative reference doesn't really matter to me. As President Truman once said: "I don't care what you write about me. Just spell my name right." As much can be learned from mistakes as from successes. Truth emerges honor bright like the rising sun despite our best and worst efforts. May it be so for humor and all its applications. It has been around a long time. The sun knows it well.

My advice to you is to kick off your shoes, keep a bookmark handy and enjoy reading this book. Take your time. Don't rush it and don't make it "work." Set it aside when interrupted. Let it help lighten your mood. Through it may you casually converse with Plato and with your favorite comic. It can be a guided tour of the world of humor, a fun experience. There's a fee, an obligation! When your tour is complete, you're expected to pass it on. That means you must add more humor to your life and to the lives of others. If you don't, my curse on you will be that you will be haunted by all the comedians you dislike, with all their friends throughout history, who will tell you every bad joke you ever heard—again and again. So let go, loosen up, lighten up, and laugh!

CONTENTS

HUMOR

Theory • History • Applications

CHAPTER 1

WHAT'S FUNNY?

> *Different things*
> *delight different people*
>
> *Marcus Aurelius*
> *(121-180 AD)*
> ***Meditations***

WHAT'S funny? That simple 2-word sentence opens the door to lengthy debate and discussion. It will take the remainder of this book to attempt an answer. While people have been laughing worldwide and across every language and culture for centuries, no one has as yet definitively explained why people laugh. It is today as it was for Marcus Aurelius 2000 years ago: "Different things delight different people." Humor is a multi-colored kaleidoscope of thoughts and feelings, times and places. What's funny is a complex psychological-emotional phenomenon involving a great variety of interacting variables. "Classic" funny stories and situations are those that appeal to a broad cross-section of people and transcend time and culture. Comedians who remain popular for decades can tune in to this universal frequency.

Smiles and laughter enrich daily life. Like variety, they are the spice of life. Most people would find it preferable to smile than frown, to laugh rather than cry. Voltaire wrote that "laughter always arises from a gayety of disposition, absolutely incompatible with contempt and indignation" (Eastman, 1936, p. 330). Laughter goes hand in hand with a cheerful, optimistic disposition described by E.B. White:

> Humor is a final emotion like breaking out into tears. A thing gets
> so bad and you feel so terrible that at last you go to pieces and it's
> funny. Laughter does just what tears do for you. My life as a humorist
> began in a restaurant when a waitress spilled buttermilk down my

3

neck. That great smear of white wet coming down over a blue serge suit and her words, "Jesus Christ!" were the turning point in my career (ibid, p. 343).

James Thurber elaborated further on White's idea: "The things we laugh at are awful while they are going on but funny when we look back. And other people laugh because they've been through it, too" (ibid, p. 341). In his 1922 book, *The Sense of Humor,* Max Eastman wrote:

> Laughter is, after speech, the chief thing that holds society together. . . . A smile is the universal welcome, and laughter is a greeting that we may give to any arriving friend. It is a definite affirmation of hospitality and delight. To laugh is to say "Yes." It is to say "Good!" "I agree to your emotion!" (p. 4).

Not everyone agrees that smiling and laughter are positive. Ludovici, in his book *The Secret of Laughter* described laughter as "a spiritualized manifestation of the crude snarl" (Eastman, 1936, p. 351) which Eastman characterized as "an evolutionary snarl" (ibid). This suggests a happy-sad polarity of **feeling levels** or underlying mood. Brides and beauty contest winners, obviously elated, weep. White and White (1941) describe this seeming paradox:

> . . .there is often a rather fine line between laughing and crying. . . because humorous writing, like poetical writing, has an extra content. It plays like an active child close to the big hot fire which is Truth. And sometimes the reader feels the heat (p. xviii).

Laughter and smiling are major features of humor, side effects of what's funny. Like every aspect of humor, they are multifaceted. In his book, *The Act of Creation* (1964), Arthur Koestler described laughter as "a luxury reflex" having a "rich variety of forms—from Rabelaisian laughter at a spicy joke to the rarefied smile of courtesy" (p. 30). According to Koestler, laughter can be "feigned or suppressed" into a "discrete chuckle or a leonine roar." In Koestler's view, an individual's life experience channels an innate laughter instinct and forms a unique "sense" of humor and response style: ". .habit-formation soon crystallize these reflex-plus-pretense amalgams into characteristic properties of the person." A smile is an outward sign of internal mood: amusement, affection, embarrassment, frustration or scorn: "Mood also superimposes its own facial pattern" (ibid).

With such a two-way street of emotion underlying smiling and laughter, it is unusual that experienced professional comedians have difficulty defining humor. Eddie Cantor, asked what he thought was the cause of laughter, replied: "Frankly, I don't know. Some people laugh at things that appear to me to have not the slightest vestige of humor, and vice versa" (Eastman, 1936, p. 340). He concluded: "The cause of laughter is the complete disengagement of the subject from all broader problems by means of humorous words or actions" (ibid).

THE LEXICON OF HUMOR

Eastman (1922) traced the word **fun** from which **funny** is derived to the Gaelic word **fonn.** More recent references suggest a Middle European origin from **fonnen,** to dupe, hoax or fool, which came into use in the early 1700s (Mish, 1983, p. 498). **Funnies,** to describe the Sunday comic strips, originated in the 1850s (ibid). The word **humor** is of more ancient origin, dating back to Latin and Greek, meaning a body fluid, such as the humoral theory of Hippocrates (c. 470-377 BC). He was a Greek priest-physician in the Cult of Asklipios on the island of Cos. The term **humor** crossed cultures from Greek to Latin with the spread of the Asklipian cult which in later centuries lost out to Christianity.

In those ancient days **humor** did not mean "being funny." Ascribing lighthearted joviality to the word came into use after Shakespeare, in the late 1600s. The Greeks and Romans preferred the word **comedy** (Latin **comoedia**; Greek **komoidia**), a combination of the root word **komos,** to revel, and **aeidein,** to sing as in an ode (Mish, 1983, p. 263). **Joke,** referring to "something said or done to provoke laughter. . .especially with a climactic humorous twist" came into use at about this time despite its Latin origin, **jocus,** to say or tell (ibid, p. 651). **Kidding,** to make fun of, to deceive or taunt, came into use in the early 1800s from the middle European **kide** or the Old Norwegian **kith,** for "young goat," possibly because young goats are easily led.

Koestler (1964) reported that **wit** is derived from **witan** "whose roots go back (via **videre**) to the Sanskrit **veda,** knowledge" (such as *Rig Veda,* the ancient Hindu book of knowledge). **Wit** in German is **witz** and "means both joke and acumen." Its root is **wissen,** to know. **Wissenschaft** (science) "is a close kin to **furwitz** and **aberwitz,** "presumption, cheek or jest." The French **spirituel** means "witty" or "spiritually profound"; to amuse derives from "to muse" (**a-muser**) and a witty remark is a **heu d'esprit,** a "playful and mischievous discovery." The word Jester has a respectable ancestry. The **Chansons de Geste** played a prominent part in medieval literature from the 11th to the 15th centuries. They were epics centered on heroic events. The name is derived from the

Latin **gesta** (deeds, exploits). During the Renaissance "satire tended to replace the epics of chivalry and in the 16th century the heroic **geste** turned into **jest**" (p. 50). Arieti (1976) quotes Froeschel who in 1948 defined **witticisms** as "means by which philosophical truths congenitally known but not yet expressed become 'ripe for expression'" (p. 121). The search for word origins illustrates how humor cuts across philosophy and psychology, history and literature.

This semantic excursion points up the futility of trying to discover "what's funny" from a historical exploration of word usage. A study of current word usage is also of limited value. There is a wide range of words used today to refer to verbal, written or observed humor which further frustrates the search for a simple explanation of what's funny. A sampling of words which relate to humor are: jest, joke or joking around, quip, parody, pun, mockery, ridicule, satire, sardonic, wisecrack, wit, witticism, fool, fool around or fooling, tomfoolery, horseplay, skylarking, clown or clowning (around), comic, comedic, caricature, cartoon and in the south "funnin'." These 26 terms are by no means a complete listing of humor-related words. They describe what's funny — but do not actually define it.

BASIC ELEMENTS OF EFFECTIVE HUMOR

The source material of humor surrounds us daily, available in a variety of forms: newspaper and TV cartoons; live, taped and filmed comedy shows; jokes and stories in magazines and books; comedians live, on radio, TV, or film; funny everyday situations, even humorous, nostalgic memories. With but a little effort, you can recall humorous situations in your own life, in the past and recently. What are some of your funniest memories? With a little more effort, you can no doubt think of something funny that happened within the past week.

Humor is a universal trait. It has existed in every culture, ancient and modern. It transcends language, geography and time. Everybody laughs at something. That something may vary with the individual, but it's there just the same. Everyone has a sense of humor, though it may be perceived as strange by others. People laugh more when they are happy, "and upon a less special provocation than do people who are sorrowful cry" (Eastman, 1922, p. 9). If there is any doubt, observe children burst out of the school building at recess. They slow down in junior and senior high, but the elementary school kids emit a spontaneous joy, sense of fun and appreciation for the funny. From them we learn the first of seven basic elements of what's funny: **a playful mood.** "The condition in which joyful laughter most continually occurs," Eastman wrote, "is that of play" (p. 11).

It is through a playful mood but also "poetic perception," Eastman believed, that "makes anything funny" (p. 149). In this way we experience thoughts, emotions, even instincts "as though tasting or smelling of them but not drinking them down. It is as though nature, realizing how strenuous and difficult a thing it is to live, provided for us the fairy-shadow life in which we might prepare and exercise ourselves without suffering too much and. . .refresh and restore ourselves" (pp. 11-12). The humor of children is pure, simple, and sprightly, visible more in smiles and a twinkle in the eye than in their words or meaning.

As we age we lose the spontaneity of childhood, but there are compensating factors. "Thinking, the intellect," Eastman observed, "devises games, situations real and imagined to increase the harvest of pleasure" (p. 13). This introduces the second basic element of what's funny: **it is experiencing pleasure.** We prefer to experience pleasure to pain and this has been a common element in personality theory from Freud to the behavioral therapists, demonstrated consistently in animal and human research.

Positive humor is balanced between pain and pleasure, failure and success, inspiring and insulting. By "word magic," by semantic manipulation, psychological pain is diminished and failure becomes more tolerable. This transformation can occur very quickly, with rapidity as to be the envy of a Zen Master, mystic guru or medieval alchemist. It can be a lightning flash of insight, a moving "Ahah!" experience. It is a quick flip of the coin of mood from tails **down** to heads **up.** It can soften the hard or rigid, smooth differences and warm the cold. It has tremendous potential for good and is available to us daily. The third basic element of what's funny is its **transformational power.**

A fourth basic element is humor's **ephemeral, transitory quality,** what Eastman described as its "fairy-shadow life." He elaborated further: "There is no flower in nature more fragile to transport, more rooted in the specific. . .every jest has its season; it flourishes and dies" (p. 31). White and White (1941) felt that humor which teaches has a longer life but it, too, is limited:

> Humor is only a fragrance, a decoration. Often it is merely an odd trick of speech and of spelling. . . .Humor must not profoundly teach, and it must not professedly preach but it must do both if it would live

forever. By forever I mean thirty years. With all its preaching it is not likely to outlive so long a term as that. The very things it preaches about and which are novelties. . .cease to be novelties and become commonplace in thirty years. Then that sermon can thenceforth interest no one (p. xxii).

A fifth basic element of humor is its **"gem-like," fragile quality** "created by the exact coincidence of a playful shock or disappointment with a playful or genuine satisfaction" (Eastman, 1922, p. 28). This fragile quality requires that it be presented with a significant level of skill. Potentially hilarious material can die prematurely, "bomb" or "backfire" if not presented well. This is true for visual humor such as cartoons, silent movies or slapstick humor without dialogue or any sound at all as well as verbalized or written verbal humor:

> A joke is not a thing to be mauled and tinkered and revamped and translated about like an old trunk, from one nation, race, tribe, family, generation or language into another. It is a chemical gem, a delicate and precarious contexture of non-affirmative qualities, likely to go off at the touch of a feather in appropriate circumstances, or to lie flat and mute as a pancake (ibid, p. 30).

There are many exceptions (unhappily, in the study of humor there are many!). The humor and wisdom of *Aesop's Fables,* written in the 6th century B.C. allegedly by a slave, still retain their quality and effectiveness. The same is true for many of the writings which follow in this book, from the most ancient sources to those of recent generations. Humor survives because of the sixth basic element of what's funny: its **universality.** There are certain subjects and situations which have universal appeal, and applying humor to them is more likely to increase their laughter potential.

A seventh basic element of what's funny is its **timelessness.** According to Eastman (1922):

> . . .the comic itself in its origin does not mean lampoonery, or satire, or ridicule, or anything else either so scornful or so intellectual as that. It means village revelry or merrymaking and has relics in its aroma of wine-drinking in the evening and of ribald song and organized conviviality after the day's work is done (p. 126).

Summary of Basic Elements of Effective Humor

1. **Playful mood.** The listener/observer must be in a playful and therefore receptive mood.
2. **Experiencing pleasure.** The process and its result must facilitate a feeling of pleasure.

3. **Transformational.** It changes, elevates the mood.
4. **Short-lived.** It has a brief, ephemeral "fairy-shadow" life.
5. **Fragile.** It has a delicate, gem-like fragility requiring significant skill to effectively deliver.
6. **Universality.** It is a common trait and therefore of potentially universal appeal or appeals to a broad cross-section of people, across language and culture.
7. **Timeless.** What's **really** funny is funny for all time.

JOKESMITHING: FUNNY SUBJECTS

Studying the subjects most used by comedians and humorists will help us understand what's funny. Steve Allen is an experienced and established comedian and humorist who has been studying what's funny for decades. In his 1987 book *How to Be Funny,* Allen observed that "the comedian's experiences are probably no more amusing than others; he or she simply has a certain sensitivity to the environment and circumstances and so perceives humor that a more serious person might miss" (p. 5). Max Eastman (1936) added another ingredient, the broadest possible appeal: "It is necessary to play upon impulses that are common at least to a considerable group and can be relied upon to be in a situation of appetite almost all the time" (p. 31).

Steve Allen described the subject matter of jokes according to the formulations of two experienced "jokesmiths": David Freedman, joke writer for Eddie Cantor, and Sidney Reznick, radio and TV jokewriter. Freedman improved on his earlier classification and his categories are labelled **earlier** and **later** to differentiate them:

David Freedman's (Earlier) Categories

1. Literal English (puns)
2. Insults
3. Sex
4. Domestic jokes
5. Underdog theme
6. Incongruity
7. Topical humor

David Freedman's (Later) Categories

1. Insults
2. Anatomical reference
3. Kissing
4. Marriage
5. Dumb jokes
6. Children's mistakes
7. Truth (of life)

Sidney Reznick's 15 Categories

1. Marriage
2. The excuse
3. Old maids
4. Liquor or drinking
5. Whiskers
6. Seasickness
7. Death
8. Boardinghouse
9. Thrift
10. The fat man
11. Cute kiddy sayings
12. Underdog turnabout
13. Mother-in-law
14. The bride

15. Talkativeness

Steve Allen's Addendum to Reznick's Categories

16. Religion
17. Smoking
18. Driving
19. Swimming
20. Cowardice
21. Television
22. Drugs
23. Homosexuality

Let's consider a joke and review it according to the Freedman, Reznick and Allen criteria:

A little girl asks her mother: "Mommy, where did I come from?" Mother sits down with some apprehension and concern and explains love, marriage, the mechanics and chronology of having babies, and concludes with: "Does that answer your question, dear?" The child, bewildered, replies: "No, Mommy. Johnny, the boy next door says he's from Chicago. I was just wondering where I came from."

This joke could fit into either or both the **literal English** and the **sex** categories of Freedman's earlier categories and either or both **children's mistakes** and **truth of life** of his later categorization. The best fit is Reznick's **cute kiddy sayings,** but it's more a kiddy question. Even so, this one joke crosses five categories. None of them fit perfectly. The joke involves a child's perceptual processes (directly), sex (only indirectly), parent-child relations, a generation gap, semantics (meaning of words), interpersonal communications or a communications gap. That's six more categories. If you choose any one, from Freedman's first or second list, Reznick's, Allen's addendum, or mine, the joke is forced arbitrarily into one mold, typing and labelling it. Analyzing humor so precisely can diminish its appeal and its effect.

Much, perhaps all humor is multifaceted, multidimensional. This joke has more than one unique, appealing feature. There is the innocent charm of a little girl; her sensitive, well meaning but ineffectual mother;

a parent's responsibility to teach and guide the child; the little girl's unique, individual need and her readiness level to understand. All these factors are intermingled in the brief, warmly humorous joke which teaches as well as entertains and with the added boon of little or no embarrassment or ridicule for either mother or child. There is far more to it than any simple label could identify. Every joke has its own gestalt which can exceed the sum of its component parts. No classification system can capture a joke's quality.

Attempts at listing **the** subject matter of jokes is as futile as knowing what's funny from a study of the words used to describe humor. Doing so is reminiscent of the early literature on needs and phobias. Textbooks and journals discontinued such itemization when the lists grew so long and cumbersome as to be of little use to clinicians and a nightmare to students. While there are subjects more likely to be of interest to the broadest cross-section of an audience, what's funny can involve any subject. Steven Allen concedes this: "The number of types of jokes is limited only by the number of things there are in the world for us to discuss" (p. 29). Listing major subject areas of jokes does describe mines from which those gem-like jokes are most likely to be found.

Classifying a joke or any other kind of humor by its subject matter does not explain **why** it's funny. There are many interacting variables, each with its own **valence** or relative influence on successful outcome:

Factors of a Funny Joke

Premise (funny situation or conditions)
Context (location and its implied meaning, value and perceptual set, expectations)
Persons in the joke story
Person(s) telling the joke
Person(s) hearing the joke (effect varies if told to one, two, three or a group)
Technique (time, timing, semantics, verbal and nonverbal behaviors and qualities)

There are interpersonal variables as well which are involved in a joke's effectiveness:

1. The **listener must be interested** (Eastman, 1922, p. 99). A "dirty" joke told to most teenage boys arouses more interest than, let us say, a political or current events joke. They lean forward so as not to

miss a word, with fixed eye contact and attention. As we will see in a later chapter, Freud believed that there was vicarious experiencing in many "dirty" jokes, as if the speaker and listener lived some or all of the joke's action and situational dynamics.

2. The **listener's opinions or feelings must not be too strong** or the joke "goes too far" and is likely to "bomb" or "go flat." As Eastman observed: "There is a general incompatibility between humor and the deep experience of passion" (p. 99).

3. **Feeling tone must flow naturally,** casually, congenially and not forced or artificial.

4. The **punchline/point must be delivered cleanly.** Eastman maintains this exceeds the old maxim that brevity is the soul of wit. "The soul of wit," he admonishes, "is more than brief, it is instantaneous" (ibid).

5. **Optimal content only (in words and ideas),** through word economy, not over-explained, and only pertinent content to make the point, not overly elaborated. "Nothing in this world," Eastman wrote, "is more remote from the cause of humorous laughter than the perfect comprehension of an explained joke" (ibid).

These are by no means definitive listings of the mechanical and interpersonal variables involved in what's funny. They illustrate the complexities of humor which must be included in any systematic analysis.

COMEDIANS AS PERSONS

Steve Allen (1987) maintains that comedians are "by and large" intelligent and most, "the truly funny ones, anyway, are quick-minded." These traits make comedians uniquely qualified to react with humor to the realities of daily living: "It is impossible, in today's world, for quick-thinking, intelligent people not to be endlessly frustrated by the ineptitude, the slow thinking, the ignorance, the stupidity, the inefficiency by which they are daily surrounded" (p. 203).

A frequently asked question of comedians is when they first realized they were funny and Allen reports that "the real ones usually know very early. The world told them. It was not something they calculated; you don't plan to be funny at age 6" (p. 195). While comedians can use the same basic type of humor, there are differences: "No two individuals are funny in exactly the same way. Certain comedians have some factors in common but never everything" (Allen, 1987, p. 196). It is also true that no two audiences are alike, though they may look like the same general assortment of men and women. Allen feels it is "easier to get laughs from women. Men tend to be more socially inhibited" (p. 79).

Comedians can be effective and successful despite what many would be likely to perceive as negative or unappealing personality traits. Steve Allen describes himself as basically shy and inhibited in his earlier years when hosting the *Tonight Show* (p. 209). He describes Rodney Dangerfield as "tremendously, openly, unashamedly hostile, despite the fact that he himself is the butt of most of his funny lines" (p. 205). Of the late Lenny Bruce, Allen observed: "Lenny spoke very directly, although I never objected to his use of that sort of language because he never did it for an easy cheap laugh. He was always making a philosophical point" (p. 211).

Allen characterizes Phyllis Diller as showing "more sadness than anger although the two are intertwined since despair often masks anger" (ibid). He points out how difficult it is for female comics to be funny. If she does not project herself as feminine, women no longer identify with her and men lack interest. Women who have successfully retained a strong female identity without losing humorous impact, according to Allen: Lucille Ball, Mary Tyler Moore, Elaine May, Phyllis Diller, Goldie Hawn, Whoopi Goldberg and Gracie Allen.

TYPES OF COMEDIANS

There are distinctive types of comedy routines or subject matter each with its own distinctive type of comedian:

Standup comedians, as the title implies "stand up" and talk in a monologue to or dialogue with the audience. Examples of standup comedians: Bob Hope, Johnny Carson, Richard Pryor, Lily Tomlin, Robin Williams, Joan Rivers, Whoopi Goldberg, Buddy Hackett, George Carlin, Bill Cosby, Billy Crystal, Eddie Murphy, George Burns, Don Rickles, Redd Foxx, Bob Newhart, Sam Kinison, Steve Martin, Jay Leno and David Brenner. Some standup comedians specialize in **political humor** such as Mark Russell, Mort Sahl and Dick Gregory. Bob Hope blends quite a bit of satire with his comedy routine. Some comedians use **family situation humor** such as Bill Cosby and Sam Levinson. Some have a more **cerebral humor** such as Alistair Cooke, David Frost, Steve Allen, David Letterman and Dick Cavett.

Character comedians can be stand up or typecast in a unique role, personality or character such as Walter Matthau, Jack Lemmon, Carol

Channing, George Segal, Lucille Ball and Carole Burnett (as several different characters in their TV series), Peter Sellers (Inspector Clousseau in the *Pink Panther* series), George Burns, Jack Benny, Fred Allen, and Bob Hope. There are comic characters who are more in the role of clowns, involving costume, props and exaggerated delivery verbally and/or with mime: Red Skelton, Red Buttons, Soupy Sales, Pee Wee Herman, Sid Ceasar, Jerry Lewis, Milton Berle, Jackie Gleason, Jonathan Winters, Rip Taylor, Buster Keaton, Charlie Chaplin and Ed Wynn.

Physical comedians are active and animated, usually with slapstick type humor and "hands on" physical touching of others, such as: Harold Lloyd, Laurel and Hardy, Abbott and Costello, Marx Brothers, Three Stooges, Keystone Cops, Our Gang, Milton Berle, Monty Python, Buster Keaton, Ed Wynn, Charlie Chaplin and Rip Taylor. The overlap is noted with the duplication of Berle, Keaton, Wynn, Chaplin and Taylor who are also well defined character comedians. As we have seen in our efforts to analyze what's funny earlier in this chapter, this attempt to type comedians into simple, mutually exclusive lists is also fraught with disaster. They "cross over" in their subject matter, style and delivery.

Cartoon comedy characters are animated, usually animal characters, with an identifiable appearance and a distinctive, usually good-natured lovable personality. Some have enjoyed popularity for decades such as Mickey and Minnie Mouse, Bugs Bunny, Donald Duck, Yogi Bear, and others. There are also character groups such as the Seven Dwarves and the Smurfs. The comedic content of these cartoon characters is similar to that of "live" entertainers, the chief difference being that they are animated drawings with added human voices.

Mimes. Pantomine, humor using body motion or body language without any speech, is increasing in popularity. It is not unusual to see white-faced, white-gloved mimes at shopping centers and major events. Some stand statue-like, others mimic passersby or do everyday tasks with invisible objects such as peeling a banana, opening jars, and such. Some combine magic tricks or juggling. Marcel Marceau and Shields and Yarnell are leading proponents of this form of humor. Break dancing is rich in mime techniques.

Clowns. Clowns are typed by character and settings. The more classic **whiteface clowns** wear brightly colored 1-piece costumes with frilly ruffles around the neck, sleeves and cuffs and full white-face makeup. **Character clowns** such as a Charlie Chaplin, Keystone Cop, hillbilly, sailor, baby or others are unique comic personalities and most are

auguste clowns wearing flesh makeup on the face with large white ovals around the eyes and mouth. Traditionally, the whiteface clowns instigate trouble and auguste clowns work it through but "zap" the whiteface with a pie in reprisal. A third clown type originated in the United States and is the **hobo** or **tramp** type. Costuming varies from **Fifth Avenue** with threadbare tuxedo, battered top hat, fingerless gloves and toes protruding from shoes, to the **railroad** or **junkyard** types. All these clowns are made up to look dirty and dishevelled and are either sad or "what the hell" carefree. Emmett Kelly and Box-car Willie were of this type.

With such a wide variety of comedy it should come as no surprise that some of it is controversial or considered to be "in bad taste." Don Rickles and Joan Rivers have a caustic wit and their humor is offensive to some. Dudley Moore has been criticized for enacting the role of a drunk in the movie *Arthur*. In *Lovesick* he was a psychiatrist who had an affair with a patient. Sam Kinison's comedy routine involves bizarre, psychotic-like behaviors. Franky Fontaine got laughs in the role of a fictitious person with a speech defect and whose behaviors were typical of the mentally retarded. Jonathan Winters and Robin Williams use a manic style but which is less exaggerated than these others. These comedians walk the fine line between good and bad taste.

HUMORISTS

Usually the term **humorist** describes a writer, speaker or popular personality known for her or his wit and humor such as Art Buchwald and Jimmy Breslin. Humorists are thinkers, conceptualists. **Comedians** are doers, practitioners, humorous actors or actresses onstage saying or doing comedy routines. What an actor is to a playwright a comedian is to a humorist. George Bernard Shaw, George S. Kaufman, Alexander Woolcott, Oscar Wilde, Ogden Nash, P.G. Wodehouse and James Thurber were humorists, not comedians. Some humorists have been successful onstage comedians and Mark Twain and Will Rogers are two examples. Occasionally leaders in the arts or sciences are quoted or become known for humorous sayings, such as Ralph Waldo Emerson, Alfred North Whitehead and Bertrand Russell (philosophy), Albert Schweitzer (medical missionary), Oscar Levant (concert pianist), H.L. Mencken (newspaper reporter), Benjamin Franklin (government) etc.

Like comedians, humorists have an imaginative sensitivity for the world about them, the physical environment and the people. Don

Herold described a humorist as one who "feels bad but feels good about it" (Eastman, 1936, p. 335). White and White (1941) observed that "one of the things commonly said about humorists is that they are really very sad people, clowns with a breaking heart." The authors point out that "there is a deep vein of melancholy running through everyone's life." They suggest that the humorist is "perhaps more sensitive of it" and "compensates for it actively and positively" (p. xviii).

Humorists have what Eastman (1936) calls a "lovable honesty" which can be perceived as inappropriate and they themselves as uncouth:

> It was in America, I think, that the poetic "humorist" as a professional character was first baptized with that name. He is not a satirist. . . clown. . .comedian nor in any sense a resurrected court fool or jester. He has not enough wit or agility for that. He is a man of naturally droll mind and rather uncouth magnetism, who simply stands up and talks. He makes everything he talks about seem funny without cracking jokes about it. It seems funny because he is funny. He is inappropriate. Everything he does. . .is inappropriate. The harlequin dresses himself up. . .to make people laugh but the humorist, knowing that all mankind is dressed up, achieves the same end by coming out in his own clothes. If there is any point in his humor it is a kind of lovable honesty which underlies all that inappropriateness. . .a profound honesty. . .honest provincialism in a society much overstraining. . .to escape it (p. 84).

COMEDIANS' CHOICE OF WHO'S FUNNY

The *American Comedy Awards* were presented for the first time in 1987, based on voting by professional comedians. The winners and runners up provide a good indication of the choice of comedians as to what's funny:

- *Best standup female comedian:* Lily Tomlin
  Runners up: Joan Rivers, Bet Midler, Whoopi Goldberg
- *Best standup male comedian:* Robin Williams
  Runners up: Billy Crystal, Eddie Murphy, Richard Pryor
- *Funniest female performer of the year:* Bet Midler
  Runners up: Whoopi Goldberg, Lily Tomlin, Betty White, Carol Burnett
- *Funniest male performer of the year:* Robin Williams
  Runners up: Woody Allen, David Letterman, Eddie Murphy, Jay Leno

- *Funniest TV star in a special:* Robin Williams in *Evening at the Met.*
  Runners up: Carol Burnett, George Carlin, Billy Crystal,
    Gary Schandling
- *Best newcomer:* Woody Harrelson
  Runners up: Sam Kinison, Roseanne Barr, Mark Linn-Baker
- *Best record or videofilm: Mud will be flung tonight* with Bet Midler
  Runners up: Dan Ackroyd, George Carlin, Whoopi Goldberg,
    Steve Martin

In 1987, the *Mary Tyler Moore Show* was rated the best all-time TV situation comedy with *Cheers* as the best current TV sitcom based on nationwide ratings.

NEGATIVE ASPECTS OF COMEDY

Asked to comment on negative aspects of comedy routines, Steve Allen referred to the inevitable "dead" audience which sits passively stone-faced and doesn't laugh. Most professional comedians have a "doom's day routine" for such unhappy occasions, lines like:

"Is this an audience or an oil painting?"

"Is this an audience or a jury?"

"Are you here for the show or to read a will?"

"Just because the last act was lousy, don't take it out on me!"

"Is this a funeral?"

"Did I say something sad?"

Allen is critical of inexperienced newcomers who use awkward language in their routines, words such as: ". . .uh. . .y'know. . .I mean. . .right?. . .yeah!. . .OK. . .know what I mean?" or who fidget with their hands. He provides an illustrative example of how such expressions detract from meaning:

"Our Father, who art in Heaven, Okay?

Hallowed be Thy name, you know what I'm saying?" (p. 198)

Commenting on current TV comedy Steve Allen concludes: "One distinguishing trait of today's TV humor is a lack of originality" (p. 264). Allen Funt, the creator of the popular *Candid Camera* TV series, also reports a change in audience responsivity to humor:

Viewers are more impatient, have shorter attention spans and won't tolerate buildups to humor. I think the popular and funny *Laugh-In* show changed audience expectations. The old *Candid Camera* episodes used to be almost five minutes long. Now they average 2.5 minutes. . . It's also harder to deceive people now. They are more knowledgeable about technology, more sophisticated about their rights, more cynical and assertive and, of course, sensitized to the *Candid Camera* type of experience (Zimbardo, 1985, p. 47).

Funt observed some negative aspects of human behavior during eleven years of radio, TV and film recording of 1,250,000 people. "The worst thing," he reported, "and I see it over and over, is how easily people can be led by any kind of authority figure, or even the most minimal signs of authority" (ibid). He describes how his crew erected a sign which read "Delaware closed today." Motorists not only accepted it but asked: "Is Jersey open?" Funt is concerned about this gullibility and passivity: "We need to develop ways to teach our children how to resist unjust or ridiculous authority" (ibid). He sees the *Candid Camera* format and style a possible way to achieve this goal:

> Archie Bunker made a bigot seem ridiculous but did his show reduce the level of prejudice in America? I believe *Candid Camera* could help by exposing some of the ridiculous ways in which prejudice comes out. . . I wish I could use *Candid Camera's* humorous and nonthreatening approach to help parents, teachers or salespeople reexamine what they are doing to learn from their mistakes. Sometimes just knowing how to understand one's unusual reactions can make a big difference (p. 47).

Asked what he preceives as most funny in the light of his *Candid Camera* experience, Funt's impression was that it is based on an "appeal to what is universal to human nature. . .we are essentially laughing at ourselves and our weaknesses. . .to endure those weaknesses and still get on with the business of living." He also feels it is "part of the American tradition to be a good sport, to accept a limited amount of hazing, to go along with the joke. The people we film also know that *Candid Camera* is with them, not against them." Even with more than a decade of experience, he made mistakes. He received 300,000 angry letters when he played Santa Claus for some school children the day after Christmas. "A child cried," he lamented, "because Santa was not supposed to be there on that day." Other carefully planned segments have flopped, such as the knight in full armor emerging from a New York sewer. Strangely, and still unexplained, "most people passed him right by without any sign they'd noticed" (p. 46).

On the positive side, Funt traces the appeal of his method to six basic ideas:

1. **Reversal** of normally anticipated or expected behavior, usually responding to challenging or provocative situations.

2. **Weakness** which becomes evident in a genuine, low-key manner which gently exposes universal human foibles. Such a gentle exposition reassures the audience who can safely identify with the protagonist and the situation, secretly comparing his or her reaction to "how I'd react."

3. **Fantasy** or **wish fulfillment** (Freud is smiling down on us!) where the audience can vicariously "pay back" or be assertive to authority figures such as policemen, bosses, doctors, and bureaucrats.

4. **Surprise!** Here the audience can empathically experience the coping skills of the protagonist and reflect on alternative methods of the viewer's own response style and likely reaction.

5. **Incongruity,** in Allen Funt's words "to place something that makes sense in one setting in a completely inappropriate or bizarre setting" (p. 46). He adds that an essential element quite often is that "people don't acknowledge the bizarre but it must be apparent that they've seen it" (ibid). An example is the segment where an appropriately behaved, well dressed woman shows up—with a monkey sitting on her head. Howard Brubaker is quoted in Max Eastman's 1936 book on the role of incongruity in humor: ". . .the common denominator of humor is the contact of incongruous ideas. This mixture causes a series of little explosions as in an internal combustion engine" (p. 333).

6. **Simplicity.** "Each piece was brief, self-contained, and the simple humor of the situation could be quickly understood by virtually anyone. . ." (ibid).

Asked what he considers the funniest *Candid Camera* segments, Funt chose two:

First and clearly the funniest was the "talking mailbox" on a busy New York City street. There was a concealed microphone and the mailbox "talked" to passersby. Cynical at first (as only typical New Yorkers can be!), they resorted to "helping" the mailbox communicate with them more effectively by "lifting the lid so that the box could get a better look at them." Some brought friends and even strangers over for the unique experience, at which time they were greeted with silence. The silence elicited as much laughter from audiences as the initial friendly, chatty mailbox. Funt confesses he still doesn't understand why this segment was so popular.

The second funniest segment in Funt's judgment was the "car with no engine" that was surreptitiously pushed into a gas station. Dorothy Collins, the driver, asks the attendant to change the oil while she goes to the restroom. When she returns and is told there's no engine—by a bewildered attendant—she smiles graciously and tells him to put the engine back while she again briefly leaves the scene. Funt attributes the humor in these situations to their being "closeups of people in action. . .ordinary people. . .(and the) reality of events as they were unfolding" (p. 46).

HOW WE ARE FUNNY: 32 WAYS!

From the literature review in writing this book and the author's own experience over the years, the following list emerged of the uses of humor, when and why we are funny. In whatever form, humor is used as:

1. **A direct weapon,** overt, conscious, deliberate to attack or to degrade or abuse another, impugn integrity or destroy credibility by sharp, cutting satire or sarcasm or indirectly by metaphorical or tangential humor targeted on a specific point or person.

2. **Indirect weapon,** a covert effort to degrade or discount by biased or prejudiced humor aimed at differences or minorities of race, ethnic-cultural or national origin, social status, sex, age, religion, or occupation.

3. **Repartee,** word play, a playful verbal battle of wits, between two or more persons enjoying each other or the present situation in an atmosphere of play and mutual stimulation. Groos: "Fighting play" (Eastman, 1922, p. 142).

4. **Provocation,** a direct challenge, to stop whatever is happening, draw attention from it or from person(s) involved or central to it, to yourself or to another viewpoint and thus introduce and facilitate change. Charlie Chaplin: "It is telling the plain truth of things. . .I make them conscious of life. 'You think this is it, don't you?' I say, 'well, it isn't but this is, see?' And then they laugh" (Eastman, 1922, p. 46).

5. **Probe.** To use humor to dig more deeply into a situation or process, to tease out and more closely scrutinize what is happening; done by introducing other sources, facts, attitudes, or alternatives. Though related, it differs from **intentional provocation** by motive and method, the former a skyrocket or bomb burst, the latter a carefully aimed rifle bullet.

6. **Defense.** To protect one's self against attack or involvement or to parry an attack; to avoid reality or intimacy; to avoid relating to a person or dealing with a problem. "Generally we laugh at the things we are afraid to face" (Heywood Broun, in Eastman, 1936, p. 333).

7. **Deny or avoid.** A false front, Pagliacchi-like, to laugh rather than cry, a false front to avoid psychological pain. Related to **defense** but differs in that **defense** copes with reality like a boxer bobbing and weaving in the ring but **denial-avoidance** avoids, blocks reality, refuses to see or process it.

8. **Deliberate tangent.** To outwit, distract, circumvent, to use humor to lead other person(s) astray, off on a tangent, to another subject or into absurdity.

9. **Defuse:** To use humor to relieve a tense situation and build a more relaxed atmosphere such as in negotiations, mediation, to smooth (not remove) differences and cool tempers. Cicero: Humor "very often disposes of extremely ugly matters that will not bear to be cleared up by proofs" (Eastman, 1922, p. 95).

10. **Disarm,** to lessen the antagonism of an adversary in good faith and build trust preventing or lessening offensive action from an adversary.

11. **Improve coping skills.** A coping mechanism to increase toleration, lessen one's stress threshold, continue functioning at an optimal level with less frustration and discomfort.

12. **Control mechanism** for negative emotions (anxiety, fear); to maintain emotional control in catastrophic situations (war, crisis); to prevent anxiety escalating to panic or despair; to "plateau" emotions.

13. **Facilitate change.** To ease the frustration and psychological pain from inevitable change such as on the job (new boss, new job, computerization, layoffs), romantic or marital problems or divorce, empty nest syndrome, loss.

14. **Attitude change.** Blurs the painfully sharp black-on-white focus of problem situations or people; encourages flexibility, movement of opposing sides toward a mutual center; conducive to "what's important, really?" or "what the hell, so we each give a little" outlook.

15. **Mood change.** Lightens the mood, overcomes anxiety, lessens fear, guilt and apprehension; transformational like medieval alchemists changing lead to gold, transforming sad to happy, pessimism to optimism, frozen frustration to warmly positive expectancy.

16. **Vent emotion,** an emotional steam valve to release tension in high stress situations; once vented a more relaxed, cooperative, less stressful mood results.

17. **Affection.** Warm, supportive "pat on the back" kidding; "puppy dog" playful, positive strokes ("warm fuzzies"); often done with "baby talk."

18. **Seduction.** To charm, tantalize, bend values, ethics or morality, relax rules, overlook practicalities in a "come on, let's have fun" or "the water's fine" approach.

19. **Manipulative.** Artificial "plastic fuzzies," ingratiating and gamey, insincere mechanical humor used by unscrupulous sales types, con artists and similar phonies "brick by brick" to build a receptive attitude toward their own goal.

20. **Cerebral.** Dry, intellectual wit, haughty, droll, condescending, snobbish, elitist, cold, distancing.

21. **Facilitate intimacy.** A verbal warm hug with a sincere intent to join together and with no other ulterior motive; laughing WITH and not AT others as an equal, sharing partner.

22. **Taunting-teasing.** Like the little boy who punches the girl he likes on the arm to show affection; a childish form of humor well intentioned but poorly delivered; reaction formation in clinical terms.

23. **Give permission,** use of humor to send the message: "It's OK" — to "take a break, take it easy, be human, be you, be a kid again, to have fun."

24. **Elation-joy.** "Getting off" in a strong blast of joy; crowing (similar to babies who can't yet talk); that "victory cheer" or "rebel yell" feeling of uninhibited joy.

25. **Facilitate creativity.** Using humor to free the mind, to clean the mental palate; unlock brain circuits and allow them free and open discharge (stimulates brainstorming).

26. **To speak the truth.** Artemus Ward: "I have always meant the creatures of my burlesque should stab Error and give Right a friendly push" (Eastman, 1936, p. 354). "I don't think I agree that humor must preach in order to live; it need only speak the truth — and I notice it always does" (White and White, 1941, p. xxii).

27. **Teach/learn** the uses of humor, how to laugh, how to "let go" and "loosen up"; to learn about humor as the natural trait it is and use it with skill and understanding.

28. **Acceptance** of pain, even death; to face and cheerfully accept the inevitable. "And when the heart in the body is torn," Heine wrote, "torn and bleeding and broken, we still have laughter beautiful and shrill" (Eastman, 1922, p. 171). Abraham Lincoln: "I laugh because I must not cry — that's all. That's all" (Eastman, 1936, p. 331). Lord Byron: "If I laugh at any mortal thing 'tis that I may not weep" (Eastman, 1936, p. 330).

29. **Personal growth.** Robert de Lamennais: "The self which discovers the ridiculous in one of the inferior regions of its being, separates itself from that at which it laughs, distinguishes itself from it and rejoices

inwardly at a sagacity which elevates it in its own esteem" (*Esquissen d'une Philosophie,* IX, Chapter 2, in Eastman, 1922, p. 140).

30. **Therapy,** to help learn life's hard lessons with a little less pain; to help forgive yourself and accept weaknesses; to close the book on the past with a smile—of regret but also relief it's over; to practice "good humor" and "good cheer" as new attitudes of the new you, to help you more easily become the real you. By taking an occasional "laugh break" you can also more effectively cope with stress or illness.

31. **Transcendence.** At the 1987 annual American Comedy awards, Norman Lear described humor as a mystic or spiritual experience. He recommended developing an attitude that "life is a love in." Zen Buddhists have laughed at their enlightenment for centuries. Humor can facilitate a mental tune-up freeing the mind, a Shangrila transcendent experience.

32. **Natural function,** a genetic, instinctive trait across species, the playful mood in animals and humans, "puppy dog" lighthearted, spontaneous funloving and good cheer, "singing in the rain" or "whistling in the dark."

As is true for most behaviors and traits, there is overlap in these applications. The following listings group these numbered applications by their positive-neutral-negative polarity and whether they occur mainly in a group or social setting or are personal:

External Applications (Social-interpersonal)

NEGATIVE POLARITY (offensive, negative effect)

1. Direct attack   2. Indirect attack

AMBIVALENT (positive or negative effect)

3. Repartee	8. Tangent
4. Provocation	10. Disarm
5. Probe	18. Seduction
6. Defense	19. Manipulation
7. Denial-avoidance	20. Cerebral

22. Taunting-teasing

POSITIVE POLARITY (constructive, supportive)

9. Defuse	23. Permission/approval
14. Attitude change	24. Elation/joy
15. Mood change	25. Facilitate creativity
17. Affection	26. Speak truth
21. Intimacy	27. Teach/learn

32. Natural function

Internal Applications (intrapersonal)

11. Improve coping
12. Control emotions
13. Facilitate change
14. Attitude change
15. Mood change
16. Vent emotions
20. Cerebral

23. (Self) permission
24. Elation/joy
25. Facilitate creativity
28. Acceptance
29. Personal growth
30. Facilitate therapy
31. Transcendence

32. Natural function

SO WHAT'S FUNNY?

This chapter was a quick overflight of that territory known as humor. Newly named (c. 1700 AD), it has existed unnamed since ancient times. The Greeks and Romans enjoyed comedy, evidence that they valued a sense of humor. Our detective work to explore "what's funny" began with a review of words used to describe humor. We reviewed the elements of humor, the signs and symptoms of what's funny: playful mood, experiencing pleasure, mood elevation, brevity, fragility, universality and timelessness. We considered several lists: factors of "funnyness": reversal, fantasy, wish, surprise, incongruity and oversimplification; subjects with highest humor potential according to professional jokesmiths; the "best" comedians chosen by their peers; 32 uses of humor. Despite this extensive sampling we have not arrived at a definition of humor nor with a simple statement of what's funny. Is it possible to do so?

Maurice Charney (1978) observed that "comedy may not be a single identifiable subject for which any individual theory or set of data will be adequate" (p. 3). T.A. Ribot wrote in 1896 that "laughter manifests itself in such varied and heterogeneous conditions that the reduction of all these causes to a single one remains a very problematical undertaking. After so much work on such a trivial phenomenon the problem is still far from being completely explained" (in Koestler, 1964, p. 32). Eastman (1936) joined this chorus, admonishing us that

> . . .to make precise, through an experimental study, the distinction between the laughter of pleasure and a comic laugh, to determine just what is the state called playfulness or being-in-fun and what are its conditions, and so gradually, in an empirical and verifiable manner, to narrow this generalization which as it stands is about as wide and as high as the universe (p. 355).

More recently, Steve Allen (1987) agreed that "no all-inclusive definitive answer has yet been found" and that humor is "a gift of the gods, a potentiality of the mind that because it varies from individual to individual will never be completely understood" (pp. 7 and 10). Still, as Aristotle observed 2000 years ago, "all men by nature desire knowledge" (Bartlett, 1968, p. 97). We must have working hypotheses even though they may be primitive charts of largely uncharted oceans and continents. Research has been described as "successive approximations of truth." T.S. Eliot summed it up well: "We shall not cease from exploration, and the end of all our exploring will be to arrive where we started—and know the place for the first time." The remaining chapters will continue to explore humor and what's funny. The exploration is not limited to psychology but is a Taoist search for truth regardless of source, touching on literature and history, philosophy and science, from earliest history to recent books and journals. Humor has enormous scope. So must any valid study of it.

For now, we can say that "what's funny" is whatever makes you smile or laugh. That varies with the individual and with group values. We will continue our exploration of the world of humor from ancient Greece and Rome, later even Sumer the oldest known source of humor, moving to the present with brief visits with philosophers, behavioral scientists and writers, all detectives of the mind who had much to say about humor and what's funny. THEN we'll return to T.S. Eliot's exploration theme and try to "know the place for the first time."

CHAPTER 2

CLASSICAL THEORIES

Heavy years go by,
Heavy hundreds of years,
Till a shroud and mask drop. . .

Carl Sandburg (1879-1967)
The people, yes (1936)

JUST AS there is no single, universally accepted explanation of **what** is funny, there is also no agreement as to **why** anything is funny. There are several theories of humor, some dating back more than 2000 years, some emerging only in the 19th and 20th centuries. "Many of the great minds of history have brought their powers of concentration to bear on the mystery of humor," Steve Allen observed, but "their conclusions are so contradictory and ephemeral that they cannot possibly be classified as scientific" (1987, p. 9). In 1941, White and White cautioned against overanalyzing: "Humor can be dissected, as a frog can, but the thing dies in the process and the innards are discouraging to any but the pure scientific mind" (p. xvii). But it is also **powerfully** true that we "by nature desire knowledge" and "learn by doing" (Aristotle, *Metaphysics*). We all laugh. We have a very strong innate drive to know why.

From a review of world literature, ancient to modern, eight major theories of humor emerge, two ancient or classical, four neo-classical and two modern, one emerging in the 1960s, the other introduced in this volume. In descending rank order from ancient to modern these theories are:

1. Derision or superiority
2. Disappointment or frustrated expectation
3. Pleasure-pain and learning-conditioning

4. Instinct-physiological
5. Sympathy-empathy
6. Creativity and change
7. Semantics and content analysis
8. Syzygy (polarity, power, process theory)

In this chapter the first two theories will be described, derision/superiority and disappointment/frustrated expectation theories, termed "classical" because they are the oldest, dating back to Plato and Aristotle respectively. Pleasure-pain, instinct-physiological, sympathy and empathy, and creativity and change theories, termed "neoclassical" because they emerged after Platonic and Aristotelian theories, are described in Chapters 3 and 4. The remaining two theories, semantics and syzygy, are termed "modern" because they originated in the 20th century and the most recent, are described in Chapter 5.

HISTORICAL-CULTURAL CONTEXT

To better understand and appreciate classical theories of humor it is helpful to examine the historical and cultural context from which they emerged. This is especially true since more than 2000 years have elapsed since these two classical theories were first described and also since they arose in a people and a land where language, lives and times differed from our own.

In his *Essay on Comedy,* George Meredith (1828-1909), the English novelist and poet, wrote: "Comedy was never one of the most honored of the muses. . .it rolled in shouting under the divine protection of the Son of the Wine-jar, as Dionysus is made to proclaim himself by Aristophanes" (Sypher, 1956, p. 5). Comedy and tragedy are two limbs of the same tree, and that tree is deeply rooted in the history of civilization, long before even Plato and Aristotle, both of whom had the luxury of examining both in the context of the Golden Age of Greece, rich in both comedy and tragedy.

Sypher (1956) referred to Aristotle's observation that both comedy and tragedy "begin as improvisation." Comedy arose from "phallic songs" which Aristotle reported were "still sung in many of our cities" and which depict people as "worse than they are." Tragedy arose from ancient cult rituals (Dionysian, Eleusinian and their forerunners) involving hero worship and death-rebirth themes presenting people "better than they are." Comedy evolved from "invective" into "dramatizing the ridiculous." In ancient satyric dramas, poetry was recited, chanted, then danced, in fertility rites, largely Dionysiac or phallic, involving feast and sacrifice, a give and take, have and have not duality. "Art is born of ritual," Sypher wrote, "and comic and tragic are themselves archetypal symbols for characters in rituals such as killing the old year (or aged king) and bringing in the new (resurrection or initiation themes)" (p. 216). Remember New Year's Eve? In our "rituals" we are not so different than those ancient Greeks!

Another ancient ritual described by Sypher is "expelling a scapegoat." By this ritual, the tribe was purged. In *The Golden Bough,* the classic study of cults and ritual by Sir James Frazer (1854-1941), there is an apt description of Mardi Gras-like celebration:

> The time of year when the ceremony takes place usually coincides with some well-marked change of season. . .this public and periodic expulsion of devils is commonly preceded or followed by a period of general license, during which the ordinary restraints of society are thrown aside and all offenses, short of the gravest are allowed to pass unpunished (Sypher, p. 216).

According to Sypher, comic and tragic poetry evolved from this very ancient ritual of sacrifice-feast. "Elemental folk drama" emerged from the poetry, then "action myths" so typical of the Athenian theatre. Comedy was associated with erotic action, from its roots in phallic songs, and the "disorderly rejoicing" that accompanied it. Sacrifice (tragedy) and feast (comedy) were "dual and wholly incompatible meanings. . .cruelty and festival, logic and license." Aristophanes play *Clouds* "is an argument between Right Logic and Wrong Logic. . .logic and passion appear together in the primal comic formula" (p. 218).

"Comic action is a Saturnalia, an orgy," Sypher wrote, "an assertion of the unruliness of the flesh and its vitality. . .triumph over mortality by some absurd faith in rebirth, restoration and salvation." In ancient times carnival rites "were red with the blood of victims" because the "archaic seasonal revel brought together the incompatibilities of death and life." This kind of humor defies reason: "No logic can explain this magic victory of Winter, Sin and the Devil." And humor **is** magic: "The comedian can perform the rites of Dionysus and his frenzied gestures initiate us into the secrets of the savage and the mystic power of life. Comedy is sacred and secular" (ibid, p. 22).

The "scorpion-philosopher" Friedrick Nietzsche (1844-1900) maintained that truth is discovered "in the excesses of the Dionysian orgy which is ecstasy as well as pain." Greek drama, Nietzsche believed, was played "at a point of conflict between our Apollonian and our Dionysian selves." Reason (**logos**) is the Apollonian self and song (**melos**), evolving from the songs and chants of the Greek chorus, is the Dionysian self. The Dionysian self is a satyr-self, an otherwise "natural being madly giving out cries of joys and sorrow that arise from the vast cosmic night of primordial existence." And so, according to Nietzsche, "our deepest insights must and should appear as follies." Sypher concluded that against this profound backdrop "the Dionysiac theatre consecrates truth by outbursts of laughter. Comedy desecrates what it seeks to sanctify" and therefore the "comic perspective can be reached only by making game of 'serious' life" (pp. 223-224).

This was the context within which first Plato, then his student Aristotle, sought to interpret the **why** of humor. Plato's contribution was **derision theory** which some call **superiority theory**. Aristotle's contribution was **disappointment theory** which has also come to be known as **frustrated expectation**.

DERISION/SUPERIORITY THEORY
Exemplar: Plato (c. 427-347 BC)

This is the oldest known theory of humor. Plato is credited with founding it with his observation that "at the sight of tragedies the spectators smile through their tears. . .even at a comedy the soul experiences a mixed feeling of pain and pleasure. . .pleasure of seeing other people humiliated" (Eastman, 1922, p. 123). Aristotle, Plato's student, agreed that the source of humor was "enjoyment of the misfortune of others due to a momentary feeling of superiority or gratified vanity that we ourselves are not in the predicament observed" (Allen, 1987, p. 10).

Plato wrote *Symposium,* the story of an imaginary night-long debate featuring, among others, the comedy playwright Aristophanes, the tragedian Agathon and "the goat-faced Socrates, the philosophic clown." In *Symposium,* Alcibiades tells Socrates he looks "exactly like the masks of Silenus" and his "face is like that of a satyr." Socrates, "resembling a caricature of a man. . .makes the dissolute Athenians care for their souls." By daybreak Socrates ends the debate by concluding that "anyone who can write tragedy can also write comedy because the craft (**techne**) of writing comedy is the same as the craft of writing tragedy" (Sypher, 1956, p. 214). In his book *Comedy,* Wylie Sypher observed: "Perhaps the most important discovery in modern criticism is the perception that comedy and tragedy are somehow akin" (ibid, p. 193).

Derision theory is based on the premise that we laugh **down** at others. Its basic drive is to humiliate, to subjugate, to disparage. The feeling tone is hostile and aggressive, its attitude negative and pessimistic. The joke teller and the listener get a "kick" from it, an emotional "high" which the British philosopher Thomas Hobbes (1588-1679) described as "a feeling of sudden glory" (Eastman, 1922, p. 33). The psychologist Alexander Bain, wrote: "Not in physical effects alone, but in everything where a man can achieve a stroke of superiority in surpassing or discomforting a rival, is the disposition of laughter apparent" (Koestler, 1964, p. 53).

According to derision theory, humor substitutes a verbal attack for physical violence. If you can't strike out physically at someone or something, you can do so "in the spirit of fun." Its goal is to realize superiority over others through an Adlerian "will-to-power." It arises from a pessimistic, fatalistic view of life typified in the tee-shirt motto, "life's a bitch, then you die." Eastman (1922) used the following joke to illustrate derision theory:

In the Old West a group of hard-drinking cowboys are creating a disturbance in the town saloon. The sheriff stands outside on the street and says to the townspeople: "I'm gonna go in there and clean'em out. You count'em as they come flyin' through the door." He strides proudly into the saloon. Moments later the sheriff comes flying through the door shouting: "Stop countin'—it's me!"

In this joke law and order does not prevail and the "good guy" loses. Most people who hear this joke consider it to be funny. Eastman suggested this is because the hero is a braggart and doesn't deserve to win. Though he fails, he has a sense of humor which provides a quick change of attitude while being thrown through the doorway and that becomes the punch line of the joke. It is a tragicomic balance with humor in failure. Derision/superiority theory would say of it: "You can never win." In the words of Roseanne Rosanadanna, humorous Hispanic character created by Gilda Radner on *Saturday Night Live:* "There's always something."

Stephen Crane (1871-1900) wrote *The Red Badge of Courage* (1895), one of the first novels describing the realities of war. He served as a war correspondent in Cuba and in Greece 1896-1898. Crane wrote the following which illustrates derision/superiority theory on a grand, cosmic level:

A man said to the universe: "Sir, I exist!" "However," replied the universe, "that fact has not created in me a sense of obligation."

Any joke that ends in or in its meaning or effect is a "put down" satisfies the criteria of derision theory. Even when the punch line is not disparaging, any joke which in its telling has negative connotations, directly or indirectly, is malicious and destructive. For example, Plato defined love as "a grave mental illness." As Thomas Hobbes put it: "Jokes are always on somebody. . .comic emotion is the same thing as scorn or the feeling of one's own superiority" (ibid). A generation later, the French satirist Voltaire (1694-1788) observed that "a mistake is the only thing that ever awakens violent peals of universal laughter" (Eastman, 1922, p. 155).

The following are opinions from experienced observers and analysts of humor who subscribe to derision/superiority theory. All are excerpted from Max Eastman's 1936 book *The Enjoyment of Laughter:*

From J.P. McEnvoy, cartoonist-creator of the comic strip character *Mister Noodle:* "People don't want to laugh so much as they want to feel superior to somebody else. They want to be taller, or richer, or better looking than the people they associate with, and the only places most newpaper readers can find such people to gloat over are in the comic strips" (p. 93). A colleague cartoonist-humorist, George Ade: ". . .all laughter at the expense of someone else is really founded on a 'feeling of superiority' on the part of the amused person over the victim" (p. 335).

Henry A. Murray, the Harvard professor and psychologist who studied needs and need states wrote that "the enjoyment of derisive humor is associated with. .egocentric, individualistic, aggressive and world-derogatory sentiments. . . An intense enjoyment of crudely disparaging jokes was chiefly an indication of repressed malice. . .an unconscious need for destruction" (p. 352). Murray's comments are suggestive of the Freudian **id,** the primitive beast within, lurking in the shadows of the mind, watchful and ready to pounce on the unwary, with the sharp blade of wit, using humor as a well-honed weapon. It is the *Adapted Child* or *Not OK Kid* of Eric Berne's transactional analysis, pouting, selfish and cruelly sadistic, eager to complete a **kick me** game with a joke's payoff line.

James Thurber: "The closest thing to humor is tragedy. I think humor is best that lies closest to the familiar, but that part of the familiar which is humiliating, even tragic" (p. 342). Thurber is describing the "funny potential" of what in reality would be very dangerous situations such as in the old silent films, *The Perils of Pauline,* when the villain ties her to the train tracks and the steam engine approaches at high speed, or huge buzzsaws, bombs, crashing airplanes or Keystone Kops chaotically chasing crooks.

W.C. Fields: "I never saw anything funny that wasn't terrible. If it causes pain, it's funny; if it doesn't, it isn't. I try to pretend that it isn't painful. I try to hide the pain with embarrassment and the more I do that, the better they like it" (p. 336). Slapstick comedy and circus clown skits would be physically painful or dreadfully embarrassing situations in real life but are made into caricatures, exaggerated in action and overdramatized with garish clothing and grotesque props. Clown magic is funnier when the tricks seem to fail. In all these examples, we laugh **at** and not **with** the characters.

George McManus, cartoonist: "Yes you've got to make fun of somebody. People laugh when they see somebody fall down. That's the typical laugh. But if he doesn't get up they stop laughing" (p. 335). McManus is pointing out the delicate balance between "good" and "bad" humor. Excessive "practical jokes" hurt feelings. The victim "takes a fall" psychologically just as someone who slips and falls and is injured physically. In such instances laughter instantaneously changes to a strained embarrassment, a self-conscious "electric" silence.

The French philosopher Henri Bergson (1859-1941) described the precarious balance between laughter and shame: "In laughter we always find an unavowed intention to humiliate." But the humor dissolves quickly, according to Bergson, if compassion is evoked in the audience: "Depict some fault, however trifling, in such a way as to arouse sympathy, fear or pity; the mischief is done and it is impossible for us to laugh" (p. 148).

In his 1964 book *The Act of Creation*, Arthur Koestler observed that "cruelty and boastful self-assertion are much in evidence" in humor that appeals to "children and primitives" and the same is true of historically earlier forms and theories of the comic" (p. 52). He gave a capsule history of derision/superiority theory:

> As laughter emerges with man from the mists of antiquity it seems to hold a dagger in its hand. There is enough brutal triumph, enough contempt, enough striking down from superiority in the records of antiquity and its estimates of laughter to presume that original laughter may have been wholly animosity. In the Old Testament (according to Mitchell) there are 29 references to laughter. . .13 are linked with scorn, derision or contempt and only two are 'born of joyful and merry heart.' A survey among American school children between the ages of 8 and 15 led to the conclusion that mortification or discomfort or hoaxing of others very readily caused laughter while a witty or funny remark often passed unnoticed (pp. 52-53).

Koestler maintained that even more sophisticated humor is basically hostile even though it "evokes mixed and sometimes contradictory feelings." Regardless of the context "it must contain one ingredient whose presence is indispensable: an impulse, however faint, of aggression or apprehension. It may be manifested in the guise of malice, derision, the veiled cruelty of condescension, or merely as an absence of sympathy with the victim of a joke" (ibid).

CRITIQUE: Derision/superiority theory is reductionistic, seeking to reduce all humor into one simple category with a simplistic common motive: superiority. It does not include all the varieties of humor. It is negativistic and depressive, seeing humor as malicious and destructive, an attack on the individual's dignity. It denies positive aspects of sharing pleasure, empathy and emotional support. Having studied this theory in considerable depth and written two books on humor (1922 and 1936) Max Eastman concluded: "It seems as though these authors never enjoyed a moment of hilarity and I am sure that they never came into cordial relations with a baby. For either of these experiences would have taught them more than all they have said in their discourses about laughter" (1922, p. 148).

DISAPPOINTMENT/FRUSTRATED EXPECTATION
Exemplar: Aristotle (384-322 BC)

Galett Burgess described derision and disappointment theories as "two main divisions" of the "several varieties of the Comic": "The first. . . is **frustrated expectation**. . .as if a train jumped the track arriving at an unexpected terminus. (The second) and undoubtedly the first cause in psychological development is the sense of superiority and cruelty" (Eastman, 1936, p. 339).

As Plato is generally credited with the first formal identification of derision theory, Aristotle is associated with disappointment theory or the theory of frustrated expectation. In the fifth chapter of his *Poetics,* Aristotle described the seeming contradiction in humor: ". . .in some defect or ugliness which is not painful or destructive. . .for example, the comic mask is ugly and distorted but does not imply pain" (Eastman, 1922, p. 124). This theory of humor best explains the "fun" of Hallowe'en with its "false faces," frightening costumes and gruesome "make believe" creatures. The terms "false face" and "make believe" characterize disappointment theory.

According to this theory, disappointments or frustrated expectations are perceived as funny. We know it's all "put on" or that we or others have been "set up" but "all in good fun." In this way amusement and theme parks remain popular "for children of all ages." Preschoolers and golden agers equally enjoy "the rides" and "thrills." Disney's Haunted House isn't really haunted, though for a few brief moments we indulge the child within and believe so, to be playfully frightened then suddenly released into reality again. Those of all ages walking from a "thrill ride" show all the body language of children "having fun": spontaneous smiles, animated gestures, bright-eyed and sprightly gait. We "make believe" it's terrifying (it is — tell the truth!) but we know we're really safe and it will end well.

W.C. Fields was a master at this type of humor and he described it as follows:

> It seems in general as though people laugh only at the unexpected and yet sometimes they laugh still harder exactly because they expect something. For instance, I play the part of a stupid and cocky person who has invented a burglar trap. I explain to the audience how I shall make friends with the burglar and invite him to sit down and talk things over, and I show how the instant his rear touches the chair bottom, a lever will release a huge iron ball which will hit him on the head and kill him instantly. From then on the audience knows what's coming. They know that I am going to forget about my invention and sit down in the chair myself. They begin laughing when I start toward the chair and their laugh is at its peak *before* the ball hits me. How do you explain that? (Eastman, 1936, pp. 93-94).

Derision theory would explain that by his own admission Fields enacted the role of "a stupid and cocky person" who, like Max Eastman's sheriff, "has it coming to him." The audience is shown what is **supposed** to happen **to the burglar,** a logical expectation. But the inventor's ego changes the expectation, frustrates it and transforms it into a wish for the inventor to get "zapped." The audience knows no one will be killed, that it's all "make believe." This is the secret of circus clown "pie in the face" humor and W.C. Fields's skit is more clownlike than the usual standup comedian routine, especially with its use of props and an absurd situation. Absurdity, costumes and props contribute to an unreal fantasy quality that allows an unpleasant theme (death, murder, violence) to become funny. The climax is anticipated with increasing laughter and arrives suddenly at peak excitement, concluding the action. Time and timing are critical. Anticipation spices the process, ensures interest and attention and builds emotional tone and excitement. As Eastman commented about practical jokes, much depends on "the abrupt collapse of an expectation and laughter follows the collapse" (1936, p. 94).

Johnny Carson's *Karnak the Magician* routine is a recurrent theme, reassuringly predictable. The audience expects Ed McMahon to be put down by *Karnak*—and they are not disappointed. They also know that the jokes and punch lines will be simple and require little concentration or close following to be understood. Abbott and Costello's "who's on first" routine, Ernie Kovac's *Nairobi Trio* skit, Jackie Gleason's "one of these days, Alice, POW!" line, like the weekly repeated radio routines of Jack Benny, Fred Allen, Fibber McGee and others involved frustrated expectations delivered much like W.C. Fields's silly invention in action and development. These redundant absurdities remained popular for years on radio and later on television, evidence of a common factor: as Aristotle hypothesized, the universal appeal of a frustrated expectation.

Monty Python, John Cleese, Gene Wilder, Richard Pryor and Mel Brooks continue this tradition. The essential ingredients are a funny (absurd or unusual) situation, with funny characters (exaggerated normals or bizarre), costumes and props which enrich the visual effect, growing expectation of mock danger or disaster, increasing excitement—and the critical mass is reached and the joke naturally goes to conclusion: BLAM! More experienced comedians have a gift of good timing, using silences, pacing of words, appropriate tone of voice and gestures and mannerisms which shape the action on stage and audience response and involvement. This is a Space Age explanation of what Aristotle described 2000 years ago: ". . .that is stated which we did not expect and we acknowledge it to be true" (Eastman, 1922, p. 129).

The ancient Greeks such as Plato and Aristotle were not alone in theorizing about the ultimate cause or origin of humor. Marcus Tullius Cicero (106-43 BC), orator (a "wordsmith"), statesman and philosopher, was aware of both derision and disappointment theories. "A joke, to be really amusing," he wrote, "has to be at someone's expense." Derision theory. "The funniest jokes are simply those in which we expect to hear one thing and then we hear another" (Allen, 1987), Disappointment/ Frustrated Expectation Theory. Across 2000 years, Cicero remains an able politician, a gifted contortionist who can sit on the fence but with both ears to the ground!

Eastman (1922) described a 3-step process of humor adapted from the work of the German psychologist A. Zeising:

1. **Shock** of "an object which seems to amount to something and yet does not."
2. **Countershock** in which we are "freed from the deception and recognize the nothingness of the object."
3. **Climax!** A "happy sense of superiority to that nothingness which makes us burst out laughing" (p. 141).

The philosophers Immanuel Kant (1724-1804) and Arthur Schopenhauer (1788-1860) preferred disappointment theory.

Kant wrote in his *Critique of Judgment* that "laughter is an affection arising from the sudden transformation of a strained expectation into nothing" (Eastman, 1922, p. 154). Kant told the story of a wealthy, snobbish merchant travelling on the ship carrying his goods. The ship was caught in a storm and sank. All the goods were lost but the merchant survived but "his wig turned white overnight." This tragedy is made tragicomic in the same way as Max Eastman's sheriff and W.C. Fields's burglar "hot seat." The protagonist is pompous and rich enough to sustain the loss of his goods. He got what he deserved, like the sheriff and inventor W.C. Fields. In 1819, Schopenhauer observed that "all laughter is occasioned by a paradox and therefore by unexpected subsumption. . .in words or actions. This, briefly stated, is the true expectation of the ludicrous" (ibid).

The following are excerpts of the opinions from others who supported disappointment/frustrated expectation theory, taken from Max Eastman's 1922 book *The Sense of Humor:*

The Scottish philosopher, Francis Hutcheson (1694-1746), commented that laughter is caused by "bringing together the images with contrary ideas as well as some resemblances to the principal idea" (p. 145). In his essay *On Wit and Humor* William Hazlitt observed that "we laugh at what only disappoints our expectations in trifles" (p. 164). Leon Dumont wrote: "We laugh every time our intelligence finds itself in the presence of facts which are of a nature to make us think of one and the same thing, that it is and that it is not" (p. 157). Charlie Chaplin as we learned in Chapter 1 described his technique as "telling the plain truth of things. . .I make them conscious of life. 'You think this is it, don't you?' I say, 'well, it isn't but this is, see?' And then they laugh" (p. 46).

Art Young: ". . .we laugh generally because we have seen or heard something that is at variance with custom. . . Of course, to enlightened imaginative people a sheeplike acceptance of custom is sometimes funnier than a departure from it, but enlightened, imaginative people are a small minority" (Eastman, 1936, p. 338).

Al Frueh: "I describe what I call humor this way. . .the 'possible impossible' or 'practical impractical'. . .you think it's going to work all right but it won't" (Eastman, 1936, p. 337).

Raskin (1985) described disappointment theory as an **incongruity-related** theory which requires two seemingly incompatible premises which humor suddenly bridges or fuses. He offers an example from

Woody Allen: "I don't know if I believe in an afterlife but I'm taking a change of underwear" (p. 39).

Eastman summarized the dynamics of disappointment theory:

> A word or series of words which seems and pretends to be heading toward a certain meaning and which 'leads us on' in the direction of that meaning, fails abruptly and with playful intent to get us there at all. It let us down. It leaves us flat. It April fools us. . .we find in failing a comic pleasure (1936, p. 53).

In addition to the slapstick, absurd level of humor described here, disappointment or frustrated expectation theory also includes a more sophisticated type. According to Eastman, it is a "mature and pointed wit, besides failing to arrive where we seemed to be going, we arrive somewhere else. And we find that somewhere else an interesting place to be. . ." (ibid).

EXAMPLES

In the first person (self-derision): "I'm troubled. I'm dissatisfied. I'm Irish" (Marianne Moore, last line of *Spencer's Ireland,* 1941, In Bartlett, 1968, p. 996).

In the second person (public at large): "To wear the arctic fox you have to kill it" (Marianne Moore, *The Arctic Ox (Or Goat),* 1959, ibid).

In the third person: "Tomorrow night I appear for the first time before a Boston audience — 4000 critics" (Mark Twain, letter to Pamela Clemens Moffet, November 9, 1869, in Bartlett, 1968, p. 759).

CRITIQUE: Disappointment theory is a better "fit" to slapstick visual "sight gags" and some other forms of verbal humor than derision theory and broadens the scope of derision theory with this added versatility. It is the first theory of humor to describe the "one two punch" of first impression (expectation) and surprise realization (disappointment or frustration) repeated though in greater detail by neoclassical and modern theories. It is, however, still basically negative, focussing on human weaknesses and foibles. It describes a 2-step process of integrating opposing premises (expectation followed by a surprise opposite) but it does not define the special relationship between them. It does not include all types of humor.

CHAPTER 3

NEOCLASSICAL THEORIES: PLEASURE-PAIN
AND INSTINCT-PHYSIOLOGICAL

Why did the Lord give us agility
If not to evade responsibility?

Ogden Nash (1902-19)
The face is familiar (1941)

PLEASURE-PAIN

Exemplar: Sigmund Freud (1856-1939)

SINCE 1900 two related theories of behavior have emerged: the **psychoanalytic theory** of Sigmund Freud and the **behavioristic theory** of John Broadus Watson, further developed by B.F. Skinner. Freud was a physician, Watson a psychologist. Neither was in the mainstream of their professions when they made known their ideas and both were confronted initially with considerable resistance. Freud commented: "to be proscribed from the compact majority a certain independence of judgment was obtained." Watson reported that his psychologist colleagues reacted to his work by "asking what it had to do with psychology!" The study of humor is in much the same state today, not in the mainstream of either psychiatry or psychology research.

Watson's work was a reaction to Freud's psychoanalytic theory and its reliance on "instinct" and "insight" and the theory of the **unconscious.** These were useful constructs for clinicians because they explained much of human motivation and behavior. They were resisted by researchers and behavioristic psychologists because they were untestable by laboratory methods and eluded statistical analysis. Freudian theory is still criticized for its lack of an empirical research basis compared to other psychotherapy systems. Watson focussed only on overt observable behavior. Nothing existed in the mind, he maintained, except overt observable behavior, which could be objectified, quantified, statistically analyzed and compared.

For Watson, Skinner and their followers, what's funny is learned, conditioned, reinforced from early life experience to the present. It is all external and accessible. Freud taught that much of behavior, including what is perceived as funny, is hidden and not readily accessible to us. He pictured the mind functioning like an iceberg, the majority of its contents below the level of consciousness (in the unconscious), inaccessible except by dream analysis, and, in his later writings, by analyzing wit and humor. What's funny is intuited from the dark lagoon of the mind. The conflict between Watson and Freud is reminiscent of the similar polarity between Locke and Leibnitz, between the **tabula rasa** "blank slate" mind and the nativist **monad.**

Both Watson and Freud agreed that the pursuit of pleasure and avoidance of pain is a powerful motivating force. For the behavioral psychologists, this provided the foundation of learning, conditioning, and reinforcement theories and they have amassed an impressive body of animal and human research in these areas. Freud focussed on "the pleasure principle," and showed mainly by case studies and his conclusions of them how we seek gratification and avoid discomfort in an "if it feels good, do it" regressive, instinctive pursuit. The psychoanalyst's concept of **regression** (to infantile pleasure) seems quite similar to behavioral psychologists **early learned behavior.** Instinct, a genetic factor, is still widely accepted by the "medical model" but remains quite unpopular with behavioristic psychologists. Psychoanalysts search for more insight while psychologists seek to neutralize and overcome reinforced behaviors. There is a bias in these two models inherent (no pun intended!) in the professional orientation and training of each.

There were antecedents to pleasure-pain theory before Watson and Freud. It is probable that throughout history people reacted with humor to the constraints of parents, authority figures, society or even rationality. Eastman (1922) quotes Charles Renouvier in observing that humor represents "deliverance from the constraints of rationality" (p. 185). In 1711, Lord Shaftesbury wrote an essay entitled *The Freedom of Wit and Humor* and in it commented:

The natural free spirits of ingenious men if imprisoned or controlled, will find out other ways of motion to relieve themselves in their constraint; and whether it be in burlesque, mimicry or buffoonery, they will be glad at any rate to vent themselves and be revenged on their constraints. . .'tis the persecuting spirit has raised the bantering one (Eastman, 1922, p. 184).

"The Comic," Alexander Bain wrote in his *The Emotions and the Will*, "starts from the Serious. The dignified, solemn, and stately attributes of things require in us a certain posture of rigid constraint; and if we are suddenly relieved from this posture, the rebound of hilarity ensues, as in the case of children set free from school. . . It is always a gratifying deliverance to pass from the severe to the easy. . .the comic conjunction is one form of this transition" (Eastman, 1922, p. 185).

In 1873, the physiologist Ewald Hecker described humor as "a rapid oscillation back and forth between pleasure and pain" (Eastman, 1922, p. 219). "The simultaneousness of the birth of the two feelings constitute the so-called point, without which the comic effect even of a joke or an anecdote is lost" (p. 221). Several examples come to mind from World War II. It seems a valid generalization that the death, destruction and privation of war clearly represents pain and oppose and are antagonistic to pleasure. The popularity of the cartoons of Bill Mauldin portraying two combat infantrymen using humor to cope confirms Hecker's pleasure-pain oscillation theory. Jokes of the time are also consistent with it:

Moments after an air raid alert in London, with everyone off the street and in underground shelters, an air raid warden called into the shelter doorway: "Is there anyone pregnant down there?" A woman's voice returned: "Give us a chance, Love, we've only been here a few minutes." Many of the British, frustrated over the inconveniences of the war and further irritated by the influx of so many American GIs, lamented that the "Yanks" were "overpaid, oversexed and over here." Much humor does oscillate between pleasure and pain.

In his book *Psychology, A Study of Mental Life*, R.S. Woodworth unknowingly moved toward a synthesis of the pleasure-pain approaches of Freud and Watson: "While laughing is a native response we learn what to laugh at, for the most part, just as we learn what to fear" (Eastman, 1936, p. 354). Both Freud and Watson agreed to the role and effect, the great power of pleasure and pain in changing behavior. In both animals and humans the strong tendency to pursue and prolong pleasure and to avoid pain is easily observable and clearly demonstrated. Psychoanalytic

and behavioristic theories are more similar than dissimilar with respect
to pleasure-pain aspects of humor.

Freud provided more descriptive information on humor than Watson
or Skinner, producing his 170-page *Wit and Its Relation to the Unconscious*.
It was written, fifteen years after his major work *The Interpretation of
Dreams* which described dreams as "the royal road to the unconscious."
He felt that humor was also a direct link to the unconscious. Certainly
vulgarisms and colloquialisms confirm more than deny Freud's oral,
anal and genital phases. Common oral activities are gum chewing,
nailbiting, smoking, drinking from soda or beer bottles, and oral sex.
The anal phase is evident in expressions such as "Oh shit" (fact: frequent
last words of pilots before crashes! Not "Oh God!" significantly), "up
yours. . .bullshit. . .what's the poop. . .my ass is draggin'. . .bowels in an
uproar. . .shit disturber. . .don't give a shit. . .lower than whale shit" and
the French preference for **merde** rather than "cussing" in the name of deity. Dirty jokes daily illustrate our preoccupation with sex and directly
connects to the pleasure principle.

In his 1956 book *Comedy,* Wylie Sypher wrote that "comedy unerring-
ly finds the lowest common denominator." He maintained that this is especially true for the so-called "dirty joke." Humor is, according to
Sypher, a "reducing-agent that sends us reeling back from our properties
to the realm of Old Pan." He suggested that "any group of men and
women, no matter how refined, will sooner or later laugh at a 'dirty'
joke, the question being not whether they will laugh but when or at precisely what. . .under exactly what coefficient of stress a code of 'decency'
breaks apart" and we "fall steeply down to the recognition of our inalien-
able flesh" (p. 208).

Freud was, despite criticism of the bias in some of his work, a keen
observer and a skilled reporter of human behavior. He continues to be a
major influence in psychiatry. Ads and TV commercials apply his orientation to the pleasure principle and to covert sexuality to sell a great variety of products. That these strategies succeed lends credibility to
Freudian theory, as do "Freudian slips" and oral-anal-genital references
in everyday life. The film classic *Spellbound* and more recently *Brazil,* are
rich in Freudian symbolism and dreamlike imagery and further attest to
Freud's continued influence on the arts, the marketplace, and our attitudes and behaviors. Alec Guinness does a masterful and humorous
enactment of Freud in the film *Lovesick,* with Dudley Moore as psychiatrist, Elizabeth McGovern as his patient and the late John Huston as his
mentor. *Spellbound* is more serious than humorous, *Brazil* about 50-50

and *Lovesick* more humorous than serious, demonstrating the variety and versatility of humor.

The historical and theoretical significance and the influence of Freudian theory merits a more detailed review. Arieti (1976) observed: "Of all the discussions of the phenomenon of wit, the one by Freud seems to me the most illuminating and the most far-reaching in its implications" (p. 102). What follows is taken from A.A. Brill's 1938 translation and all page references are to Brill's *Basic Writings of Sigmund Freud* (Modern Library). Care has been taken to use Freud's own words to describe his ideas.

Freud began his analysis of humor by noting its importance and also that it has been ignored: "our philosophical inquiries have not awarded to wit the important role that it plays in our mental life" (p. 633). He defines wit as "playful judgment" then applies it to the arts where the esthetic attitude is playful, free to express itself. He quotes from the humorist Jean Paul that "freedom begets wit and wit begets freedom. Wit is nothing more than the free play of ideas." He observes that "since time immemorial the definition of wit is the ability to discover similarities in dissimilarities, hidden similarities" and that wit "expresses itself in words that will not stand the test of strict logic or of the ordinary mode of thought and expression. . .(but) more by leaving its truth unstated" (pp. 633-636).

He provided an overview of other definitions of wit. He credited Vischer with adding the element of "surprising quickness," Fischer who claimed it involved more contrast than similarities and Kraepelin for contrast through speech associations. He focussed on the sense to nonsense transformation of Lipps who wrote that "what we accept one moment as senseful we later perceive as perfect nonsense." Lipps maintained that this is the origin of "the comic element." We accept a meaning, interpretation, or perceptual or value set which is suddenly decisively changed or challenged, resulting in another meaning, several meanings or no meaning at all.

At this point definitions other than from Freud are inserted because of their relevance. Arieti (1976) referred to J.C. Gregory's 1924 definition of wit as "quick, vivid illumination of truth" and that of E. Froeschels in 1948: ". . .the means by which unexpressed philosophical truths that actually have been known to us from the time of our birth become ripe for expression" (p. 102). Eastman (1922) quoted a reference to wit as "assembled with quickness and variety" from John Locke (1632-1704), the British philosopher. Locke also theorized the mind as a "tabula rasa" or blank slate empty at birth and devoid of meaning except for the learning and conditioning in one's life, basically a behavioristic construct. He and the German mathematician and philosopher, Gottfried Wilhelm von Leibnitz (1646-1716), debated the nature of mind and consciousness.

Leibnitz believed everything and everyone is a **monad** and reflects the universe whether or not that thing or creature is conscious of it. This is more similar to Freud's unconscious. Here we see how philosophy as well as psychology relates to a study of humor. Ironically, we laugh at jokes without such in-depth analysis, and Freud also observed this: "When one laughs very heartily about a joke he is not in the best mood to investigate its technique" (p. 658).

Freud tended to analyze in great depth and it should not be surprising that he coined terms such as **wit-work,** the process or mechanics of wit formation, **understanding-work,** wit conception and meaning, **word-wit** based on humorous use of words, **thought-wit** humor from subjects made funny or funny situations, **harmless-wit,** just for fun and **tendency-wit,** wit with an ulterior motive or hidden agenda. He classified wit as a part of humor, humor being more global. Wit can be analyzed by its effect and the following differentiates **harmless-wit** from **tendency-wit:**

> It is easy to guess the character of the witticism by the kind of reaction that wit exerts on the hearer. Sometimes wit is wit for its own sake and serves no other particular purpose; then again, it places itself at the service of such a tendency and it becomes tendentious. Only that form of wit. . . runs the risk of ruffling people who do not wish to hear it (p. 688).

"Wherever wit is not a means to its end, i.e., harmless," Freud wrote, "it is either **hostile wit** serving as an aggression, satire for defense, or it is **obscene wit,** wit serving as a sexual exhibition" (p. 693). Wit can also be used aggressively to neutralize hostility, such as Brill's story of a Kentucky abolitionist on a train to Ohio. "You tryin' to free the niggers?" a prejudiced country preacher asked. "Yes," the abolitionist replied. "Why you doin' that here? Why don't you do that in Kentucky?" the preacher charged. "Are you trying' to save souls from Hell?" the abolitionist asked. "I sure am," came the proud reply. "Then," the abolitionist said, "Why don't you go there?" (p. 698).

Freud listed the "techniques" of **thought-wit:**

displacement
faulty thinking
absurdity
indirect expression
representation through the opposite

Especially noteworthy is Freud's comment that "each and all of these are also found in the technique of dreams. The dream is indebted to displacement for its strange appearance which hinders us from recognizing in it the continuation of our waking thoughts" (p. 686). He elaborated this idea:

> Indirect expression, the substitution of the dream-thought by an allusion, by a trifle or by a symbolism analogous to comparison is just exactly what distinguishes the manner of expression of the dream from our waking thoughts. Such a far-reaching agreement as sound between the means of wit-work and those of dream-work can scarcely be accidental (p. 687).

After defining and analyzing wit, Freud considered humor and he characterized it as "one of the highest psychic functions. . .a means to gain pleasure. . .and to liberate painful affects" (p. 797). He reflected on the varieties of pleasure humor provides:

> I can enjoy the pleasure of humor originating in myself without feeling the necessity of imparting it to another (or for) certain insight. . . sympathetic understanding. . .coarsest gallows or grim-humor. . . In the case of the rogue who did not wish to take cold on the way to the gallows we roar with laughter (p. 798).

He felt that "the forms of humor are extraordinarily varied according to the nature of the emotional feeling which is economized in favor of humor" (p. 800). He saw humor as a potential weapon against obstacles to pleasure when "fused with wit or any other form of the comic" (p. 801).

Freud's summary of the techniques of wit:

I. Condensation
  (a) with mixed or fused words
  (b) with modification or substitution
II. Application of the same material
  (c) The whole and the part
  (d) Change of order
  (e) Slight modification
  (f) Same words used in full or colorless sense
III. Double meaning
  (g) Name and verbal significance
  (h) Metaphorical and verbal meaning
  (i) True double meaning (play on words)
  (j) Ambiguous meaning
  (k) Double meaning with allusion

Condensation with substitutive function by mixed or fused words.
Freud described Heine's character, Hirsch Hyacinth, who boasts that the

Baron Rothschild "treated me just as I were an equal, quite **famillionaire**" (p. 640-641). It's a play on words based on **condensation** of **familiar,** the way he was treated, and **ionnaire** from millionaire, to connote treatment as an equal. From Disraeli: "Old persons are apt to fall into **anecdotage.**" The Christmas season is the **alcoholidays** (p. 642).

Condensation with modification and substitution. A person critical of another says "Yes, vanity is one of his four Achilles heels" (p. 644). The implication is that he is not only weak but more animal than human. Of a retiring Minister of Agriculture: "Like Cincinnatus of old he retires to his place **in front of** the plow" (p. 645). He's more an ass, an ox, than a person.

Application of the same material. A convicted thief laments that one has to be a "lively hood for a livelihood" (p. 647). "How goes it?" the blind man is asked. "As you can see" the blind man replies. To the question "Do you call it kind when debts go unpaid?" comes the response "I call that **unremitting** kindness." And finally, the aphorism: "The undertaker always carries out what he undertakes" (pp. 647-649).

Double meaning, play on words. From Shakespeare, *Henry IV:* "Discharge thyself of our company, Pistol" and "for Suffolks' Duke may he suffocate." Freud comments: ". . .no violence is done to the word. It is not torn into syllables. It need not undergo any modifications. . .it can express two meanings just as it stands." Other examples: A doctor to the husband of an ailing wife: "I don't like her looks." The husband's reply: "I haven't liked her looks for a long time." A man who "forever sang one tune" was asked why he did so. "Because it haunts me," he replied. "No wonder," the questioner responds, "you're continually murdering it." Dr. Johnson, referring to a university "poor in purse but prolific in degrees" wished that "it persevere in its present plan that it may become rich by degrees" (pp. 650-651).

Ambiguous meaning. Comment on an apathetic student who "could pass nothing but water."

Freud described examples of the variety of forms of humor (enumeration mine):

1. Puns	8. Outdoing-wit
2. Displacements	9. Indirect allusion
3. Nonsense	10. Omission
4. False logic	11. Comparison
5. Automatic errors	12. Peculiar attributes
of thought	13. Reproduction of old
6. Unification	liberties
7. Contrast	14. Smutty (dirty) joke

1. **Puns,** Freud observed, were "generally counted as the lowest form of wit." Fischer described a pun as "a bad play on words, for it does not play with the word as a word but merely as a sound." Freud offers the example of Agassiz, the great naturalist, who when presented by his students with an insect deliberately assembled from parts of many others and asked to identify it replied: "It's a humbug." Brill refers to a critic who described a play as "so poor the first act had to be rewritten. Now it's rerotten" (pp. 655-656).

2. **Displacements.** To "have you taken a bath?" the reply: "Why, is one missing?" (p. 657). A salesman trying to sell a horse said it was so fast "you can leave home at 4 AM and be in Monticello at 6:30." The prospective buyer replied: "What'll I do in Monticello at 6:30?" (p. 662).

3. **Nonsense.** Freud tells the story of Ike, a bright young man serving in the artillery but who wasn't doing well with military duties. His superior tells him: "Ike, why don't you buy a cannon and make yourself independent?" (p. 663). The nonsense here allows the superior to comment on Ike's ineptitude at military tasks but also to acknowledge his abilities in other areas better suited to civilian pursuits.

4. **False logic** or in Freud's words "Sophistic faulty thinking." There was a great religious leader in Cracow who, while praying, had a vision of a colleague dying in Lemberg, a distant city. He turned in mid-prayer to the congregation and announced what he had seen. They went into deep mourning until word came from Lemberg that the man was alive and well. Confronted with this fact, a loyal follower observed: "Ah, but to look from Cracow to Lemberg was wonderful anyhow" (p. 668).

5. **Automatic errors of thought.** A matchmaker and prospective husband visited the home of an eligible young lady. The matchmaker pointed to a "handsome silver set" as a sign of the family's wealth. The prospective husband suggested it may have been borrowed just for the occasion. "What an idea," the matchmaker replies, "who would lend them anything?" (p. 669).

6. **Unification.** Fischer described this technique as one in which "experience consists in experiencing what one does not care to experience." Rousseau wrote a poem "to posterity." Voltaire reviewed it and commented: "It will not reach its destination." A baker said to a tavernkeeper who had a sore finger: "I guess your finger got into your beer." The tavernkeeper replied: "No, I got some of your bread under my fingernail." The Emperor Augustus saw a man in the crowd "who bore a striking resemblance to himself." He asked him: "Was your mother ever employed in my home?" The reply: "No Sire, but my father was." The Duke Karl of Wurtemberg asked a dyer: "Can you color my white horse blue?"

The reply: "Yes, Sire, if the animal can stand the boiling." And Fischer observed that "human life is divided into two halves: during the first one looks forward to the second and during the second one looks backwards to the first" (pp. 670-672). Freud observed that "it is essentially unification which forms the basis of the so-called repartee of wit. . .using the defense for aggression and 'turning the tables' " (pp. 670-672).

7. **Contrast,** what Freud referred to as "representation through the opposite," and he offers three examples. Frederick the Great summoned a Silesian clergyman who reportedly could communicate with the dead. "Can you call up ghosts?" the Emperor asked. "At your pleasure, Majesty," the clergyman responded, "but they won't come." A child visiting the Wax Museum saw the figure of the Duke of Wellington on a horse. "Which is the Duke and which is the horse?" the child asked. "Just as you like, my child," the guide answered, "you pay your money and you take your choice" (pp. 672-673). Lichtenberg allegedly gave this eulogy:

> The attributes of the greatest men were all united in him. Like Alexander, his head was tilted to one side; like Caesar, he always had something in his hair. He could drink coffee like Leibnitz and once settled in his armchair he forgot eating and drinking like Newton and like him, had to be awakened. He wore a wig like Dr. Johnson and like Cervantes, the fly of his trousers was always open (p. 673).

8. **Outgoing-wit.** In this technique "contradiction takes the place of an exaggerated confirmation." Freud referred to Mark Anthony's speech at the death of Caesar which by repetition of contradictory remarks built to the crescendo of paradox in the line "For Brutus was an honorable man." Freud summarized this technique as "the only technique that is characteristic of irony is representation through the opposite" (pp. 674-675).

9. **Indirect allusion.** Two wealthy businessmen enjoyed great success through questionable means. They commissioned an artist to paint their portraits which were hung side by side on the wall. Entertaining a great art critic, they asked his opinion of the paintings. He studied them, nodding as if something was missing, and then pointed to the empty wall between the paintings and said: "Where is the Saviour?" (p. 676).

10. **Omission.** This is comparable to condensation without substitutive formation and a form of allusion, according to Freud. He considers the following as a "genuine and correct allusion-witticism": "A wife is like an umbrella, at worst one may also take a cab." Heine's Hirsch Hyacinth's "twisting of words" provides "a veritable wasp's nest of stinging

allusions" such as "I am a practicus and you are a diarrheticus" and "he has the same experience as the ostrich. . .when it sticks its head into the sand so that only its backside is visible. . .would have done better if he had stuck his backside into the sand and shown us his head" (pp. 678-680).

11. **Comparison.** In this technique, "comparisons are strikingly grouped, often in absurd combinations." As Lichtenberg observed, "it is almost impossible to carry the torch of truth through a crowd without singeing somebody's beard." Another example from Lichtenberg: "Everyone has a moral backside which does not show except under the stress of necessity and which is covered as long as possible with the pants of good breeding" (pp. 682-684).

12. **Peculiar attributions.** From Heine: "Her face resembles a kodex palimpsestus where under the new block-lettered text of a church father peel forth the half-obliterated verses of an ancient Hellenic erotic poet" (p. 685).

13. **Reproduction of old liberties.** Student sprees and "skylarking," college cheers and songs, class reunions and scientific congresses fall in this classification. "The student attempts to preserve that pleasure which results from freedom of thought," Freud wrote, "a freedom of which he is more and more deprived through scholastic discipline." Freud characterized graduates returning for nostalgic reunions and reminiscences of "the good old times" as feeling themselves students again, compensating for "added mental inhibitions" after graduation (p. 718).

14. **Sense in nonsense.** Freud held that there are "two firmly established points in the determination of wit—its tendency to carry through the pleasureful play, and its effort to guard it against the criticism of reason—make it perfectly clear why the individual witticism, even though it appear nonsensical from one point of view, must appear full of meaning or at least acceptable to another." A joke is "missed" when the punch line meaning is missed or misunderstood and it is then "relegated to the category of 'nonsense.' " Freud concluded:

> The psychogenesis of wit has taught us that the pleasure of wit arises from word-play or from the liberation of nonsense and that the sense of wit is meant not only to guard this pleasure against suppression through reason (p. 721).

15. **Smutty (dirty) jokes.** "The smutty joke," Freud wrote, "is directed toward a certain person who excites one sexually and who becomes cognizant of the speaker's excitement by listening." The speaker hopes the listener also becomes sexually excited: "There is no doubt that

the original motive of the smutty joker was the pleasure of seeing the sexual displayed." But Freud points out "the listener may react with shame and embarrassment." If, on the other hand, a woman yields to a man "smutty speech is short-lived for it gives way to the sexual act." If the woman resists there is likely to be a "defense reaction" and "sexually exciting speech changes into obscene wit. . .becomes distinctly hostile and cruel and utilizes the sadistical components of the sexual instinct against the hindrance" (pp. 693-694).

Alcohol. While not classified a technique of humor, Freud commented on the effect of alcohol on the humor process: "Reason, which has stifled the pleasure in nonsense, has become so powerful, that not even temporarily can it be abandoned without a toxic agency. . .hilarious humor, whether due to endogenous origin or whether produced toxically weakens the inhibiting forces among which is reason and thus again makes accessible pleasure sources" (p. 718).

THE PLEASURE MECHANISM

Wit, according to Freud, eludes, overcomes and disinhibits "inner resistances" and obstacles to pleasure. "Wit makes use of a means of connection which is rejected by and carefully avoided in serious thinking." The pleasure mechanism finds something familiar, acceptable, permissible in what is being discussed. "To discover the familiar," Freud commented, "is pleasurable and it is not difficult to recognize such pleasure as economy-pleasure and to refer it to the economy of psychic expenditure" (pp. 712-714).

Sypher (1956) wrote that comedy is its own catharsis, that "after discharging our inhibited impulses in folly we regain the sanity that is worn away by everyday gestures" (p. 222). Using derision theory as a referent but moving into Freudian theory, Sypher held that malice is "one of the many obscure motives for laughing" but laughing is "a release from restraint. . .our hysteric effort to adjust our repulsion from and our attraction to a situation" (p. 202).

PLAY

As Freud saw it, before wit there was play or jest. Play appears in children "while they are learning how to use words and connect thoughts." This pleasure originates in "repetition of similarities, the re-discovery of the familiar, sound associations, etc. which may be ex-plained as an unexpected economy of psychic expenditure." Its symptom is laughter and the laughter is, in behavioristic psychology terms, rein-forcing: "These resulting pleasures urge the child to practice playing and impel him to continue without regard for the meaning of the words or the connections between sentences." Word-play is the "first step of wit" and is curtailed by criticism and reason "rejected as senseless (and). . .by reason it becomes impossible." Only accidentally "it is possible to derive pleasure from those sources." In adults it slips through and is "merged into a playful mood which, as in the case of merriment in the child, re-moves inhibitions." Adult wit development is driven by two impulses, to elude reason and to "substitute for the adult an infantile state of mind" (p. 719-720).

JEST

"The object of jest," Freud wrote, "is to bring about the resultant plea-sure of playing and at the same time appease the protesting reason which strives to suppress the pleasant feeling." To achieve this, "the senseless combination of words or absurd linking of thoughts must make sense." According to Freud, "jest makes use of almost all the technical means of wit." He differentiates jest from wit by the "pith of the sentence . . .does not need to be valuable, new or even good. . .though what it may say is obsolete, superfluous and useless. The most conspicuous fac-tor of the jest is the gratification it affords by making possible that which reason forbids. . .from the beginning its object is to remove inner inhibi-tions and thereby render productive those pleasure-sources which have become inaccessible" (p. 720). Freud offered these examples of jest: Phy-sics Professor Kastner at Gottingen in the 16th century, welcomed a stu-dent names Warr who was 30 years old with: "So I have the honor of seeing the Thirty Years' War?" Rokitansky, asked his sons' vocations: "Two are healing and two are howling" (two were physicians and two were singers).

JEST AND WIT

The "essential character" of wit, Freud taught, "could almost be ex-plained by means of the jest." Effective wit provides a "general feeling of satisfaction without our being able to decide offhand which part of the pleasure comes from the witty form and which part from the excellent thought contained in the context." Wit "sets itself up against an inhibiting and restrictive power or against critical judgment." Jest "serves to produce pleasure only" whereas "wit is never purposeless even if the thought contained therein has no tendency and merely serves a theoretical, intellectual interest" (pp. 721-722).

Freud considered wit "a powerful psychic factor. The great tendencies and impulses of our psychic life enlist its services for their own purposes." The "original purposeless wit" of early childhood "which began as play becomes related in a secondary manner to tendencies from which nothing that is formed in psychic life can escape for any length of time." This playfulness drive, as in all humor according to Freud, "overcomes inhibitions of shame and decorum by the pleasure premium it offers." When used aggressively it "changes the original indifferent hearers into active haters and scorners." When cynicism and skepticism are used "it shatters the respect for institutions and truths in which the hearer had believed."

WIT, DREAMS AND THE UNCONSCIOUS

Dream-work is a "structure of thoughts, mostly very complicated. . . built up during the day and not brought to settlement — a day remnant (which). . .threatens to disturb sleep." It is "transformed into a dream by the dream-work and in this way rendered harmless to sleep. . .cast into the form of a wish" (p. 746).

Condensation is the dream-work process which allows representation only of the "raw material" of ideas and not the "thought-relations." It "reserves the freedom of leaving the latter out." The material of dream-thought "experiences an extraordinary compression or condensation." Words used "combine different meanings in their sounds." Newly formed "common points of condensation become manifest" (pp. 748-749).

Displacement. "What occupies the center of the manifest dream is endowed with vivid sensory intensity" becomes "peripheral" or "secondary" (or vice versa) and causes the dream to appear "out of proportion" (p. 749).

Freud described "transformation into expressive activity, condensation and displacement" as "the three great functions of dream-work."

WIT AND DREAMS

Dreams are personal and asocial. They have "nothing to tell anyone else, having originated in an individual as a compromise between conflicting psychic forces and it remains incomprehensible to the person." A dream "must guard against being understood as it would then be destroyed; it can only exist in disguised form. . .in undecipherable distortions." Wit, on the other hand, is "the most social of all those psychic functions whose aim is to gain pleasure." It is therefore more intelligible than dreams. Sometimes its condensation and displacement are "to no greater extent than can be deciphered." Wit and dreams are "different spheres of the psychic life. . .widely separated categories of the psychological system" (p. 761).

The dream is a wish; wit is developed play. Dreams relate to the great interests of life, "a regression detour of hallucinations." Wit "seeks pleasure from free and unencumbered activities." Dreams "guard against pain" while wit "serves to acquire pleasure' in these two aims all our psychic activities meet." Nonsense or absurdity in dreams "stands for the judgment: 'it's pure nonsense.'" In wit, nonsense and absurdity "is an end in itself. . .reviving the old pleasure" (pp. 758, 761). Both dreams and wit tap the unconscious, dreams in a more cleverly disguised form and wit as a "peculiar unconscious elaboration (of). . .the infantile type of the mental process" (p. 754).

Sypher (1956) offered several examples from art and drama relevant to Freudian theory: Picasso's *Guernica,* "a shocking comic strip in black and white. .like a bad dream," Kafka's novels were "nightmares." Shakespeare: "In the language of the sleeping self," Banquo warned MacBeth, "the instruments of darkness tell us truths." Surrealism is "dream play. . .involuntary 'free associations' of the hidden life which have their own absurdity and improbability." Caricature "employs a dreamwork charged with the spell of mania" and Van Gogh, "one of the most potent forms of caricature as Michelangelo's unfinished sculptures." Many artists, Sypher contended, exploit their dreams into art. "The dream is nonsensical and free, having none of the logic and sobriety of our waking selves; the very incongruity of the dream world is comic. Freud interprets the dream and the jest as a discharge of powerful psychic energies, a glimpse into the abyss of the self" (pp. 198-199).

WIT AND THE COMIC

Freud traced the origin of the comic to the clown, an "immoderate and inappropriate" character with "excessive energy." He suggests that the spontaneous motions made by a bowler after releasing the ball represents "ideational mimicry." The same is true for professional mimes, puppets, making faces and playfully wiggling one's ears (pp. 768-769). The brevity of wit is a "marked and distinctive characteristic feature. . .a tendency to economize. . .sign of the unconscious elaboration which the thought of wit has undergone. . .condensation. . .localization in the unconscious" (pp. 752-753).

HUMOR

Freud saw humor as a defense and a change agent to transform pain to pleasure, temporarily regressing us back to the joy of childhood when we could unabashedly experience pure pleasure. He considered humor the "loftiest of the defense functions." It seeks ways to withdraw energy from painful material and "through discharge" change it into pleasure. It is a "connection to the infantile" because it was in childhood we experienced "intensively painful affects over which today as grownups we would laugh." It is "elevation of ego evidenced by humoristic displacement. . .in the neurotic process of repression" (pp. 801-802).

Sypher (1956) concluded "man cannot live by reason alone or forever under the rod of moral obligation, the admonition of the superego. . . The comedian is the self behaving as prodigal and bohemian. . .Comedy is a momentary and publicly useful resistance to authority and an escape from its pressures; and its mechanism is a free discharge of repressed psychic energy or resentment, through laughter (p. 241).

BEHAVIORISM — A PARTING SHOT!

According to B.F. Skinner (1987) behavioristic psychology remains strongly opposed to introspectively derived rules and theories of mental life or those attributed to any organ (like the brain), organ system or to body chemistry. The ancient Greeks believed the heart **(thumos)** was the body's center for thoughts, feelings and survival needs. We know this is not so but we still use the heart as a symbol of life and references can still be heard ascribing thought and emotions to it: "broke my heart. . .in your heart you know I'm right. . .love with all your heart. . .pull heart strings. . .broken heart," etc. If there is any doubt about this, check the greeting cards before Valentine's Day.

Loeb's 1916 research on tropism, an organism's movements reactive to external stimuli, the work of Mach in 1915 and Bridgman in 1927, Bertrand Russell's 1927 book *Philosophy* and Skinner's 1931 paper on the reflex were all precursors of a logical positivist approach to the study of behavior. Other researchers moved from this central path: Watson into habits, then conditioning, Lashley into the nervous system, Tolman to cognitive maps, and Clark Hull into neurophysiology. The Loeb to Skinner connection is pure behaviorism. The others drifted toward a more internal locus, in the brain, physiology or neurophysiology.

Skinner's orientation is entirely external as it has always been just as Freud's was and remained entirely internal. For Skinner there is no response without a stimulus and a response is a "function of variables in the fields of conditioning, motivation and emotion. . .**outside** the organism" which he termed "third variables" but which Tolman called "intervening variables" (p. 781). Skinner maintains that both verbal and nonverbal behaviors are formed by contingencies of reinforcement, that these can be studied by operant analysis. There are two promising fields for such study: "self-observation," the way verbal contingencies reinforce private events; "self-management or thinking in which problems are solved by manipulating either contingencies (as in practical problem solving) or rules (as in "reasoning") (p. 782).

Skinner sees "three formidable obstacles" which block the path of "an experimental analysis of behavior":

1. **Humanistic psychology,** because "operant analysis replaces creation with variations and selection" and "there is no longer any need for a creative mind or plan, or for purpose or goal direction."

2. **Psychotherapy,** which speaks "everyday English which is heavy laden with references to internal causes. . . Instead of investigating the early lives of their patients or watching them with their families, friends or business associates, they ask them what has happened and how they feel about it. . .then construct theories in terms of memories, feelings and states of mind. . .and say that an analysis of behavior in terms of environmental events lacks 'depth.' "

3. **Cognitive psychology** or **cognitive science** because of its preference for rule-governed and not contingency-shaped behavior and its

consequent emphasis on information theory, computer technology and brain function as models for memory retrieval and thinking.

Skinner attacks humanistic psychology as an "antiscience stance," psychotherapy as having "practical exigencies," and cognitive science as a modern version of the ancient Greek belief in a single organ. He concludes:

> For at least 2500 years philosophers and psychologists have proceeded on the assumption that because they were themselves behaving organisms they had privileged access to the causes of their behavior. But has any introspectively observed feeling or state of mind yet been unambiguously identified in either mental or physical terms? Has any ability or trait of character been statistically established to the satisfaction of everyone? . . .has anyone ever explained how the mind works on the body or the body on the mind? (p. 785).

CRITIQUE. Pleasure-pain theory analyzes humor in greater scope and detail than derision or disappointment models. There is an empirical research base from behavioristic psychology to substantiate learning and conditioning aspects of humor. Freudian theory is substantiated from readily available observations of everyday behaviors. There is much to be said for humor as a pursuit of pleasure, as early learned behavior (Skinner) or regression to infantile gratification (Freud). Its major contribution is its attempt to trace the origin of humor in the joy of infancy and systematically classify the varieties of humor by type, form and technique. It is also the first theory of humor that can be empirically demonstrated in both animals and humans. But unlike animals, humans think, do and say funny things and this theory does not satisfactorily explain why this is so. It explains much but not all humor and in this respect it is narrow and oversimplified.

INSTINCT-PHYSIOLOGY THEORY
Exemplar: Charles Darwin (1809-1882)

Pleasure-pain theory is psychophysiological, involving both thoughts (cognition) and feelings (affect). **Instinct,** as used in terms of this theory traces humor not to overt behavior or an unconscious mind but to a specific genetic-physiological trait. **Playfulness** is most often used to qualitatively describe the outward or behavioral manifestations of that genetic trait. Sypher (1956) wrote that "we have, in short, been forced to admit that the absurd is more than ever inherent in human existence;

that is, the irrational, the inexplicable, the surprising, the nonsensical — in other words, the comic" (p. 195).

Max Eastman devoted an entire chapter of his 1922 book *The Sense of Humor* to applying Darwinian theory to humor. Eastman credited Lactantius with associating laughter with "satisfactions of the social instinct, asserting that animals as well as men are endowed with this faculty and express their 'mutual love and indulgence' with 'a kind of smile'. . .this obvious truth disappeared out of literature and all the philosophers began to identify laughter with comic enjoyment. They all followed in the footsteps of Aristotle" (p. 206).

Charles Darwin "with his gift of pure observation. . .rediscovered the obvious truth that men laugh when they are happy and laid a new basis for the understanding of this whole subject" (ibid). In Darwin's own words:

> Laughter seems primarily to be the expression of mere joy and happiness. We clearly see this in children at play who are almost incessantly laughing. With young persons past childhood, when they are in high spirits, there is always much meaningless laughter. The laughter of the gods is described by Homer as "the exuberance of their celestial joy after their daily banquet". . .Idiots and imbecile persons likewise afford good evidence that laughter or smiling primarily expresses mere happiness of joy (ibid, pp. 206-207).

Darwin also described a secondary "laughter at the ludicrous. . .an expression of human pleasure and satisfaction." He suggested that these expressions are "surviving remnants of complete acts which were useful to the species at some point in its earlier history." These "acts" were to Darwin "primary or essential" and emotions were "the interior quality which belongs to them." Eastman differentiated acts from feelings in a Darwinian context: "We no longer say that the attitude of alertness and a preparation for flight 'expresses the emotion' of fear. We say that fear is a feeling which attends this attitude and those preparations" (ibid, pp. 207-208).

Initially, Darwin had difficulty confirming this theoretical construct. He could not isolate "any useful instinctive activity which occurred at moments of special satisfaction" which would account for innervation of all the various muscles employed in smiles and laughter." He had to "discover what instinct it is" which differs so markedly from hostility and attack and instead produces an "agreeable" neuromuscular response (accepting eye contact, facies, gestures, mannerisms) sometimes with vocalized sound. Eastman's interpretation: "To exchange a smile is to do something, and short of kissing or devouring one another, nothing more with these particular muscles can very well be done." These behaviors suggest a **social instinct** or an **instinct of playfulness** which "finds its stimulus in mere companionship or friendly meeting" (ibid, p. 209). According to Darwin:

> We can see in a vague manner how the utterance of sounds of some kind would naturally become associated with a pleasurable state of mind; for throughout a large part of the animal kingdom vocal or instrumental sounds are employed either as the means for a joyful meeting between the parents and their offspring and between the attached members of the same community (ibid, pp. 209-210).

Eastman was an enthusiastic proponent of the instinct theory of humor. He considered laughter a "means of social communication of pleasure" which has "acquired almost a kind of identity in our nervous sytems with the state of joy or satisfaction in general. . .one of the most necessary gifts we have." He maintained that "the fortieth day. . .is the birth of laughter. . .not an act of rejection but of acceptance. It is not pain but pleasure. It is not derision but delight. . .a smile of dawning welcome. . .the native original of all smiles and all laughter" (ibid, pp. 7-9).

According to instinct theory play and playfulness are by observation in animals and humans "more spontaneous and instinctive than conscious and deliberate. . .a hereditary gift." Eastman described the active hand muzzling of a dog "in playful mock attack" an everyday example of how the dog "will perceive and adopt the play-attitude without previous instruction and with hardly the possibility of error. . .just as early and just as mysteriously well as he can fight." The dog doesn't bite because he achieves "full satisfaction without it" (ibid, pp. 12-13). In the wild, on the farm and in zoos the playful mock attacks of birds and animals with their peers, especially among the young, is readily observed. The same is true for dolphins and whales. These behaviors are suggested as evidence that a playful instinct exists.

Instinct theories claim affection is as powerful a drive as the predatory instinct. "Playful failures don't cut or destroy," Eastman commented, "instead of hurting they make us laugh. . .an act of welcoming a playful shock or disappointment. . .the character of mortal combat without suffering" (ibid, p. 14, 17). Playfully attempting to wrest a favorite object from one's dog is met with firmly clenched jaw and snarls but—important for instinct theory—both pet and owner know it's "all in fun." In his *Descent of Man,* Darwin wrote that "dogs show what may be fairly called a sense of humor as distinct from mere play" (ibid, p. 192). He referred to feigning a ball throw and a mock attack receiving mock defensive behavior. Humans at some spirited sports events exhibit "mock combat" behaviors in their nonverbal (jumping up, clenched fists) and verbal behaviors ("kill'em"). Eastman described this as "the fighting-glory theory of laughter: Men would like to think. . .they are ferocious gorillas, gnashing their teeth and thumping their chests and exulting over a broken foe" (Eastman, 1936, p. 352).

Eastman also cited the early onset of humor as an example of its hereditary origin: "laughter. . .appears so early and so spontaneously. We never have to teach children when to laugh; we have to teach them when not to laugh." The more primitive and spontaneous humor of early childhood becomes more sophisticated as children grow older. "If some little argument is required to show them the superiority of clever jokes over crude humor," Eastman observed, "that is because their gift of laughter is lustier than ours and they are not so agile in perception and the apprehension of meanings" (ibid, p. 227). A child's sense of humor is "more primed and violent than ours, more close to its true purpose and that is why they laugh so lavishly. . ." (ibid, p. 28). Childrens' humor has not changed since the centuries-old *Punch and Judy* puppets to today's TV cartoons, from funhouses and thrill rides and the amusements of theme parks and travelling carnivals. They are all "make believe" facilitating playfulness. The thrill is mock violence (pain); the result, relief, laughter and shared affection (pleasure). Most of it is simple, unsophisticated, even crude and primitive.

Tickling is cited by Eastman (1936) as evidence of a physiological component to humorous emotion. "Although we continue to fight it off," he wrote, "we still continue to invite it. We experience thus a confused sense of pain combined with pleasure or at least the dread of pain with humorous delight which since the day of Plato the psychologists have vainly taxed their science to explain" (p. 16). These are elements of pleasure-pain, derision and disappointment theories but placed in a genetic-physiological context. Early onset agrees with Freudian theory as a regressive trait and behavioristic theory as presocial or unsocialized behaviors.

"The sense of humor is a primary instinct of our own nature" Eastman concluded, "originally only in the state of play and related remotely in its development to that gregarious instinct of which smiles and smiling laughter appear to be an inherent part." It is spontaneous and universal, personally and socially perceived from infancy with intensity which weakens with increased sophistication and socialization. In the words of Honore de Balzac (1799-1850): ". . .when we travel onward laughter sinks down and dies out like the light of the oil-lit lamp" (1922, p. 228).

The psychologist and Harvard professor William McDougall (1871-1938) suggested that an instinct must have three characteristics:

1. Emotional excitement
2. Occurs both in animals and humans
3. There is evidence of morbid exaggeration

Hilarious laughter satisfies the first, playfulness (playbiting, romping, teasing) to instinct theorists satisfies the second, and the hysterical (now termed histrionic) laughter and "inappropriate" or "exaggerated" affect in certain forms of mental illness satisfies the third.

THE PHYSIOLOGY OF HUMOR

If you stop now and recall the last time you had a really good laugh, uncontrollable as a sneeze, gasping for breath, tears in your eyes, about to wet your pants, you'll realize and more fully appreciate the physiological component of laughter and that it can be a profound and powerful physical experience. Sypher (1956) referred to Baudelaire's laughter "heard in the dark bohemian world of Paris" as "a nervous convulsion, an involuntary spasm." Here's Josh Billings's observation—and advice:

> Genuine laughing is the vent of the soul, the nostils of the heart and it is just as necessary for health and happiness as spring water is for a trout. . .I say laugh every good chance you can git but don't laugh unless you feel like it, for there ain't nothin' in this world more hearty than a good honest laugh, nor nothin' more hollow than a heartless one.
>
> When you do laugh, open your mouth wide enough for the noise to get out without squealing, throw your head back as though you was gonna be shaved, hold on to your false hair with both hands and then laugh till your soul gets thoroughly rested (Eastman, 1936, p. 331).

In his 1964 book *The Act of Creation*, Arthur Koestler flatly stated that "laughter is a reflex" but conceded that there is considerable dispute as to the definition of a reflex and "this has in fact been the central battleground of psychology for the last fifty years." Laughter requires "the coordinated contraction of fifteen facial muscles in a stereotyped pattern accompanied by altered breathing" and Koestler reminds us, "as Darwin and others" pointed out there are gradations "from the faintest and most decorous smile up to the full explosion of the laugh" (p. 28). Koestler claimed the continuum of scale from faint smile to "Homeric laughter" was "confirmed by laboratory experiments" (p. 30). He maintained that humor is the "only domain of creative activity where a stimulus on a high level of complexity produces a massive and sharply defined response on the level of physiological reflexes" (p. 31).

He referred to electrical stimulation of the zygomatic major, the lifting muscle in the upper lip, by varying current, producing a range of responses from smile to facial movement clearly typical of laughter. Films have been made of tickle responses in babies and in "hysterics" to whom tickling "was conveyed by suggestion." Both groups "showed the reflex swiftly increasing from the faint facial contraction to paroxysms of shaking and choking" (ibid, p. 30).

Koestler termed laughter a "luxury reflex" since "it serves no apparent biological purpose." He speculated that "its only utilitarian function" seems to be "to provide temporary relief from utilitarian pressures. On the evolutionary level where laughter arises," he theorized, "an element of frivolity seems to creep into a humorous universe governed by the laws of thermodynamics and the survival of the fittest." It is a complex response as Koestler suggested by analogy:

> It strikes us as a reasonable arrangement that a sharp light shone into the eye makes the pupil contract, or that a pin stuck into one's foot causes its instant withdrawal because both the stimulus and the response are on the same physiological level. But that a complicated activity like the reading of a page by Thurber should cause a specific motor response on the reflex level is a lopsided phenomenon which has puzzled philosophers since antiquity (ibid, p. 31).

In his 1860 essay *The Physiology of Laughter,* Herbert Spencer suggested that laughter is a neurophysiological discharge mechanism: "nervous energy always tends to beget muscular motion when it rises to a certain intensity. . .the channels of least resistance are the muscular movements of laughter" (Koestler, 1964, p. 55). "The details of Spencer's theory (parts of which Freud incorporated) have become obsolete," Koestler conceded, "but its basic thesis that emotion tends to beget bodily motion has not only been confirmed but has become commonplace in contemporary neurophysiology." The "peculiar" breathing while laughing, Koestler suggested, "seems designed to 'puff away' surplus tension in a kind of respiratory gymnastics." He identified "self-assertive" and "aggressive-defensive" emotions as those which involve the sympathico-adrenal system but only the aggressive-defensive type flows into the comic because it has "greater inertia, persistence and mass momentum than reason. . .frequently our emotions are incapable of keeping step with our reason. . ." (ibid).

Koestler identified the sympathetic branch of the autonomic nervous system and adrenalin and noradrenalin from the medulla of the suprarenal glands as "chief mediators" of the laughter reflex. This neuropsychological circuit is enervated when "emotion is deserted by thought." This is because emotion has "greater mass momentum" and cannot track or follow sudden changes of ideation to a different logic or "rule of the game." Comparing thought vs. feeling, quick cognition to sluggish heavy emotion in terms of Shakespeare's *Tempest,* Koestler wrote: "Ariel leads Caliban on by the nose. She jumps on a branch, he crashes into the tree" (ibid, pp. 57-58). Much of slapstick humor emphasizes this thinking-emotion mismatch.

But what of laughter from a quip, a pun, a quickly stated very funny joke? How can such a brief, flatly stated verbal stimulus elicit such a profound response? Koestler explained these as due to "an echo, however faint, of situations that held a threat. . .in the remote past of the species which once were biologically relevant. . .(which) lag by many milennia behind the conditions in which we live." He offered everday examples: "We jump at a sudden sound; we develop gooseflesh to a screeching noise. . .overstatements of the body" (ibid). Glandular and autonomic functions "and the emotion-controlling centers in the midbrain are much older than the Paleolithic Age. . .when the struggle for existence was more deadly. . .when any unusual sight or sound had to be answered by jumping, bristling, fight or flight" (ibid, p. 62).

As society grew, it provided more safety and security to its members and "the affect-generating emergency mechanisms of the sympathico-adrenal system gradually became an anchronism. . .but not at the rate they became redundant." As a result, our thinking increasingly was "at odds with emotions," out of proportion with biologically or socially appropriate reactions which "cannot be worked off through their original channels." Laughter and weeping became "overflow mechanisms" to discharge at least part of the redundant emotions. Laughing and crying are "twin reflexes" because laughter discharges aggressive emotions **denied** by the intellect while crying discharges "participatory emotions accepted by the intellect" (ibid).

Animals don't laugh, Koestler explained, because laughter can only arise in "a biologically secure species with redundant emotions and intellectual autonomy." Some pets and zoo animals "seem capable of a humorous expression. . .and teasing activities" which Koestler saw as "evolutionary forerunners of laughter" (ibid, p. 63). Humor, almost exclusively human, "is the only domain of creative activity where complex. . . intellectual stimulation elicits a sharply defined. . .physiological reflex" (laughing) (ibid, p. 95).

In his 1945 paper *The Psychology of Humor*, Cyril Burt described laughter as a "safety valve" for the "overflow of emotional energy, instinctively excited by the perception of some specific situation which automatically tends to stimulate the instinct but on closer examination is seen not to require energetic action" (Koestler, 1964, p. 97). Stimuli which lead to laughter "thus involves a double-entendre: there is first the superficial or manifest meaning" of emotion appropriate to threat "momentarily disturbing equilibrium" and secondly the "deeper or latent meaning" which "contradicts the first impression" and laughter results "to give immediate relief to the superfluous emotional excitement" (ibid).

Arieti (1976) reported that "various authors have stressed that humor in all its aspects has a healthy influence on the human organism." He referred to a 1972 study by Patricia Keith-Spiegel in which she summarized the views of authors from Herbert Spencer in 1860 and Charles Darwin in 1872 to Menon in 1931. She concluded that laughter and humor "have been hailed as 'good for the body' because they restore homeostasis, stabilize blood pressure, oxygenate the blood, massage vital organs, stimulate circulation, facilitate digestion, relax the system and produce feelings of well being" (p. 123).

Ewald Hecker was the physiologist previously quoted in this chapter who proposed the **oscillation principle** in pleasure-pain theory. Inspired by the earlier work of Wilhelm Wundt (1832-1920) in Leipzig and Emil Kraepelin (1856-1926) in Berlin, Hecker in 1873 suggested that response to humor stimulated the autonomic nervous system, the sympathetic more than the parasympathetic. Wundt and Kraepelin were (still are!) recognized authorities and very serious researchers. Wundt, physiologist-psychologist, founded the world's first experimental psychology laboratory and is regarded as the "father of psychology." Kraepelin, physician-psychiatrist, was the first to differentiate affective from thought disorder and is known as the "father of psychodiagnostics."

Hecker observed that when someone is tickled there is a dilation of pupils of the eyes, constriction of blood vessels and a lowering of blood pressure, symptoms common to stimulation of the sympathetic branch of the autonomic nervous system. If you think this is simple, then try this from Eastman's 1936 book: "He inferred that a lowering of the blood pressure in the brain is what enervates the muscles of the diaphragm which cause laughter and that the function of laughter in tickling is to compensate for that dangerous brain condition by narrowing the thoracic cavity, submitting the heart and lungs and greater blood vessels to a strong pressure and so increasing the force of the circulation" (p. 219).

ANIMAL-HUMAN RESEARCH

Domjan (1987) described the complexity and current "state of the art" of research on comparative animal and human behavior. In a review of the literature, he cited Darwin's 1871 observation that animals showed "wonder, curiosity, imitation, attention, memory, reasoning and a sense of beauty — all of which had been considered to be uniquely human" (p. 556). George Romanes in 1881, C. Lloyd Morgan in 1894, Edwin Thorndike in 1911 and Dollard and Miller in 1939 continued and expanded Darwin's original work and on that of Pavlov in Russia and Watson in the United States suggesting "an interplay between animal and human research (to) complement one another in the development of a general theory of behavior" (p. 557).

Domjan traced three major themes which "continue to guide contemporary research": comparative cognition; animal models of human behavior; animal models of the neurobiology of learning. There are human behavior models based on animal research: systematic desensitization and flooding treatments of phobias; token system of behavior modification; programmed instruction; aversion therapy; biofeedback; learned helplessness theory of depression (p. 559).

In the 1980s Amsel and Stanton and Vogt and Rudy researched the "ontogenetic development of instrumental conditioning phenomena to postnatal brain development." They found in rats that reward system effects are influenced by the ongoing development of the limbic system, the area of the brain below the cortex, below what was believed the "thinking" hemispheres. If true for humans, learning involves subcortical as well as cortical brain areas and there is physical, structural tissue growth to accommodate and reinforce what's learned. Some learnings become so strongly reinforced they become "ingrained" or "second nature" or "automatic" and "on call" so that when something "strikes" us as "funny" — POW! A laugh! Impressive? In the Old Testament it is written: "To everything there is a season and a time to every purpose under the heaven" (Ecclesiastes 3:1).

Other research notably Garcia et al. in 1974 and Kiefer in 1985 demonstrate **selective association.** Rats chose between cues such as taste or sound to cope with what they perceived as internal or external threats. These experiments may demonstrate a neurophysiological basis for the ancient observation that there is "a time to weep and a time to laugh; a time to mourn and a time to dance" (Ecclesiastes 3:4).

These studies show that the simplest behaviors under closer examination turn out to be complex, multicausational and involve psychological and physiological components. To trace any behavioral trait to neural pathways in the brain is even more difficult, as Domjan observed:

> Simple associative learning mechanisms have turned out to be anything but simple. Reflecting this complexity Minetka titled a recent review of fear conditioning *The frightful complexity of the origins of fear.* . . . One might well talk about the frightful complexity of conditioning and learning generally (p. 562).

Such is the case for humor and all its varieties. It is not so simple, despite centuries of study from Plato to the present. Conditioning is not as simple as Pavlov thought when he paired a conditioned stimulus (bell) to an unconditioned stimulus (salivating to meat powder) to produce a conditioned response in dogs (salivating to the bell). It was a beautiful experiment — and a gross oversimplification. We know now there are "hierarchical associative controls." And so also for humor. Not everyone laughs at something offered as funny. Much depends on the time and place, the person telling and listening, verbal and nonverbal behaviors, individual differences, other reinforcers (mood, subject, interest, others present or absent) to name but a few. One researcher refers to such variables as "the causal texture of the environment" (p. 562).

Formerly instrumental or operant conditioning was seen as a direct causal relationship between a stimulus (like food) and a behavior or response (like pressing a button or lever). Today the stimulus is seen as representing "an opportunity to engage in certain behavior, eating" (p. 562). There are choices, alternatives, more variables. We now study "what factors determine how organisms choose among their various response options" (p. 563). Philosophers such as Plato and Aristotle have been telling us for more than 2000 years that life means choosing among relative truths. Psychologists tell us choosing forms personality. Philosophy and psychology may at least speak the same language. Domjan provides the psychologist's view:

> Biological theory suggests that organisms select among their various options so as to get the most out of life in some sense. Thus, choice be-

havior must reflect attempts at some form of organization. Questions about what is being optimised and whether and how optimization is achieved dominate contemporary research on instrumental contingencies (p. 562).

CRITIQUE. Instinct theory is more easily said than proven. Animals unfortunately do not talk or laugh, not in the same way as people. They can't tell us what they think or what they think is funny. People talk and laugh but they can't agree universally as to what's funny. Animal and human playfulness are more similar than dissimilar and both emerge in infancy. Animals and humans show many of the same signs typical of a genetic predisposition, primary innate pattern or instinct of playfulness. There is still a great gap of conclusive evidence to clearly establish an instinct of humor. As anthropologists search for the "missing link" between ape and man, we also search for the missing link of humor, to confirm it as instinct, animal and human, between infantile playfulness and the intricate complexity of adult humor.

CHAPTER 4

NEOCLASSICAL THEORIES: SYMPATHY AND EMPATHY; CREATIVITY AND CHANGE

Here's to those who love us;
Here's to those who don't
A smile for those who love us.
A tear for those who don't.

Anonymous

SYMPATHY/EMPATHY
Exemplar: Will Rogers

IN THE world's literature on humor there are enough specific references to the active and direct involvement of sympathy and empathy
to constitute a significant body of data in support of them as a major
dynamic of humor. This altruistic motive is in contradiction and contra-
distinction to the theories of derision/superiority and disappointment/
frustrated expectation and the pain component of pleasure-pain theory.
Sypher (1956) traced the onset of this theory of humor to the "genial ro-
mantics of the early 19th century" such as Charles Lamb who believed
that "laughter is an overflow of sympathy, an amiable feeling of identity
with what is disreputably human, a relish for the whimsical, the odd, the
private blunder." Carlyle (of all people!) cheerfully supposed that the
man who smiles is "affectionate" (p. 204).

Eastman (1922) offered this quote from the usually caustic Carlyle:

True humor springs not more from the head than from the heart; it
is not contempt, its essence is love; it issues not in laughter but in still

67

smiles which lie far deeper. It is a sort of inverse sublimity, exalting as it were into our affection what is below us while sublimity draws down into our affections what is above us (pp. 168-169).

In his 1804 book *Vorschule der Aesthetik*, the popular French comedian Jean Paul wrote that "when we laugh at others it is because we have 'loaned' them our insight and thus see differences between a minimum and maximum of such insight. . .one often experiences with the pain the subjection of others. . . Laughers are good-natured and place themselves often in rank and file with those they laugh at; children and women laugh most; the proud self-comparer the least. . ." (pp. 169-170). Eastman reported that he had studied thirty theories of humor to "distinguish it from the rather hard, reptilly thing they had conceived the comic in general to be." He concluded that "there is an absence of scorn in humor, a presence of emotion, and humor is an excellent thing" (p. 168).

Sympathy/empathy is, according to Sypher (1956), "at the radiant peak of 'high' comedy" and "laughter is qualified by tolerance and criticism, modulated by a sympathy that comes only from wisdom. . .a victory over our absurdities. . .won at a cost of humility. . .in a spirit of charity and enlightenment" (ibid, p. 212). Even in the Golden Age of Greece slavery was not unusual, wars common and women had no rights. It may be that the realities of life barely allowed for the philosophic reflections of Plato and Aristotle, little or no time for sympathy and empathy. Let's remember that Socrates was tried, convicted and executed for values and effort we prize today, or say we do.

Since Socrates, world history has recorded the rise and fall of many kings, in many wars, with little time for compassion. The rise of sympathy/empathy theory suggests that civilization evolves into greater realization and valuing of personal freedom, rights and the pursuit of happiness. Sympathy (compassion for others) and empathy (seeing one's self in others) walk hand in hand with freedom. Cervantes' *Don Quixote*, Shakespeare's *Tempest*, Goethe's *Faust*, Lewis Carroll's *Alice in Wonderland* and Mark Twain's *Tom Sawyer*, and many others have an underlying compassion which lingers after the material is read or acted.

In his *Ethics IV*, the philosopher Baruch Spinoza (1632-1677) criticized derision theory because its effect is painful: "Derision is an evil thing. . .jests should promote well being" (Eastman, 1922, p. 152). In his 1936 book, Max Eastman agreed: "Jests which slap in the face are not good jests." These and other observers point out that not all humor is nor needs to be based on derision or disappointment. Some humor is clearly pleasurable, personally and socially accepting, approving and supportive. Even pleasure-pain and instinct theories recognize the pursuit of positive feelings for the self and for others.

Koestler (1964), presented with a duality of emotions seeking release, self-assertive aggressive and self-transcending accepting, saw the aggressive as leading to derisive humor, the accepting toward sympathetic humor. He referred to compassion and identification as factors of self-transcending emotions which "mediated by physiological processes. . . discharge not in laughter but in tears." But he still maintained that even in the "more affectionate varieties of humor there is an element of aggression — a drop of adrenalin" (p. 95)

Walt Disney pioneered in creating animal characters in stories rich in humor, pleasurable across generations. He observed that "people are often sympathetic when they laugh." He reported that "sometimes children sympathize too much and have to shut their eyes during a cruel scene" (Eastman, 1936, p. 341).

Exaggeration to absurdity, of characters, in dialogue or contrived situations is another aspect of sympathy. Doing so distances us from reality and takes off the track of anxiety and worry. It renders reality less painful. Thomas Hobbes, in his essay, *Human Nature,* wrote that for laughter to be inoffensive "it must be absurdities and informities abstracted from persons" (Eastman, 1922, p. 140).

The following is a sampling of quotes which support sympathy/empathy theory, all taken from Eastman (1936):

From John Erskine (1879-1951), Columbia English professor and author of many books on English literature: "Humor is the art of adapting oneself to another temperament. If you acknowledge the right of all your fellows to survive, even though they disagree with you, you must learn how to bend to their peculiarities without surrendering your own pet queernesses" (p. 339).

Charlie Chaplin: "Of course, they are often sympathetic with me while they laugh! Playful pain. . .that is what humor is. The minute a thing is overtragic it is funny" (p. 331). Chaplin's belief in playful pain links him with pleasure-pain theory but his stronger belief in audience sympathy extends beyond it.

Rube Goldberg may not be remembered by younger readers, but his bizarre cartoon inventions were so popular that any absurd solution to a problem was often termed "a Rube Goldberg." Like Chaplin, he recognized the appeal of negative aspects of humor but he also considered sympathy/empathy important: "To get a belly laugh you have to destroy something, either in the object or in the person who appreciates the joke. But humor has to have a background of sympathy, too" (p. 331).

Eddie Cantor also acknowledged the existence of hostile motives in some but not all types of humor. "Satire is barbed and malicious and likely to hurt," he said, "whereas the genuine quality of humor is founded on tenderness and gentleness. It is my belief. . .the most pleasant type of laughter is rarely evoked by touching on human follies or deformities" (p. 340).

Anita Loos, co-author of the hit comedy *Gentlemen Prefer Blondes* (1925): "I never feel superior when a hero or villain stubs his toe and falls on his fanny — I only hark back in memory to times when I have done the identical thing." She felt an audience collectively reacts in much the same way "not sitting in superior amusement but is rather translating its own activities into those of the futile little souls on the screen and laughing at them with brotherly understanding and sympathy. In my own case, every pie that hit Chaplin has also hit me. This is certainly not superiority" (p. 332).

Dorothy Parker, whose trademark in her poetry, short stories and off-the-cuff sayings was her sharp wit, wrote: "The funny people you like the best are the ones you laugh **with.** There's Benchley, for instance. You live through his troubles with him — they are your own troubles — and that is why you enjoy them so particularly. A humorist, I think, is just balancing on the edge of the dumps" (p. 331). The hobo or tramp type of circus clown specializes in evoking this kind of sympathy from the audience, with an exaggerated sad face, dejected mannerisms and tattered clothing. This is a uniquely American innovation in clowning, born in the hard times of the 1930s Depression, and its continued popularity confirms Parker's observation.

"Laughter can be sympathetic," Milt Gross wrote, "and the really great humorists laugh at themselves" (p. 335). His comment reminds me of Mark Twain's "opinion" of how stupid he felt his parents were when he was a teenager and how much they had learned by the time he reached adulthood. The joke, on him, is also on each and every one of us who grows **up** instead of just growing **old,** and the nostalgic vision looking back over those awkward, formative years.

Groucho Marx: "There are all kinds of humor. Some **is** derisive, some sympathetic and some merely whimsical. That's what makes comedy so much harder to create than serious drama; people laugh in many different ways and they cry only in one" (p. 336).

Thomas Mitchell described how in *Tom Sawyer Abroad* "their balloon landed in a desert somewhere and some lions came after them. They just barely got away and Tom looked back down at the disappointed lions: 'I couldn't help seeing their side of it,' he said" (p. 336).

"Mark Twain was my model," Irvin S. Cobb confided. "I studied his method. I concluded that what Mark Twain was saying to mankind as a humorist was this: 'Look what fools we are and I at the head of the procession.' I concluded that a man who can't laugh and doesn't laugh fundamentally at himself is not a humorist in the full sense" (p. 337). Frank Sullivan expressed a similar opinion when he wrote: "Maybe humor is refusing to take yourself, or anyone else, too seriously" (pp. 340-341).

Will Rogers, exemplar of sympathy/empathy theory, with characteristic kick-off-your-shoes down-to-earth honesty, observed: "I don't know what humor is. Anything that's funny, tragedy or anything, it don't make no difference, if you happen to hit it just right." Rogers then freely self-discloses his own involvement in sympathy/empathy: "There's one thing I'm proud of. I ain't got it in for anybody. I don't like to make jokes that hurt anybody" (p. 338).

Mae West, one of the first sex symbols but also a humorist, writer and director: "Ridicule is just one phase of humor and is not always the basis for a laugh, although it's a sure-fire short cut. In ridicule, too, all those who laugh are not necessarily amused. Sympathy may be aroused for the poor fellow who is the object of ridicule" (p. 337).

Circus and parade clowns wear garishly colored costumes and face makeup which gives them a large degree of anonymity. Their exaggerated actions are childishly playful. They portray "make believe" problem situations and "sight gags" that strike harmonic sympathetic chords in the audience. The clown's problems are overcome laughingly, usually in some absurd way and with a happy ending, many times evoking an "Ah yes!" or affirmative nod of the head of spectators in an instant of insight. The funniest clown routines, true also for other types of humor, touch on universal frustrations and an underlying sympathy for the frailties and follies of the human condition. Regardless of their costume, character, makeup and the ridiculous absurdities they act out, clowns demonstrate a great deal of sympathy and empathy.

In his 1978 book *Creativity*, psychiatrist Silvano Arieti agreed with Freudian theory that "most jokes are motivated by gratification of an inhibited wish." Arieti acknowledged other motives such as restating an old truth or habitual situation in new ways or "even to lead people to experience brotherhood and compassion. . .we also find an attempt to sympathize with our fellow men for their inadequate attempts to get out of one or another of the many kinds of human predicaments." He described the main character in a joke as "often a poor fellow like the rest of us. . .caught like a fly in the web of a complicated situation. Let us laugh at him. . .(he is) one of us; laughing at him we laugh at ourselves since we cannot escape from our human limitations" (pp. 122-123).

CRITIQUE. Sympathy/empathy theory offsets the negative polarity of classical humor theories and relates more to the pleasure side of pleasure-pain theory. It rounds out and further completes classical and other neoclassical theories. But its emphasis only on positive factors excludes derision, disappointment and pain, factors that have been demonstrated for 2000 years. It is a reaction against and antagonistic to the crudity and veiled or direct hostility of classical theories. Because of this reactive stance, it tends to equate with its opposite and is as narrow and incomplete as its adversary. It excludes and seeks to replace other theories. It seeks to add positive emotions of acceptance, approval and affection to classical and neoclassical theories but it does not embrace the content of them.

CREATIVITY-CHANGE

Exemplar: Henri Bergson (1859-1841)

Sypher (1956) referred to Henri Bergson as "the most celebrated modern philosopher of intuition." From 1907 to 1935 Bergson authored books and essays "protesting against the mechanical, seeking to discern (and) protect what is inward and spontaneous from what is automatic" (ibid). His ideas became quite influential and in 1927 he was awarded a Nobel prize in literature. Sypher described Bergson's basic message as: "Life is vitality, a spontaneous, changing personal response to each situation. . .inward discoveries and intensities. What is alive is not mechanical" (ibid). He was strongly opposed to "coarse logic" and "positivistic thought" and believed in a dualism of what he termed **elan vital** (life spirit or life force) and matter (everything else). According to Bergson, we know matter through intellect but only through intuition can we realize **elan vital.** It cannot be understood by reason alone.

Duration was a term used by Bergson to describe the "true nature of time," not mechanical clock time but rather dynamic, ongoing personal growth and individual experiencing, an unfolding, becoming, blossoming. "Duration," Bergson wrote, "is the continuous progress of the past which gnaws into the future and which swells as it advances" (Commins

& Linscott, 1947, p. 274). He emphasized "continuity of change in the process of growth and growth itself is unending creation, with freedom as its ultimate goal" (ibid). In his essay *The Evolution of Life* he described **duration** in greater detail:

> The universe *endures*. The more we study the nature of time, the more we shall comprehend that duration means invention, the creation of forms, the continual elaboration of the absolutely new. The systems marked off by science endure only because they are bound up insepara-bly with the rest of the universe. It is true that in the universe itself two opposite movements are to be distinguished   descent and ascent. The first only unwinds a roll ready prepared. In principle it might be ac-complished almost instantaneously, like releasing a spring. But the as-cending movement, which corresponds to an inner work of ripening or creating *endures* essentially, and imposes its rhythm on the first, which is inseparable from it. . . .The present contains nothing more than the past, and what is found in the effect was already in the cause (Commins & Linscott, p. 283).

Relevant to our search for a definition of humor and the "true" theory of humor, in this same essay Bergson cautioned against attempting the "perfect definition." He admonished: "The perfect definition applies only to a completed reality.   .vital properties are never entirely realized though always on the way to become so" (ibid, p. 285). This conclusion should not be unsettling since we still have no universally accepted defi-nitions for personality, intelligence or memory. Though worlds apart, Bergson like Freud preferred to speak in terms of "tendencies": "ten-dency achieves all that it aims at. . .if it is not thwarted by another ten-dency" (ibid).

In his 1907 essay *Creative evolution,* Bergson differentiated the function of intellect from intuition:

> Consciousness, in man, is pre-eminently intellect. It might have been, ought, so it seems, to have been also intuition. Intuition and in-tellect represent two opposite directions of the work of consciousness: intuition goes in the very direction of life and intellect goes in the in-verse direction. A complete and perfect humanity would be that in which these two forms of conscious activity should attain their full de-velopment. A different evolution might have led to a humanity either more intellectual still or more intuitive. In the humanity of which we are a party intuition is in fact almost completely sacrificed to intellect. Intuition is here but vague and discontinuous. It is a lamp almost ex-tinguished, which only glimmers now and then for a few moments at most. But it glimmers wherever a vital interest is at stake (Leavens & Leavens, 1962, p. 72).

Bergson discounted intelligence as "the faculty of making artificial objects, especially tools to make tools" (Bartlett, 1968, p. 849). As Harlow and later Goodall demonstrated, chimpanzees make tools, suggesting that intuition and not intelligence better differentiates humans from animals. Humor, also, is more human than animal and in Bergson's frame of reference relates more to intuition than to intelligence. "Consciousness," Bergson maintained, "corresponds exactly to the living being's power of choice; it is synonymous with invention and with freedom. In the animal, invention is never anything but a variation on the theme of routine. With man, consciousness breaks the chain. In man, and in man alone, it sets itself free" (Leavens & Leavens, 1962, p. 70).

As we have seen, Bergson was an enemy of mechanistic routine, of rigidity and artificiality. Whatever people did that was artificial and mechanical was funny: "Rigidity," Bergson wrote, "is the comic, and laughter is its corrective" (Sypher, 1956, p. 74). "Automatism, inelasticity, habit that has been contracted and maintained are clearly the causes why a face makes us laugh" (p. 76). When inelasticity "plays on people as an instrument or pulls strings as if they were puppets, it is a kind of automatism that makes us laugh, closely akin to absentmindedness and comic characters — is generally comic in proportion to his ignorance of himself. The comic person is unconscious. . .becomes invisible to himself while remaining visible to all the world" (p. 71).

In Sypher's introduction to Bergson's essay he further defines automatism as that "of the business code, the egoism of the expert, professional callousness, inelasticity, pride, automatic responses, like a ready-made product, absent-minded, insensitive, incapable of authentic personality, those who live by formula, whose behavior is a series of repetitions" (p. xi). The popularity of puppets and ventriloquists, slapstick comedy routines, and man vs. machine skits tend to confirm Bergson's theory of humor. From *Punch and Judy* to *Pinocchio*, Charlie McCarthy to the Muppets and Sesame Street, *Petrouchka* and the inanimate-made-animate characters from the *Nutcracker Suite* to Disneyland, these are consistent with Bergson's ideas.

Bergson's 1900 essay, *Laughter*, contains the three basic elements of his theory of humor (Sypher, 1956):

1. **The comic is uniquely human** and "does not exist outside the pale of what is strictly human. A landscape may be beautiful, charming and sublime, or insignificant and ugly; it will never be laughable. You

may laugh at an animal but only because you have detected in it some human attitude or expression. You may laugh at a hat but what you are making fun of. . .is not the piece of felt or straw but the shape that men have given it" (p. 62).

2. **Comedy is objective, indifferent.** "An absence of feeling usually accompanies laughter. . .as though it fell on the surface of the soul that is thoroughly calm and unruffled. Indifference is its natural environment, for laughter has no greater foe than emotion. . .look upon life as a disinterested spectator and many a drama will turn into comedy. . .stop our ears in a room where dancing is going on and the dancers at once appear ridiculous. How many human actions would stand a similar test? To produce the whole of its effect, the comic demands . . .a momentary anesthesia of the heart" (pp. 63-64). This aspect of humor can be demonstrated by turning off the sound of a movie or TV show or commercial as Bergson suggested or "stopping our ears" and watching people in everyday pastimes. Much of the humor in *Candid Camera* involved such casual eavesdropping.

3. **The comic is social.** The comic "appeals to intelligence (which) must remain in touch with other intelligences. . . You would hardly appreciate the comic if you felt yourself isolated from others. Laughter. . . needs an echo. . .laughter is always the laughter of a group" (p. 64). Bergson gave an example of a man who sat unmoved while others wept at a moving church service. Asked why he did not weep he replied: "I don't belong to this parish." Bergson observed that "What he thought of tears is still more true of laughter. However spontaneous it seems, laughter always implies a kind of secret freemasonry, or even complicity, with other laughers, real or imaginary" (ibid).

CREATIVITY AND CHANGE

Humor can be used as a creative outlet and to facilitate change. Will Cuppy (1884-1949), humorist-critic and author of *How to Be a Hermit* (1929) and *How to Tell Your Friends From Apes* (1931) wrote that "humor is meant to blow up evil and make fun of the follies of life" (Eastman, 1936, p. 337). Artemus Ward (1834-1867), the American humorist of great popularity on the lecture circuit and who died on tour in England, described his comedy technique: "I have only drifted with the current which has carried me gaily on of its own accord. . . I have always meant the creatures of my burlesque should stab Error and give Right a friendly push" (ibid, p. 354).

Eastman (1922) described two paths of change through humor: positively, by "imaginative sympathy" or negatively by "corrective hostility" (p. 127). Bergson emphasized the negative: "In laughter we always find an unavowed intention to humiliate and consequently to correct our neighbor if not in his will, at least in his deed." He felt that emotionality kills humor: "Depict some fault, however trifling, in such a way as to arouse sympathy, fear or pity: the mischief is done and it is impossible for us to laugh" (ibid, p. 148). Cicero, Horace and Moliere shared this view. Marianne Moore (1887-1972) described humor's positive effects: "Among animals, none has a sense of humor. Humor saves a few steps; it saves years" (*The Pangolin*, stanza 8, 1941).

In his book *Motivation and Personality* (1970), Abraham Maslow described how children unknowingly — and creatively — solve problems:

> A child overwhelmed by repeated stories in which wolves figure will in some cases tend to come back to the problem again, e.g., in play, conversation, questions asked, making up stories and in paintings. The child may be said to be detoxifying or desensitizing the problem. This result comes to pass because the repetition means familiarization, release, and catharsis, working through, ceasing to respond with emergency reactions, slowly building up defenses, trying out various mastery techniques, practicing successful ones, etc. (p. 140).

This is a phenomenon easily observed and validated. Children on amusement park rides are subjected to frightening experiences yet many of them are eager to repeat the experience.

In his 1968 book *Toward a Psychology of Being*, Abraham Maslow itemized sixteen characteristics of self-actualized persons which he termed "B-values," those facilitating "Being." In contrast, "D-values" detract from personal growth and are "deficiency" related. One of Maslow's sixteen "B-values" is playfulness: "I very strongly feel that playfulness of a certain kind is one of the B-values. . .it is fairly often reported in peak experiences." Maslow lamented that "it is very hard to describe this B-playfulness since the English language falls far short here (as in general it is unable to describe the 'higher' subjective experiences)." Despite this difficulty, he offered this description:

> It has a cosmic or a godlike, good-humored quality, certainly transcending hostility of any kind. It could as easily be called happy joy, or gay exuberance or delight. It has a quality of spilling over as of richness or surplus (not D-motivated). It is existential in the sense that it is an amusement or delight with both the smallness (weakness) and the largeness (strength) of the human being, transcending the dominance-subordinance polarity. It has a certain quality of triumph in it, some-

times perhaps also of relief. It is simultaneously mature and childlike. It is final, Utopian, Eupsychian, transcendent in the sense in which Marcuse and Brown have described it. It could also be called Nietzschean (p. 112).

Maslow viewed this trait as "in itself an integrator as beauty is, or love or the creative intellect." It is a "resolver of dichotomies, a solution to many insoluble problems. . .teaching us that one way of solving a problem is to be amused by it. It enables us to live simultaneously in the D-realm and in the B-realm, to be at the same time Don Quixote and Sancho Panza, as Cervantes was" (ibid, p. 113). In his book, *Motivation and Personality* (1970), Maslow described "one aspect of the healthy love relationship that was very clear in my subjects: namely, fun, merriment, elation, feeling of well-being, gaiety" (p. 194).

Freud, champion of pleasure-pain theory, observed aspects of spontaneity, and even inspiration, in the production of wit. He did so in the context of his theory of the unconscious: "Wit also evinces a peculiar behavior along the lines of association of ideas. Frequently it is not at the disposal of our memory when we look for it. . .it often appears unsolicited . . .where we cannot understand its presence" and these, Freud contended, "point to their unconscious origin." He then acknowledged the possibility of creative expression: "Wit shows in a most pronounced manner the character of an involuntary 'inspiration' or a sudden flash of thought. . .something indefinable" with "a sudden drop of intellectual tension." He concluded that "in wit-formation a stream of thought is dropped for a moment which then suddenly emerges from the unconscious as a witticism" (Freud, 1938, p. 752).

Arieti, trained in Freudian theory, was supportive of creativity-change theory: "It may seem surprising that a study of the creative product should give first consideration to wit and the comic. . .yet even for researchers as different in background and methodology as Freud and the essayist, Arthur Koestler, the study of wit has been the path to a better understanding of the creative process" (p. 101).

Arieti saw comic situations, games and children's play as interrelated: "They are all pleasant and imply a special attitude toward life." They "promote an evasion of reality" and in this way "show their similarity to dreams." Arieti concedes that funny situations, games and play can go beyond evasion: "They substitute a bit of creativity for what they replace or temporarily suspend from the focus of consciousness." Make-believe is the "main characteristic common to both children's play and wit" but "are based on different mechanisms." Reality is suspended in child's play or "kept at the periphery" and wit is very short-lived: "As soon as the faulty logic reacquires the upper hand, make-believe disappears in a wake of laughter." The pleasure of wit, according to Arieti, is not solely in enacting fantasy but in "realizing how astounding it would have been had we been able to accept the story" (p. 127).

In 1892, Karl Gross described this denouement effect as an "esthetic consciousness between the shock of deception and the countershock of enlightenment." He saw this as occurring in three phases: "In the first phase my ego is repelled from the object, in the third phase it emerges from it laughing." During the second phase it "must have been in the object and just this transporting of oneself into the object is the characteristic of esthetic perception." Gross considered this esthetic aspect of humor voided Plato's derision theory: "Superiority is an absurdity which we previously believed" (Eastman, 1922, p. 141).

In his book, *The Act of Creation* (1964), Arthur Koestler acknowledged inspirational, transcending experiences as facilitating creativity: "Listening to Mozart, watching a great actor's performance, being in love or some other state of grace may cause a welling up of happy emotions which moisten the eye or overflow in tears." It can be happy, sad or bittersweet and "compassion and bereavement may have the same physical effect. Emotions of this class, whether joyous or sad, include sympathy, identification, pity, admiration, awe and wonder." He claimed there is a "common denominator of these heterogeneous emotions" and that is "a feeling of participation, identification or belonging; in other words, the self is experienced as being a part of a larger whole, a higher unit which may be Nature, God, mankind, universal order or the Anima Mundi; it may be an abstract idea or a human bond with persons living, dead or imagined" (p. 54).

Koestler saw "a common element" in the emotions as the "common denominator" of "the participatory or self-transcending tendencies." He explained that "this is not meant in a mystical sense (though mysticism certainly belong to this class of emotion); the term is merely intended to convey that in these emotional states the need is felt to behave as part of some real or imaginary entity which transcends. . .the boundaries of the individual self." Together with self-asserting tendencies "emotions are complex mixtures in which both tendencies participate. Thus the emotion called 'love' whether sexual or maternal usually contains an aggressive or possessive, self-asserting element" (ibid).

Graves' definition of humor was the "faculty of seeing apparently incongruous elements as part of a scheme for supralogical necessity. . .an economical equating of concepts which are by definition inequitable." It does this with "metaphysical pitilessness." He believed the funniest comedians and humorists "force their audiences out of control by bullying them with some small shred of humor, the smaller and sillier the better." Popular skits of the past confirm this view: Abbott and Costello's "who's on first" routine, the repetitive skits of the *Keystone Kops,* Ernie Kovac's *Nairobi Trio,* and typecast behaviors of Charlie Chaplin, Buster Keaton, Harold Lloyd, W.C. Fields, Jackie Gleason, Sid Caesar, Phil Silvers and groups such as Our Gang, Marx and Ritz Brothers, and The Three Stooges. Graves differentiated humor from hysteria, both involving laughter but that of humor is voluntary, reasonable and proportioned but in hysteria laughter is involuntary, unreasonable and exaggerated (Graves, 1974, pp. 55-58).

ARCHETYPES AND HUMOR

Carl G. Jung (1876-1961), one of Freud's original "inner circle" and the only early follower who was a psychiatrist, was fascinated in the immediate and ancient roots of behavior. His major contributions which relate to humor are: **primordial archetypes,** mental imagery common to all humanity in a **collective unconscious,** most relevant to humor being *The Trickster* and *The Telesphoros* of Asklipios; the symbolization and meaning behind **alchemy** and such constructs as **the shadow.**

Telesphoros is a tiny cloaked human figure, a child or dwarf, holding a lantern up in one hand as if to light its way or to help others find him or her or to find their own way. Jung (1970) described this as an archetypal figure, "a pointer of the way." This imagery came to Jung while inscribing a stone for his garden. "I dedicated a few words to him," Jung wrote, "which came into my mind while I was working." Here is the inscription which begins "with a fragment from Heraclitus," the next sentence "alludes to the Mithras liturgy and the last sentence to Homer (*Odyssey,* Book 24, verse 12)":

> Time is a child — playing like a child — playing a board game — the kingdom of the child. This is *Telesphoros,* who roams through the dark regions of this cosmos and glows like a star out of the depths. He points the way to the gates of the sun and to the land of dreams (1970, p. 227).

The Trickster "haunts the mythology of all ages sometimes in quite unmistakable form, sometimes in strangely modulated guise." It occurs "in carnivals and revels, in magic rites of healing, in man's religious fears and exaltations." It is "a **psychogem** of archetypal psychic structure of extreme antiquity. . .that has hardly left the animal level. . .a faithful reflection of an absolutely undifferentiated human consciousness" (Jung, 1969, p. 260). *The Trickster* is "man and animal at once. . .both subhuman and superhuman, a bestial and divine being whose chief and most alarming characteristic is his unconsciousness" (p. 263).

Both *Trickster* and *Telesphoros* symbolize the Eternal Child easily observed wherever there is laughter. Another of Maslow's sixteen characteristics of self-actualization resembles Jung's *Trickster* and also Bergson's **comic automaton.** Maslow described the self-actualized person as "more spontaneous, more expressive, more innocently behaving (guileless, naive, honest, candid, ingenuous, childlike, artless, unguarded, defenseless), more natural (simple, relaxed, unhesitant, plain, sincere, unaffected, primitive in a particular sense, immediate), more controlled and freely flowing outward (automatic, impulsive, reflexlike, 'instinctive,' unrestrained, un-self-conscious, thoughtless, unaware)." In a footnote, Maslow offered "partial synonyms" as an addendum to this description, acknowledging "slightly overlapping meanings: Unintentional, of its own accord, free unforced, unreasoning, undeliberate, impetuous, unreserved, non-withholding, self-disclosing, frank, non-dissembling, open, undissimulating, unpretending, unfeigning, forthright, unsophisticated, not artificial, unworried, trusting" (Maslow, 1968, p. 107).

Ancient rites and cult practices, the wizards and witches of the Middle Ages, today's magicians and clowns can be subsumed in Jung's *Trickster* archetype. This construct provides insight into the origins of little understood current pastimes such as bullfights in Spain and Mexico and to ancient religions such as Mithraism where Mithras, half-god and half-man was pictured slaying a bull, associating human and animal natures. *The Trickster* is not evil "but does the most atrocious things from sheer unconsciousness and unrelatedness." One wonders if this is not what inspired Bergson's **automatism** and **inelasticity** concepts. It is an effort to objectify "the fickle finger of fate" or "bad luck." *The Trickster* is a "primitive cosmic being of divine-animal nature, on the one hand superior to man because of superhuman abilities and on the other hand inferior because of his unreason and unconsciousness." Despite this paradoxical dichotomy, this yin-yang blending of extremes, it has been "a source of amusement right down to civilized times where he can still be recognized in the carnival figures of Pulcinella and the clown" (Jung, 1969, p. 264).

Trickster and *Telesphoros* are no longer outwardly manifested as in ancient times. This gradual "vanishing level of consciousness" is due to "repression (which) prevents it from vanishing because repressed contents are the very ones that have the best chance of survival (since) nothing is corrected in the unconscious." In Jung's terms "a higher level of consciousness has covered up a lower one" by "gradual civilizing" (ibid). So *The Trickster* and *Telesphoros* remain in the deep freeze of our collective unconscious, there intact, accessible under the right circumstances—a funny joke or comical situation that evokes spontaneous and forceful laughter. Our compassion for Tiny Tim in Dickens' *Christmas Carol*, *Oliver Twist, Cinderella*, and others connect us to tiny little cloaked *Telesphoros* holding the lantern that we can better see what is to be seen.

Trickster and *Telesphoros* are "a collective shadow figure which frequently appears in the phenomenology of dreams as a well-defined figure." Each is "hiding meaningful contents under an unprepossessing exterior." Because we cannot willingly and directly conjure them up in our dreams does not mean they don't exist: "If the enemy disappears from my field of vision then he may possibly be behind me and even more dangerous." To illustrate the point, Jung pointed out that we set up Christmas trees "without having the least idea what this custom means. It is really astonishing to see how many so-called superstitions are rampant. . .but if one asked 'Do you believe in ghosts? in witches? in spells and magic?' he would deny it indignantly. . .but in secret he is all for it just like a jungle-dweller" (ibid, pp. 268 and 270).

THE SHADOW

In her 1980 book, *Jung and Tarot, An Archetypal Journey,* Nichols defined **the shadow** as "a figure appearing in dreams, fantasies and outer reality that embodies qualities in ourselves which we prefer not to think of. . .because to admit to these would tarnish our image of ourselves." Because of this denial-avoidance we "project these seemingly negative qualities onto someone else" such as "an obnoxious person we never want to see again (but) who keeps popping up persistently and irrationally in our daily lives." For our own personal growth Nichols urges us to integrate the shadow so that "like in Stevenson's garden we can almost say of our shadow 'there is none of him at all' " (p. 58). Stevenson's poem illustrates Jung's **shadow** concept but also is a good example of playful humor:

My Shadow
by Robert Louis Stevenson

I have a little shadow that goes in and out with me,
And what can be the use of him is more than I can see.
He is very, very like me from the heels up to my head;
And I see him jump before me when I jump into my bed.

The funniest thing about him is the way he likes to grow
Not at all like proper children which is always very slow;
For he sometimes shoots up taller like an India rubber ball,
And he sometimes gets so little that there's none of him at all.

He hasn't got a notion of how children ought to play,
He stays so close beside me he's a coward you can see;
I'd think shame to stick to nursie
As that shadow sticks to me!

One morning, very early, before the sun was up,
I rose and found the shining dew on every buttercup;
But my lazy little shadow like an arrant sleepy-head,
Had stayed at home behind me and was fast asleep in bed.

(Opie & Opie, 1955)

HUMOR AS ALCHEMY

The Medieval alchemists sought to transmute lead, a base metal, into gold, a noble metal. Transforming evil to good is just as magical but it is possible to change depressed mood into cautious optimism with a funny saying or action. This is easily demonstrated with young children. In microcosm, it is the alchemist's dream of transmuting the base into the noble, the low to the high. Jung spent many years studying alchemy. The alchemists dedicated their lives to it. Nichols connects this seemingly useless ancient science to modern life and times: "An old alchemical maxim reads: 'What the soul imagines happens only in the mind. What God imagines happens in reality.' When the Unitary World erupts into our consciousness perhaps we catch a glimpse of the world as God imaged it" (p. 67). Ralph Waldo Emerson (1803-1882), preacher, poet, prime mover of **transcendentalism** and close friend of Alcott, Thoreau, Hawthorne and Carlyle, described how the alchemist connected to the universe:

Everything in Nature
Contains all the powers of Nature
(Everything is made of one hidden stuff).

Self-reliance, Essays, First Series
(Bartlett, 1968, p. 606)

"Alchemists," Nichols wrote, "repeatedly hinted that the gold they really sought was not outer gold but rather that transcendent inner gold at the center of the psyche that Jung calls the self." In *Psychology and Alchemy,* Jung reported that alchemists referred to their science as "The Great Work." There were "stages" to this work (liquification, distillation, separation, coagulation, etc.). Jung commented that these "correspond in many ways to the various stages through which the human psyche evolves, matures and moves toward individuation." In his view, creation is a "continuous ongoing event—an eternal dialogue between the one which is our small Magician and the One which is God, the Grand Magus." Mercurious was the alchemist's exemplar, "the world-creating spirit and the spirit concealed or imprisoned in matter. . .indwelling in all living creatures. . .transformer and the element to be liberated or transformed." Nichols suggests that "our mercurial spirit (whom we might label inner Magician) also shares these ambiguities. . .concealed and imprisoned in our dark unconscious" (p. 52).

HUMOR AS PHILOSOPHY

"To be able to laugh at evil and error," Jung wrote, "means that we have surmounted them. Comedy may be a philosophic as well as psychological compensation" (Sypher, 1956, p. 246). The French existentialist, Albert Camus (1916-1960), essayist, novelist, playwright and Nobel Laureate in Literature (1957) observed that "the absurd is the essential concept and the first truth" (Bartlett, 1968, p. 882). Maslow (1970), reviewing his research on self-actualization, reported that "on a simple quantitative basis" his subjects were "humorous less often than the average of the population." Theirs was a "thoughtful, philosophical humor that elicits a smile more usually than a laugh and spontaneous rather than planned and very often can never be repeated" (p. 170). They "do not consider funny what the average man considers to be funny" and this trait was "common to all my subjects." He analyzed "self-actualizing humor" further:

> . . .they do not laugh at hostile humor (making people laugh by hurting someone) or superiority humor (laughing at someone else's inferiority) or authority-rebellion humor (the unfunny, Oedipal, or smutty joke). Characteristically what they consider humor is more closely allied to philosophy than to anything else. It may also be called humor of the real because it consists in large part in poking fun at human beings in general when they are foolish, or forget their place in the universe, or try to be big when they are actually small. This can take

the form of poking fun at themselves, but this is not done in any masochistic or clownlike way (pp. 169-170).

Maslow used Abraham Lincoln as an example of self-actualized humor: "Probably, Lincoln never made a joke that hurt anybody else,"
Maslow commented. "It is also likely that many or even most of his jokes
had something to say, had a function beyond just producing a laugh.
They often seemed to be education in a more palatable form, akin to
parables and fables" (ibid). In *Toward a Psychology of Being* (1968),
Maslow described self-actualized people as "more fully evolved. . not
fixated at immature or incomplete levels of growth (with a) full humanness." He reported that "from a few research beginnings and from countless clinical experiences" he was able to list "objectively describable and
measurable characteristics" common to them:

1. Clearer more efficient perception of reality
2. More openness to experience
3. Increased integration, wholeness and unity of the person
4. Increased spontaneity, expressiveness; full functioning; aliveness
5. A real self; a firm identity; autonomy, uniqueness
6. Increased objectivity, detachment, transcendence of self
7. Recovery of creativeness
8. Ability to fuse concreteness and abstractness
9. Democratic character structure
10. Ability to love, etc.

"There are subject confirmations or reinforcements of self-
actualization," Maslow wrote, "feelings of zest in living, of happiness or
euphoria, of serenity, of joy, of calmness, of responsibility, of confidence
in one's ability to handle stresses, anxieties and problems" (p. 157). In
the striving "perpetually toward ultimate humanness. . .we are again
and again rewarded for good Becoming by transient states of absolute
Being, by peak experiences. . .which are absolute delights, perfect in
themselves and needing no more than themselves to validate life" (p.
154).

RESEARCH DATA

Researchers have explored the relationship of humor to conflict situations, mental illness and creative problem solving.

Coping with conflict. In some cases assertiveness training can result
in increased defensiveness in others or escalation in a conflict situation.
Woolfolk (1976) described three cases where "absurd communication"

was used to introduce an unexpected disruption in recurrent patterns of conflict. Woolfolk found that the humorous intervention interrupted the established negative pattern, defused conflict and served to plateau or neutralize anger.

Mental health/mental illness. Shenderova (1972), at the Psychiatric Institute in Moscow, studied 30 families of adolescent schizophrenics and found that 36 of the 60 biological parents (19 fathers; 17 mothers) showed significant psychopathology themselves. Relevant to our study of humor, Shenderova reported that the troubled parents exhibited such behaviors which suggested they were "too serious and stern to feel a need to socialize" and they "had no sense of humor." This study suggests that a lack of a playful mood, the ability to "have fun" is consistent with significant maladjustment and psychopathology. The Woolfolk study showed how humor facilitates better communication and reduces conflict. The Shenderova study suggests how little or no humor is inimical to good mental health.

Creative problem solving. Isen, Daubman and Nowiscki (1987) conducted four separate experiments involving 325 college students to assess the relationship between positive affect and creative problem solving. To elicit good feelings and/or humor they showed short comedy films, compared with other students shown serious films, exercise without film and no intervention at all. Creative problem solving was defined as ability to see relationships between diverse stimuli. Three models of creativity were considered: Mednick's combining elements remotely associated, Koestler's bisociation of two different frames of reference, and Poincare's useful new combinations of associative elements. Creativity was measured by a 10-minute, problem-solving task across all experimental and control groups. They found that humor **is** "conducive to improved creative problem solving on simple tasks and can be facilitated by a transient pleasant affective state or induced subtly by small everyday events" (p. 1128). Conversely, humor can have a reverse effect with complex tasks and those requiring innovation.

CRITIQUE. Koestler (1964) attacked Bergson's theory that humor is based on real or imaginary artificial, mechanical attributes or when we behave like automatons. If this is so, Koestler argued, "Egyptian statues and Byzantine mosaics would be the best jokes ever invented. . . there would be no more amusing spectacle than an epileptic fit and if we wanted a good laugh we would merely have to feel a person's pulse or listen to his heartbeat with its monotonous tick-tock. If we laugh each time a person gives us the impression of being a thing there would be nothing more funny than a corpse" (p. 47). Koestler contended that Bergson omitted ingenuity and innovation: "The word **witticism** is derived from 'wit' in its original sense of ingenuity and inventiveness" (p. 28). In Bergson's defense, puppets, mechanical slapstick, funny props and contraptions, the mime of Marcel Marceau and Shields and Yarnell, Jack-in-the-box and "peekaboo" consistently elicit smiles and laughter.

There is a certain enchanting charm and delightful elegance to some forms of humor, imaginative, uplifting, carefree and joyous, conducive to sharing and personal growth. When we share in it we can all be eternal children again (like *Telesphoros!*). Here, Bergson's **elan vital** and Maslow's **self-actualization** fit well. But regrettably, the sticking point is the same for creativity-change theory as for all the previous theories: it explains certain aspects of humor but not all of them. There is still more to humor than this theory includes.

CHAPTER 5

MODERN THEORIES: SEMANTICS/CONTENT ANALYSIS; SYZYGY THEORY

Linguistics becomes an ever eerier area
Like I feel like I'm in Oz
Just trying to tell it like it was.

Ogden Nash (1902-1971)
The old dog barks backwards (1972)

LINGUISTICS, a branch of anthropology, is the scientific study of language. It is a relatively young science; **comparative** or **historical linguistics** developing mostly in Germany in the 19th century and **descriptive linguistics** largely in the United States. Its major contribution has been **generative-transformational grammar,** greatly influenced by the work of Noam Chomsky. **Semantics** is the study of words and their meanings. If it does only that it functions as a branch of linguistics. If it is an abstract study of symbolic logic in word usage and meaning it functions as a branch of philosophy. **General semantics** is the study of how word meanings influence behavior. Relevant to our study of the theories of humor is Raskin's claim that "linguists are the new boys on the humor block" (1985, p. 34), a surprisingly sexist remark for a specialist in word usage, meaning and influence. This chapter will describe two semantic theories of humor: Arthur Koestler's **bisociation theory** (1964) and Victor Raskin's **script-based semantic theory** (1985).

BISOCIATIVE THEORY

This theory is described in Arthur Koestler's 1964 book, *The Act of Creation* and page references which follow are from it. "The pattern underlying all humor is **bisociative,**" Koestler claimed and which he explained as "perceiving an event in two habitually associative contexts" (which he termed **matrices**). "This causes an abrupt transfer of the train of thought from one **matrix** to another, governed by a different logic or 'rule of the game.'" Laughter results if there is emotional energy "worked off" as a "channel of least resistance" when "certain emotions (with) greater inertia and persistance cannot follow nimble jumps of thought discarded by reason" (p. 95). That's a quick overview of Koestler's **bisociation theory.** Let's take a closer look.

THE MATRIX

Koestler chose the term, **matrix,** carefully. It is "derived from the Latin for womb," he explained, "and is figuratively used for any pattern or mould in which things are shaped and developed or type is cast." he concluded: "Thus, the exercise of a habit or skill is moulded by its matrix" (p. 50). He defined a **matrix** as a set of rules or code, a frame of reference, which develops from a skill or ability. Matrices can be "fully automatized skills" or "those of high plasticity but even the latter are controlled by rules. . .below the level of awareness. . .silent codes, condensations of learning into habit" (p. 96). All "ordered behaviors, from embryonic development to verbal thinking, is controlled by 'rules of the game' which lend coherence and stability" but flexible enough "to adapt to environmental conditions" (ibid).

Koestler proposed the concept of "matrices with fixed codes and adaptable strategies as a unifying formula (which) appears to be equally applicable to perceptual, cognitive and motor skills and to the psychological structure variously called 'frames of references, associative contexts, universes of discourse, mental sets, schemata, etc.'" (ibid). He theorized that a matrix "operates in the nervous system through 'coded signals.' We know that not only the nervous system but all controls in the organism operate in this fashion."

Koestler observed that mathematical reasoning is "governed by specific rules" and "verbal reasoning, too, is subject to a variety of specific codes." He gave the example of Napoleon's defeat at Waterloo which "can be discussed in terms of historic significance, military strategy, the condition of his liver or the constellation of the planets." These are "frames of reference getting entangled or contexts getting confused but each is governed by sets or fixed rules." Or a chess player "looking at an empty board. . .does not see the board as a uniform mosaic of black and white squares but as a kind of magnetic field with lines of force. . .the board has become patterned." **The matrix is** the pattern, "the ensemble of permissible moves. **The code** governs the matrix and can be put into simple mathematical equations which contain the essence of the pattern in a compressed 'coded' form, (the) fixed, invariable factor. **Matrix** is its variable aspect" (p. 40).

"**Matrix** and **code** do not refer to different entities," Koestler explained, "they refer to different aspects of the same activity." **A code** is tactics, "the rule of the game determining which moves are permitted." **Matrix** is strategy, "the total possible choices before you." Matrices "vary in flexibility from reflexes and more or less automatized routines which allow but a few strategic choices to skills of almost unlimited variety." But even so Koestler insisted that "all coherent thinking and behavior is subject to some specifiable code of rules. . .even though the code functions partly or entirely on unconscious levels of the mind, as it generally does. A bar-pianist can perform in his sleep or while conversing with the barmaid; he has handed over control to the automatic pilot, as it were. This applies not only to our visceral activities and muscular skills but also the skill of perceiving the world around us in a coherent and meaningful manner. Hold your left hand six inches, the other twelves inches away from your eyes; they will look about the same size although the retinal image of the left is twice the size of the right" (p. 42).

LAUGHTER AS BISOCIATIVE EXPLOSION

Laughter and what's funny are emotive and cognitive discharges, emotional venting "produced by the sudden clash of incompatible matrices: to the experienced chess player a rook moving bishopwise is decidedly 'funny' " (ibid). Stated another way, comic effects result from "the sudden bisociation of an idea or event with two habitually incompatible matrices" (p. 51). Koestler offered two jokes to illustrate his theory of bisociation, codes and matrices:

1. Two women meet. One asks how the other woman's son is doing. "The psychiatrist says he has an Oedipus complex," she confides. "So," the other woman retorts, "he shouldn't have any problem as long as he's a good boy and loves his Momma."

2. A Marquis in King Louis XIV's court discovered his wife in bed with a priest. He walked calmly to the open window and went through

the motions of blessing the people in the street below. "What are you do-ing?" the wife asked. "Since Monsignor is performing my duties," the Marquis said, "I am performing his."

The stories differ by more than a century in time, context, and comic situation but Koestler saw them as following the same pattern. In the first joke, "the cheerful woman's statement is ruled by the logic of com-mon sense. But in the context of Freudian psychiatry the relationship to the mother carries entirely different associations."

The second joke "concerns adultery," a serious situation made poten-tially violent by the husband's discovery. Koestler reminds us of Aristo-tle's observation that in such circumstances "horror and pity accomplish the purgation of the emotions and tension ebbs away in gradual cathar-sis." In this case, tension mounts but is denied climax (as was the Mon-signor!). Koestler commented that "the ascending curve is brought to an abrupt end by the Marquis' unexpected reaction which debunks our dra-matic expectations. . The narrative acted as a channel directing the flow of emotion; when the channel is punctured the emotion gushes out like a liquid through a burst pipe; the tension is suddenly relieved and exploded in laughter" (p. 33).

"When the Marquis rushes to the window," Koestler wrote, "our in-tellect turns a somersault and enters with gusto into a new game. . .the piquant expectations which the narrative carried, including perhaps an unconscious admixture of sadism and cannot be transferred to the other (and) are disposed of through channels of least resistance" (laughter) (p. 56). Koestler suggested that similar "mental gymnastics" are involved in impersonation. When children "dress up," imitating adults, comedians impersonate public figures, men as women or women as men "the im-personator is perceived as himself and somebody else at the same time. While this situation lasts the two matrices are bisociated in the specta-tor's mind." Spectators' intellects are more agile than their emotions which cannot "follow these acrobatic turns" and "they are spilled into the gutters of laughter as soup is spilled on a rocking ship" (ibid).

The "pattern" in both the Oedipus complex and Marquis' wife's infi-delity "is perceiving of a situation or idea in two self-consistent but habit-ually incompatible frames of reference (which) vibrate simultaneously on two different wavelengths as it were." The story line or comic situa-tion is in two (or more) separate contexts (**matrices**) "not merely linked to one associative context." They are **bisociated.** "I have coined the term **bisociation,**" Koestler wrote, "to make a distinction between the routine skills of thinking on a single 'plane'. . .and the creative act which always operates on more than one plane" (p. 35).

In forms of malicious humor, Koestler saw "an aggressive tendency at work which for one reason or another cannot be satisfied by the usual methods of reasoned argument, physical violence or straight invective. Regardless of the age, mood or motive of those who laugh, "humor depends primarily on its **surprise effect: bisociative shock.**" Koestler insisted that it required "originality to cause surprise." He defined originality as "the ability to break away from stereotyped routines of thought." To do this involves the ability to perceive and function on more than one place (matrix): "The caricaturist, satirist, writer of nonsense-humor and even the tickler each operates on more than one plane. . .to convey a social message or merely to entertain must provide mental jolts. . .the collision of incompatible matrices" (p. 92).

HUMOR AS CREATIVITY

Bisociation of matrices can be achieved "by a kind of 'thinking aside' or shift of attention to some feature of the situation or an aspect of the problem which was previously ignored or only on the fringes of awareness" (p. 93). This is more "caught not taught" and defies a pure intellectual quest: "The humorist may stumble on it by chance or, more likely, be guided by some intuition which he is unable to define" (ibid). "The creative act," in Koestler's view, "connects previously unrelated dimensions of experience to attain a higher level of mental evolution" (p. 96).

The "creative act of the humorist" is a "momentary fusion between two habitually incompatible matrices" and scientific discovery "can be described in very similar terms." It is "the permanent fusion of matrices of thought previously believed to be incompatible. . . The history of science abounds with examples of discoveries greeted with howls of laughter because they seemed to be a marriage of incompatibles. . . comic discovery is paradox stated; scientific discovery is paradox resolved" (pp. 94-95).

SCRIPT-BASED SEMANTIC THEORY

Victor Raskin (1985) claimed humor is of "universal nature. . .people of different cultures and backgrounds, living on different continents, share the ability to laugh" and this is verified by "research of psychologists, sociologists, anthropologists, philosophers and literary scholars" (pp. 34-35).

Raskins' **script-based semantic theory** is a linguistic theory which interposes a cognitive step in the perception of what's funny: "When you hear a joke, the important thing is to get it. Then you decide whether the joke is worth a laugh, a smile or just a shrug." Stated in more detail "humor can be set up to match the intuitive ability people have to distinguish between funny and unfunny texts" (ibid). According to Raskin, what's funny is "semantic simply because jokes are funny by virtue of what they mean" (ibid). He offered this example:

> What is the best birthday present in Moscow?
> *An onion wrapped in toilet paper.*

Raskin explained this joke is funny because of its relevance to shortages of fresh vegetables and toilet paper in Moscow. It releases tension. The "punch line," the meaning behind the answer is based on everyday realities of living in Moscow and also the gift's unusual purpose to give something useful and appreciated.

He is critical of previous linguistic theories "locked into dictionary definitions and sentence analysis." Late in the 1970s, such terms as **presupposition**, **entailment** and **implicature** were introduced to describe how, "in any unfolding text, the stage is set for every sentence by the preceding sentence and every sentence sets the stage for the subsequent sentence" (ibid). He offered this example:

> *John is Mary's brother.*

This sentence's meaning **presupposes** there is but one John (a person, not a toilet "john") and one Mary (not "merry"). It implies the additional and equal fact that Mary is indeed John's sister. They are siblings. **Implicature** (fancy word for implying or implied meaning) **changes** the literal meaning such as "Can you pass me the salt?" and implies the real request: "Will you please pick up the salt shaker and hand it to me." If John and Mary were members of a religious congregation or commune, the sentence could also mean that John feels like Mary's brother in the Biblical sense of being one's "brother's keeper."

Raskin claimed that his **script-based semantic theory** is the first semantic theory of humor and that it goes beyond previous semantic theories, is more comprehensive. He includes **presupposition, entailment** and **implicature** and adds other concepts. It is **combinatorial**: "It calculates the meaning of each sentence on the basis of the meanings of the individual words and of the ways they are combined." It includes a **lexicon** of "entries which relate a key word to other words and ideas, typical actions, time, place and other characteristics." The "total configuration of all associations is a **script**" (ibid).

For example, the word **eat** "will represent the most pertinent and widely available information about eating: who eats, what is edible, who eats what, cooking and its relation to heat, kitchen utensils, meals and their frequency and other pertinent information." According to Raskin, "every word of a sentence evokes a script and the words of the same sentence frequently evoke the same script repeatedly. . .an ambiguous sentence is fully compatible with two or more scripts" (p. 36). Here's an example:

She cannot bear children.

Raskin explained that this can mean "being infertile" (child**bearing**) or having a low stress threshold with children. **Bear** is a verb "so animal **bears** are ruled out for syntactic reasons" (ibid).

Combinatorial rules combine all scripts evoked by individual words to help perceive the meaning of an entire sentence. At the same time, additional contextual and situational information is screened and stored to apply to previous and subsequent sentences and also reflected against previously stored information. The "best fit" is found in this way. **"Script-based semantic theory,"** Raskin maintained, "looks for certain properties of meaning whose presence makes the text a joke. . . The text is a joke if it is compatible fully or in part with two distinct scripts and the two scripts are opposite in certain definite ways such as good-bad, sex-no sex, or real-unreal." Most jokes have a third element, "the trigger or punchline which switches the listener or reader from one script to another creating the joke" (ibid). This element usually depends on ambiguity or contradiction. This is especially true for simple jokes.

In Raskin's humor theory, compatibility between two different scripts is only one requirement for a joke. The two scripts must also be opposite in a special sense, usually between "actual-not actual." One script refers to the **actual,** the real, normal and possible. The other script refers to the **not actual,** the unreal, abnormal or impossible. Example:

Male patient (in a soft bronchial whisper): Is the doctor in?

Doctor's (young, pretty) wife: No. Come in!

Raskin's analysis: There are two scripts operative here, **doctors** and **lovers.** The **doctor** script is **actual** and the **lover** script is **not actual** but it integrates all the words used, "the odd pieces fall neatly into place" to produce a "funny" effect.

To produce funny ad lib humor, spontaneously and extemporaneously, Raskin says the jokester must know "which of the necessary properties are already in place and then provide the missing element or elements." Frequently this involves a "previously ambiguous statement that was meant unambiguously." Raskin referred to W.C. Fields' quip when asked if he believed in clubs for children: "Only when kindness fails" (p. 39).

CRITIQUE. All semantic analyses are limited to the spoken or written word. None of them include "sight gags" or visual humor, nonverbal slapstick routines or mime. To analyze what's funny from word meanings and their usage and combination is a step forward but ignores the many variations of meaning from one individual to another, from one group, region, nation or culture from another. Raskin's claim that there is a cognitive step when we "decide whether the joke is worth a laugh" is not consistent with instantaneous, uncontrollable outbursts of laughter. Spies have been betrayed by their sudden, uncontrollable laughter at a joke in their native language, when they were feigning an inability to speak that language. If there was a cognitive step between the punchline and the laugh they could have suppressed laughter and saved their lives. Semantic theories are like trying to define a personality based on psychological tests. The tests are but a cross-section of and not **the** total personality. Using only semantics is like trying to understand great literature by diagramming sentences, great art by examining pigments and brushes, great music by individual notes or one measure. These factors are important and helpful to our study of humor but are only parts of "the big picture" which still exceeds the sum of its parts.

SYZYGY: THE TAO OF HUMOR

Exemplars: Everyone/Everything Funny!

Syzygy is a new theory of humor introduced here, an attempt to realize Eliot's observation that "the end of all our exploring will be to arrive where we started and know the place for the first time." Syzygy theory is the first eclectic theory of humor. It includes previous theories and attempts to integrate them. It adds some new elements. The name is taken from the astronomical phenomenon that *Webster's Ninth New Collegiate*

Dictionary defines as "the nearly straight-line configuration of three celestial bodies (as the sun, moon and earth during a solar or lunar eclipse)" (Mish, 1983, p. 1199). What's funny is a syzygy or convergence of three star cluster-like forces: **polarity, power** and **process.** Without their convergence there is no humor. The closer the convergence, the greater the impact of humor. With convergence there is **joke logic** where critical judgment and reason are eclipsed and replaced by hilarious absurdity or funny nonsense. We are then regressed to the Eternal Child in playful mood having fun. Generally, the more regressive (greater the syzygy), the more impact: tearful, uncontrollable roaring laughter.

In syzygy theory there is more to humor and what's funny than derision or disappointment, more than avoiding pain and pursuing pleasure, more than expressing sympathy, effecting change or facilitating creativity. As Eastman observed, "Athenians did not throng out upon that sunny hillside to enjoy the misfortunes of others but to enjoy laughter" (1922, p. 127). Humor is, as we first perceived it at the end of Chapter 1, "whatever makes you smile or laugh" which "varies with the individual and with group values." Eliot was right, we do arrive where we began and know the place better, having explored it in depth from earliest history to the living present.

Humor is the playful, pleasurable, childlike pastime of simply and directly having fun. The evolution of humor in the individual duplicates that of civilization: "ontogeny recapitulates phylogeny." Infant play is primitive, mostly physical, stimulated by color, shape, size and sound. Preschool children laugh at being tickled, surprised, hiding and being found, even being playfully frightened: "boo, peekaboo, all fall down" and Hallowe'en costumes, magic, puppets, clowns and Santa Claus (Bergson's automatism, Jung's archetypal imagery, Koestler's bisociation). Humor development in the individual combines the physiological, flowing through neuromuscular pathways specific to smiling and laughing (Darwin was right!) and the psychological-emotional (Freud was also right!). Like all other human behavior, it is modified and conditioned, learned and reinforced (Watson and Skinner were right!). As we grow from infant to adult, humor becomes less physical and more cerebral, less childishly simplistic, more sophisticated, able to be analyzed semantically (Raskin was right!). Koestler (1964) offered examples of this graduated effect as reflected in the varieties of humor:

> At first sight there seems to be a bewildering variety of moods involved in different types of humor. The practical joke is frankly aggressive; the lavatory jokes of children are eschatological; blue jokes are sexual; the

Charles Addams type of cartoon and the "sick" joke play on feelings of horror and disgust; the satirist on righteous indignation (p. 52).

Infantile humor is predominantly slapstick-style, simple and direct, moving on to "bathroom" or "barracks" humor where (regrettably!) most dirty jokes fit, to more adult embarrassing social situations (farce) then witty word play to conceptual or intellectual gaming. The individual grows, as also civilization, from unsocialized, totally dependent to socialized, independent, hopefully creative-transcending. George Meredith wrote in 1877 that "comedy is the ultimate civilizer and the comic spirit is our united social intelligence" (in Sypher, 1956, p. 252).

Moliere used the social setting to reach up to the conceptual: "He magnified the comedy of manners to the dimensions of a criticism of life . . .whenever a society becomes self-conscious about its opinions, codes of etiquette, comedy of manners may serve as a sort of philosophic engine called the comedy of ideas" (ibid, p. 211). Shakespeare's Hamlet, philosophically reflecting on the skull of Yorick, then throwing it back to the gravedigger (incidentally, a clown!), bridged tragedy and comedy, abstract and concrete, comedy of manners and comedy of ideas. So humor functions much like a magnetic or electrical force field. In the hands of skillful writers and comedians, it has great power to influence or to transform.

POLARITY, POWER, PROCESS

According to syzygy theory, all previous theories of humor contain an element of truth, a piece of the whole. Humor is a mosaic, a multifaceted diamond, made up of all that has been observed and reported of it. Every theory has touched on the **polarity** of humor, its **power** and the varieties of rules, techniques, or factors of its **process.** What's funny is determined by these three basic principles converging like three bright stars in **syzygy.** If only two converge, though each be bright and powerful, there is no humor. Polarity, power and process function more as force fields than mechanical factors or as objects, more as verb-forms than as nouns. They are active, dynamic, sparkling stars not inert planets. For something to be funny and to cause laughter to erupt spontaneously, all three forces must be operating and fully functioning. In the *Star Wars* movie series the expression was used: "May the Force be with you." This applies as well to the confluence of the three basic forces of syzygy theory: polarity, power and process.

POLARITY

Plato emphasized a definite negative polarity in his reliance on **derision** as the prime motive for humor. Aristotle softened Plato's "hard line." Humor in his **disappointment** or **frustrated expectation** theory did not have to be negative in its intent, its content or its result. The expectation which is frustrated could be positive or negative. He broadened the scope of humor by allowing for more than one prime motive for humor. This was typical of Aristotle's love for detail, his search for the ultimate essence of everything. His theory of humor was based on whatever is perceived as funny in objects, people or situations.

The study of previous theories of humor and the varieties of humor in the writing of this book exposes a clearly defined consistent, repeated cyclic or polar phenomenon. The poles are positive or negative, judged by the feeling level or feeling tone of the humor, by its emotional effect or "payoff" in the listener-spectator. In terms of previous theories of humor, **derision** is solely negative and **sympathy-empathy** is entirely positive. **Disappointment theory** falls on either side depending on the **polarity** or **valence** of its effect. A **frustrated expectation** proceeds and/or ends positively or negatively. **Pleasure-pain** divides as either **pleasure** or **reward** reinforcing (positive) or **pain** or **punishment** reinforcing (negative). **Instinct** separates out as creative **(eros libido)** or destructive **(thanatos libido)** in Freud's terms. **Physiology** can be positive (self-transcending) or negative (self-assertive) in Koestler's model. **Semantics** relates more to **process** than content, a method of evaluating content **(content analysis)**, the flow of humor toward either of the two poles.

In syzygy theory, polarity means that humor has **direction.** It has motion, it's "going somewhere." The punch line makes a point, says something. Or the joke does, in its development, reception and response. Humor has an underlying goal, motive or intent, and a definite measurable effect. This movement is as important as the words chosen and the technique used. In terms of Eric Berne's **transactional analysis,** humor is a transaction. It originates in *The Child* which exists within each of us. The Child in transactional analysis theory exists as "the **not OK** Kid" or **adapted Child,** angry, sadistic, selfish, and "the OK Kid" or **natural Child,** happy, sharing and fun-loving (MacHovec, 1974). This construct exactly fits the polar principle of syzygy theory. The "**not OK** Kid" is "charged" negatively, the "OK Kid" carries a positive charge.

Two exemplars demonstrate the polarity of humor: Mark Twain (1935-1910) and Robert Frost (1874-1963).

Twain held that "everything human is pathetic. The secret of humor itself is not joy but sorrow. There is no humor in heaven" (Eastman, 1936, p. 331). The tragicomic story of *Pagliacchi,* the clown, falls on Mark Twain's dark side of the spectrum of humor. All the references cited for derision theory in Chapter 2 further establish a negative polarity. The following, from Twain's *Pudd'nhead Wilson's New Calendar,* Chapter 30 reflects the negative polarity of humor: "Everyone is a moon and has a dark side which he never shows to anybody" (Bartlett, 1968, p. 625).

Frost was a poet, not a comedian or humorist, but his writing demonstrates an underlying cheerful optimism and spirit of warm fellowship typical of positive humor. The following is a sample:

Astrometaphysical (1946)

Lord, I have loved your sky,
Be it said against or for me,
Have loved it clear and high,
Or low and stormy.

My love for every heaven
O'er which You, Lord, have lorded,
From Number One to seven,
Should be rewarded.

It may not give me hope
That when I am translated
My scalp will in the cope
Be constellated.

But if that seems to tend
To my undue renown,
At least it ought to send
Me up, not down.

(Lathem, 1967, p. 389)

Louis Untermeyer, poetry editor of the *American Mercury* said of Frost: "His is a poetry which contemplates and sometimes criticizes the world but regards everything about it with love, occasional amusement and tender, tolerant pity. It is a poetry which literally begins in delight and ends in wisdom." That also describes the positive polarity of humor. Mark Twain could write and speak with sympathy, despite his basically satiric view of life: "Man is the only animal that blushes—or needs to" (Bartlett, 1968, p. 625).

Perhaps there is no more powerful voice for the positive than that of Anne Frank (1929-1945) who wrote in her diary shortly before her death: "In spite of everything I still believe that people are really good at heart." The German philosopher, Moritz Lazarus (1824-1903), described humor's positive potential:

. . .the mind in humor is related to the Idea and to Reality exactly as the whole feeling of man in religion is related to God and the World . . .the humorous mind sees itself and its actual life far from the Idea, powerless to attain its goal and its desire and therefore tamed and broken in its pride and oft even condemned to the dependent fierce laughter of self-contempt and yet on the other hand elevated and purified through the consciousness that in spite of all, it possesses the Idea and the Infinite within itself and in its even so imperfect works it reveals and lives them, is itself most inwardly at one with them if only through the painful recognition they bring its own imperfection.

(Eastman, 1922, p. 170)

All humor and all theories of it can be summarized according to their polarity as follows:

Negative Polarity	Positive Polarity
Message: "You're **not** OK"	*Message:* "You're OK"
Effect: Hostile; rejecting	*Effect:* Love; accepting
Derision-superiority	Sympathy-empathy
Disappointment	Positive expectation
Pain of pleasure-pain	Pleasure of pleasure-pain
Punishment reinforcers	Praise reinforcers
Self-assertive physiology	Self-transcending physiology
Negative instinct (thanatos libido)	Positive instinct (eros libido)
Evil Magician archetype (black magic)	Good Magician archetype (white magic)
Destructive change	Creativity, positive change

Polarities Compared Solely by Feeling Tone

Positive	Negative
Love	Hate
Accept	Reject
Approval	Disapproval
Equality	Superiority-inferiority
Elevate	Denigrate
Trust	Distrust
Attract	Repel
Playful	Sadistic
Inclusive	Divisive

Any form of humor, visual or verbal, oral or written, can be classified according to its **polarity.** A joke can move from one pole to the other from its outset to its conclusion or remain at only one pole throughout its course. Humor that takes time, such as comedy movies, plays, long jokes, extended limericks and poetry, continuing cartoons or comic strips, drawings or works of art, is likely to move from pole to pole and with a varying charge moment to moment. Satire tends to remain at the negative pole. Affectionate ridicule or teasing, as long as perceived as affectionate, tends to remain at the positive pole.

The polarity of humor functions much like the sine wave, oscillating above (positive) and below (negative) a Mean (neutral) baseline. The yin-yang symbol of Taoism, an S-curve within a circle bisecting the light from the dark half is yet another graphic visualization which fits the polarity construct. Within its positive and negative forces it functions on a continuum, from most positive to most negative with a neutral zone between them for the neutral narrative which "sets the stage" and provides a background or "ground" for the "figure" of what's funny.

POWER

The positive or negative "charge" of humor varies and its variability is a measure of its **power,** its effect on the audience. Both **polarity** and **power** can be measured. The simplest measure of positive power is a sound level meter or "S-meter" graduated in decibels preferably on a scale of 0-10. The *Can You Top This* radio show years ago used a decibel meter, calling it an "applause meter." Biofeedback or polygraph instrumentation could quantify negative responsivity. There are variables to be taken into account, such as individual differences, personal and demographic, group norms (social, regional, economic, educational, etc.) and length of time, number of jokes told, and others. The same joke told sandwiched between others, earlier or later than others, told by several comedians, differences in time and timing are also variables which can affect audience response. Videotaping provides a measure of nonverbal responses such as smiling or gesturing and augment sound volume of applause or verbal responses and galvanic, respiratory, heart rate and blood pressure variables measured by instrumentation.

Power is the measure of the relative impact or effect of humor on an audience. With scientific instrumentation in the form of apparatus, questionnaires, checklists, standard measures of observation, it should be possible to quantify the power of humor on a $+10$ to -10 continuum with a neutral 0 between them. Without such precise measurement, a +3 to 0 to −3 continuum may be more practical and contribute to higher inter-rater reliability. In these ways humor, visual and auditory, written or oral, can be quantified.

When humor is successful, **polarity** and **power** are in conjunction, like two of the three stars in syzygy. There is a well defined positive or negative "charge." The "current" of words, their meaning, and the techniques or tactics of delivery build up and "spark" or "fire" in the overt, measurable behavior of smiles (visually) and laughter (audibly). The following illustrates the interaction of **polarity** and **power**:

	Effect	**Example**
+3	"Gutbuster" (highest S-meter reading).	Hysterical laughter (gasping for air; tears; wet your pants!).
+2	Involuntary muscle response (laugh).	Average positive joke response ("Yeah, yeah!).
+1	Weak muscle response (smile; nod; lowest S-meter reading).	"Hooks" into and activates a cheerful, playful mood; spontaneous funny situations.
0	Nothing! (blank stares; bewilderment; "bomb out!").	Anything expected to be funny which isn't; totally without humorous effect; dead!
−1	Weak frozen smile or poker face; blushing; mood swing to serious; mild discomfort.	Content of *I got plenty of nothin'* (Gershwin) or the ragtime song *Nobody* in its down mood; ridicule; mildly insulting jokes.
−2	Definite discomfort; moderate disagreement; some audience "grumbling."	Jokes that "backfire" with "backlash effect;" cutting inappropriate satire; insulting jokes.
−3	Violent disagreement severe agitation and discomfort in audience.	"Tar and feathers" time! loud heckling; some in audience throw things, walk out (racial, political slurs).

Polarity is judged by content, power is measured by its effect. Polarity is a qualitative measure of mood or feeling tone from none through mild, moderate and severe. Negatively, the polar continuum is from zero (no audience reaction whatever) through -1 (mild discomfort, quiet irritation, feeling unwillingly teased), -2 (feeling insulted, moderate discomfort, some look at their watches, some voiced and visual hostility) to -3 (maximum, active hostility—if you continue there may be a hanging!). Positively, the polar continuum is from zero (no reaction) through $+1$ (mild acceptance, accepted kidding—a smile, nod, soft laughter, momentary glint in the eye or enjoyment and acceptance), $+2$ (definite audible laughter, verbal or visual approval and acceptance), to $+3$ (loud, uncontrollable laughter, continuing contagious giggles, a "gutbuster" with teary eyes).

Positive polarity involves audience feeling (affect) and thinking (comprehension, intelligence). Its feeling tone is regressive and largely unconscious, a return to the playful mood and spontaneous joy of childhood, Eric Berne's *OK Kid* (MacHovec, 1974). . . Its thinking level involves conscious willingness to relax inhibitions and critical judgment, to "let go." Negative polarity is also regressive, but a return to the dark side of the yin-yang symbol, to the *not OK Kid,* vengeful, pouting, potentially destructive.

PROCESS

Process in syzygy theory is the study of the tactics of humor, its detailed mechanics, techniques, rules or codes. Whatever best explains what's funny in a given situation is valid. To make such a judgment requires a knowledge of all humor theories, considered openly, equally and without bias. To do so is to realize the **Tao of humor,** to allow it to be, to emerge of and by itself, to let its polarity flow, its power build, to the peak spark of laughter. Of the many process factors, there are several especially emphasized by syzygy theory:

Joke logic is a basic characteristic and major distinguishing feature of humor in any of its varied forms. Like dreams, humor is a direct link to the unconscious in Freudian terms or to the simple joy of childhood experiencing in behavioristic terms. Despite our intellect and social sophistication we can in a split-second regress back to the childhood joy of being on merry-go-rounds, at the circus, held high above daddy's head, warmly hugged by our mommies, affectionately teased by elders and friends, and all this by the magic carpet of humor. Koestler's bisociation and Jung's alchemical transformation constructs are but two of many examples of the transformational capability of humor. Sypher

(1956) described the magical effect of a comedian's words as "at once a stone rejected by the builder and the cornerstone of the temple" (p. 231). The most effective humor flows naturally and spontaneously at its own speed and according to its own rules and logic. It has a certain unique and classic elegance like cut glass or fine silver. That is why some jokes remain funny even after 2000 years (see Chapter 7 for examples).

Joke logic is a process factor, transformational with respect to mood, transcending in terms of its facilitating creative expression and personal growth. "Unexpectedness alone is not enough to produce a comic effect," Koestler wrote, "the critical point (is) both unexpected and perfectly logical — but of a logic not usually applied to this type of situation" (1964, p. 35). "The comic spirit," Bergson maintained, "has a logic of its own . . .a method in its madness" (Sypher, 1956, p. 62). It is "logic of the imagination which is not the logic of reason. . .one which at time is even opposed to the latter. . . something like the logic of dreams though of dreams that have been left to the whim of individual fancy, being the dreams dreamt by the whole of society" (ibid, p. 86). Here Bergson touched on Freud's idea that humor and dream similarity and also Jung's **collective unconscious.** He also approached the "rules" of the semanticists, Koestler and Raskin: "To reconstruct this hidden logic," he wrote, "a special kind of effort is needed (which) obeys laws or rather habits which hold the same relation to imagination that logic does to laughter" (ibid, p. 87).

Koestler (1964) provided an example of joke logic in the story of an art dealer who bought a picture signed "Picasso." The dealer travelled to Cannes, visited Picasso and showed him the picture. "It's a fake," Picasso said sharply. Months later the dealer showed Picasso another picture. With a quick glance Picasso snorted: "It's a fake." Upset, the dealer pointed out that he himself had seen Picasso painting the same picture. Picasso shrugged and replied: "So I sometimes paint fakes" (p. 82).

Koestler's non-joke logic version of the story pointed out that Picasso did not say: "Sometimes, like other painters, I do something second-rate, repetitive, an uninspired variation on a theme, which after a while looks to me as if somebody had imitated my technique. It is true that this somebody happened to be myself but that makes no difference to the quality of the picture, which is no better than if it were a fake; in fact you could call it that, an uninspired Picasso apeing the style of the true Picasso" (p. 84).

The listener has to use joke logic to "get" the joke. The punch line, the payoff, the "bottom line" is implied or implicit, not explicit. There must be an imaginative leap to solve the joke's riddle, its mystery, by the subtle tracking, hints or clues in the story. It "hooks" into the "hide and seek" or "peekaboo" of early childhood, a "fun game." There is freedom to playfully roam about and find the connection. "Every good joke contains an element of the riddle," Koestler maintained, "it may be childishly simple or subtle and challenging" (p. 86). If it is all explicit it loses appeal. "To a sophisticated audience," he observed, "any joke sounds stale if it is entirely explicit." In such a situation the listener thinks faster than the joke teller and "instead of tension it will generate boredom." The story line must "jump ahead leaving logical gaps" which the listener must close. This is done by **interpolation** or **extrapolation**. "Language itself," Koestler concluded, "is never completely explicit. Words have suggestive, evocative powers. . .merely stepping stones for thought" (ibid).

Joke logic is "word magic" which transforms the illogical or paradoxical into the logical and compatible, with a lightning bolt of humor and the thunder of hearty laughter. This illogical-logical switch can involve "professional with commonsense logic, of metaphorical with literal meaning, of contexts linked by sound affinities, of trains of reasoning travelling, happily joined together, in opposite directions" (Koestler, 1964, pp. 65-66). Clinical and experimental hypnotized persons, increasing their suggestibility, diminishing critical judgment, rendering bizarre and illogical ideas perceptible as reality. Trance logic and joke logic are similar in their effect on thinking and perception, though trance logic is far more powerful. They both facilitate increased suggestibility: "Suggestive techniques are essential; they create suspense and facilitate the listener's flow of associations along habit-formed channels" (Koestler, 1964, p. 83).

Content analysis. Syzygy theory accepts all the methods of classifying and analyzing humor, from Plato and Aristotle to Koestler and Raskin. Whatever best explains process is the most appropriate. Cutting satire suggests Plato's derision theory, negative polarity with a power rating of at least 2, on the polarity-power scale. A clown looking whimsical and cuddling a puppy suggests sympathy theory with at least a 2 + response.

In 1964, Arthur Koestler reported "criteria of comic technique. . . which decide whether it is good, bad, or indifferent" (p. 82). These have been adapted and synthesized into three basic criteria for effective process which converge or meet in syzygy: appeal; economy; push.

Appeal involves creative or innovative **originality** such as that of Picasso in Koestler's example. It includes skillful **selection** of subject, funny situation and its context for maximum effect. A major factor contributing to appeal is the impact of **surprise.** There are thus three **appeal** factors.

Economy refers both to words and ideas (**word economy; idea economy**). There should be just enough words used, neither too many nor too few. The best jokes are not cluttered with extraneous ideas which can mislead or confuse, but continue focussed "on target" for the climax or payoff. **Simplification** is another major criterion, meaning the use only of essential elements, most easily understood (KISS: Keep it simple, stupid!).

Push is a collective term for **emphasis, exaggeration** and **escalation.** Discussing emphasis, Koestler (1964) wrote: "The cheap comedian piles it on; the competent craftsmen play in a subtler way on our memories and habits of thought" (p. 83). Again suggesting that humor is basically a regressive trait to childhood joy and the similarity of experiencing humor to hypnotic suggestibility, Koestler wrote: "Anticipation of the type of joke or point to come do not entirely destroy the comic effect provided that we do not know when and how exactly it will strike home. . . like a game: cover my eyes and I shall pretend to be surprised" (ibid). **Push** includes the timing and pacing of the joke, a measured **escalation** to the orgastic peak. Often **exaggeration** provides more dramatic intensity, a more forceful buildup. Dialect and gestures are often used toward this end.

OVERVIEW

Syzygy theory integrates previous theories but sees all humor resulting in the convergence of three basic star clusters or forces: **polarity** (direction of feeling tone); **power** (force or valence of the feeling tone); **process** (mechanics, details of technique; how polarity and power are focussed). Polarity and power are strategic or **why** factors, measures of **effectiveness.** Process is a tactical or **what** and **how** factor based on specifics of technique, a measure of **efficiency.** Like a 3-legged stool, each star cluster or force is required for any form of humor to be effective.

CRITIQUE. Syzygy theory is eclectic, the first attempt at integrating previous theories. It includes all forms of humor, written, oral or visual. Its language is simple, its applications practical and universal. But it is new and untested and while it appears to have face validity only the test of time and use will determine its value. It appears to be a good teaching model since it does not exclude previous theories nor favor one over another.

Simplified 1040

Latest Revision

1040 Federal Income
Tax Form

Department of the Internal Revenue Service

Part 1: Income

Your Social Security Number

1. How much money did
   you make last year?............. ▶

2. Send it in .... ▶

CHAPTER 6

HUMOR SAMPLER: ITS VARIETY
AND VERSATILITY

> *Humor. . .is a personal matter,*
> *losing its virtue by diffusion.*
> *Humor in diffusion concerns ideas*
> *in diffusion and people and things*
> *in diffusion. It is type-humor. . .*
>
> *Robert Graves (1974)*
> **Mrs. Fisher or the future of humor**

THIS CHAPTER is a sampler of some of the varieties of humor. To use this chapter's humor samples as a personal, group or class study guide, read and react to them and do any or all of the following:

1. **Polarity sort.**
   (a) Classify the humor by its **dominant polarity** (positive, neutral, negative).
   (b) Did it vary in polarity from inception, through development, at climax or afterward? If it did, try writing it with the variations noted marginally.
   (c) If in a group or class, do you agree with the others on the polarity of each item?
2. **Power level (valence).**
   (a) Grade its **power** as you experienced it (+1 "Ah hah!" feeling, smile or nod; +2 motor reflex of chuckle or laugh; +3 uncontrollable, repetitive hearty laugh; 0 "bomb out" no effect; −1 feeling of dismay or disapproval; −2 muscle response (shrug, frown) or verbalized disapproval ("Hmph!" or "No, no!" etc.); −3 loud, spontaneous "eruption" (cussing, denunciation) or motor behavior (slam the book shut or throw it).

(b) Did power vary at inception, through development, at climax (punch line) or afterward? Graph it.

(c) If part of a group or class, compare your rating with others. Which items rated closest? Which were most different? Why?

(d) Which items had the most power for you? Why? This is a clue to what **you** perceive as funny. Compare with others in the group or class.

3. **Process analysis.**

(a) To which of the eight theories of humor does the item best fit? Which fits least?

4. **Evaluating your own sense of humor.**

(a) Which of the items do you like best (had the most **power** for you)?

(b) Sort only those favorite items by **polarity.** If there are more negative than positive you may want to consider toning down derision and using more sympathy/empathy or creativity/change to transform your humor (and perhaps your mood!) to be more positive, cheerful and optimistic.

There are no **right** or **wrong** answers to these questions and exercises. Responses to them do not mean one person is any **better** or **worse** because of what is perceived as funny. Humor and its perception are unique, subjective phenomena which vary from one individual to another and as every comedian knows from one audience to another. What's positive or negative also varies significantly among individuals and audiences. Mark Anthony's funeral oration swayed an audience antagonistic to him by the repeated, softly sarcastic, ridiculing, powerfully escalating "but they are all honorable men."

The humor samples in this chapter are arranged in the following categories:

Animal-human	Jobs, professions
Art	Movies-TV
Child	Music
Daffynitions	Poetry, limericks
Double meaning/entendre	Proverbs, epigrams, sayings
Essays	Puns, play-on-words
Ethnic	Riddles, conundrums
Freudian slips	Ridicule, satire
Impersonation	Sex and love

Theatre

ANIMAL-HUMAN

Koestler (1964) considered Walt Disney's animated characters as bisociation of animal and human: "Disney's creatures behave as if they were human without losing their animal appearance, they live on the intersection of the two planes" (p. 67). In terms of syzygy theory they also function on either side of positive-negative polarity. Their power is evidenced by the enthusiastic response of audiences over time. There is derision and aggression in many animated cartoons but also sympathy and support "for the little guy." This humanization of wild animals can cause problems (feeding bears in national parks) and injury (approaching wild animals as "friends"). Joke logic enables us to make this switch between animal and human, or sympathy from derision. As Koestler (1964) put it "If sympathy prevails over malice even poor Donald Duck's misfortunes cease to be laughable" (ibid).

ART

Humor is expressed in art in a variety of forms: cartoons and comic strips, drawings and graffiti, posters, painting, photographs, sculpture and statuary, and in design and decor. Music and dance are also art forms but sufficiently important for the study of humor to merit separate description in this chapter.

Examples of cartoon humor are the film characters—Mickey Mouse, Donald Duck, Bugs Bunny, Porky Pig and Elmer Fudd. Popular comic strip characters are Charlie Brown and Doonesbury. Humor in drawings, posters and painting is exemplified in the work of Norman Rockwell (1894-1978), especially the cover illustrations in the *Saturday Evening Post,* Henri de Toulouse-Lautrec (1964-1901), artist in oils, posters and lithographs, and the impressionist Pablo Picasso (1881-1973), father of cubism. *Time* and *Newsweek* photographs frequently reflect humor and continue the photojournalistic tradition of *Life* and *Look* magazines. Sculpture and statuary with a humorous flavor are common in theme parks and in garden ornaments such as gnomes, miniature animal forms and fountain figures (like the little boy "tinkling"). Theme parks, nursery and primary schools, day care centers and the children's wards in hospitals feature humorous decor in the form of posters, pictures, murals, even carpeting, pillows and blankets. Stuffed animals and toys enhance a playful mood, as do kaleidoscopes, cuckoo clocks, Jack-in-the-Box and hand puppets. Fireworks function as an art form of sound, color and pattern in the spontaneous "burst" or "Ahah!" of childhood joy.

CHILD

Young children and puppy dogs have much in common, as Koestler pointed out (1964, p. 68). The "helplessness, trustingness, attachment and puzzled expression" suggest puppy dogs are "more 'human' than grownup dogs. . .the ferocious growl of the puppy strikes us as an impersonation of adult behavior" like boys and girls playing "dress up," wearing their parents' clothing. Puppy dogs, kittens and human infants exhibit an innocence, a simple directness and a fragile naivete which is a natural "setup" for humor.

1. Mother and little daughter shopped at the supermarket. They bought a box of *Animal Crackers* (remember them?). As mother unpacked the groceries she noticed all but one cracker was gone from the box. "It was full at the store," mother said, "and you were the only one in the back seat with them." The little girl thought a moment, opened the box and took out the last cookie and said: "Well, see, this is an elephant cookie and he must've eaten up the others" (Lily Tomlin).

Kids fib a lot, it's a natural defense. The fibbing can be quite humorous, as Lily Tomlin's joke demonstrates. Kids are also pretty tough. When they really like something they keep at it — favorite games, TV shows or stories. At a transactional analysis workshop years ago the story was told of a child "caught in the act" stealing cookies from the cookie jar. Unable to blame it on the "cookie monster" (we had a ghost that would eat only junk food in the house) he was restricted to his room and denied TV for the day. Worse, he had eaten so many cookies he became ill and threw up. Now if you were his friend, confiding on equal terms, knowing no one would ever hear, the conversation would be:

YOU: Hi! How you feeling?
HIM: Not so good. I took cookies and wasn't s'posed to. I can't go out and watch TV and hafta stay here. I et so many I got sick and frew up.
YOU: Yeah. That's not so good.
HIM: Y'know what?
YOU: What?
HIM: It was worth it!

2. Mother to father: "It's time you told little Johnny about sex." Apprehensive, father approached Johnny: "I want to talk to you about sex." Johnny smiled back: "Sure, Dad, what do you wanna know?" (anon).

3. My grand-daughter Allison, but two years old at the time, had a pretty bad dose of intestinal flu. She tried as only a child could to busy herself with toys and games but the illness overtook her. She came to us looking troubled, the corners of her mouth turned down, and a bit bewildered. "My mouth is dirty," she said, a few seconds before throwing up. It may be a grandfather's doting pre-occupation, but this incident demonstrated a playful little person coping with harsh reality, reflected against the innocence of her tender age and the limits of her vocabulary, life experience and understanding. "Really sick" for the first time, she described it in her own terms.

Marjorie Fleming was born in Scotland in 1803 and died there at the tender age of eight. During her brief life, she kept a diary, written mostly when she was six. We are indebted to Sir Walter Scott (1771-1832) for immortalizing this little girl's thoughts. He named her "Pet Marjorie" and her words have all the natural charm and candor of the Eternal Child. Here's a sampling from Christianna Brand's 1963 book *Naughty Children*.

4. I am going to tell you about the horrible and wretched pleage my multiplication give me you can't conceive it the most Devilish thing is 8 times 8 and 7 times 7 is what nature itself cant endure (p. 68).

   Yesterday I behave extremely ill in Gods most holy church for I would never attende myself nor let Isabella attende which was a great crime for she often tells me that when two or three are geathered together God is in the midst of them and it was the same Divel that tempted Job that tempted me I am sure but he resisted satan though he had boils and many other misfortunes which I have escaped (p. 94).

   Today I pronounced a word which never should come out of a ladys lips it was that I called John a Impudent Bitch and Isabella afterwards told me I should never say it even in a joke but she would kindly for gave me because I said that I would not do it again I will tell you what I think made me in so bad a humour is I got 1 or 2 cups of that bad sina tea today (p. 125).

5.   ANONYMOUS CHILD'S POEM
   Debora, Debora, she liked a bit of fun—
   She went to the baker's and she bought a penny bun;
   Dipped the bun in treacle and threw it at her teacher—
   Debora, Debora, what a wicked creature! (ibid, p. 142).

Charlotte Bronte (1816-1855) wrote *Jane Eyre* in 1847. Here's an excerpt from it, a bit of childish charm more than 150 years old:

6. "Your name, little girl?"

"Jane Eyre, Sir."

"In uttering these words I looked up: he seemed to me a tall gentleman—but then I was very little; his features were large and they and all the lines of his frame were equally harsh and prim.

"Well, Jane Eyre, are you a good child?"

Impossible to reply to this in the affirmative—my little world held a contrary opinion—I was silent. Mrs. Reed answered for me by an expressive shake of the head, adding that, "Perhaps the less said on that subject the better."

"Sorry to hear it! She and I must have a talk"; and bending from the perpendicular he installed his person in the armchair opposite. "Come here," he said.

I stepped across the rug; he placed me square and straight before him. What a face he had now that it was almost on a level with mine! What a great nose! And what a mouth! And what large prominent teeth!

"No sight so sad as that of a naughty child," he began.

"Do you know where the wicked go after death?"

"They go to hell," was my ready and orthodox answer. . .

"What must you do to avoid it?"

I deliberated a moment; my answer, when it did come, was objectionable: "I must keep in good health and not die"

(ibid, pp. 204-205)

From the pen of Hector Hugo Munro (1870-1916), pen name Saki, these words from his *Autobiography:*

7. Not every afternoon did the aunts sleep, so either that or to make a marauding expedition into the storeroom via the greenhouse, equally forbidden ground, was naturally the only thing to be done.

On one occasion we emerged from the latter with a jar of tamarinds and got it safely into the night nursery where there was a large trunk in which Aunt Augusta kept spare clothes. We ate what we wanted and put the jar in the trunk between folds of a black silk dress. The jar contained a lot of juice, very sticky, and in the eating much was smeared over the sides. However, the black silk absorbed a lot.

And then Aunt Augusta had occasion to open the trunk! Broadgate resounded to her bellowings and the row was frightful. In a former life she must have been a dragon.

(ibid, pp. 238-239)

DAFFYNITIONS

(Silly satiric definitions)

Silly and satiric definitions provide an instant break from routine for a quick chuckle, psychologically and emotionally a vent from tedium and the restraints of responsibility and rigid conformity. Here's a sampling of funny definitions:

8. *Conscience* is the inner voice which warns us that someone may be looking (Mencken, 1927, p. 231)

9. *Democracy* is the theory that the common people know what they want and deserve to get it good and hard (ibid).

10. An *archbishop* is a Christian ecclesiastic of a rank superior to that attained by Christ (ibid).

11. What is a *cynic?* A man who knows the price of everything and the value of nothing (Oscar Wilde, in Bartlett, 1968, p. 839).

12. *Marriage* is the state. . .consisting of a master, a mistress, and two slaves, making in all, two (ibid, p. 986).

13. *Economic expert:* Someone who knows tomorrow why things predicted yesterday didn't happen today (Braude, 1961, p. 9).

14. *Fanatics:* People with such a large chip on the shoulder it makes them lose their balance (ibid).

DOUBLE MEANING (DOUBLE ENTENDRE)

This form of humor is based on two coexistent meanings, a manifest or obvious meaning and a latent or hidden meaning. The listener must "catch" the second, hidden meaning or miss the joke. Some well-intentioned messages have unknowingly carried a "funny" double meaning, such as "fly United" (fly **united**), "come again" on the exit door of a brothel or a sign hanging on the front door: "Closed for renovations. Beat it." In a James Bond movie, he is phoned by "M," his boss, while in bed nude with a woman. Bond smiles, looks down at himself and says: "Sorry, Chief, something's come up."

15. Hamlet: Upon what grounds did Hamlet go mad?
    Clown: Why, here in Denmark.

16. Sergeant Jones and Sergeant Smith, country boys naive to the ways of the world, approached a streetwalker "for a good time." "I'm sorry," she told them, "but I have VD." Bewildered, Jones asked: "Wal, whut's VD?" "That's a disease of the privates," she replied. "Oh, thet's awright," Jones smilingly said, "we're sergeants" (anon.).

17. A medical student was having a passionate affair with a nurse. He phoned her one day to tell her he had an opportunity to see a famous brain surgeon operate Friday night which conflicted with their date. "Well," Nurse Torrid said, "maybe you should toss a coin, heads or tails" (anon).

18. There was a Scottish fisherman who married a widow with worms (Graves, 1974, p. 9).

19. Take my wife—please! (Henny Youngman, in *Allen*, 1987, p. 32).

20. Whistler had to stop work on his famous painting because his mother was off her rocker (anon).

21. Dr. Foufou, Parisian psychiatrist, concluded his study of suicide with the finding: "People who jump in the river are often found in Seine" (anon).

22. Not to be outdone by Dr. Foufou's French psychiatric research, the American psychologist, Dr. Si Kopath, concluded that "anyone who jumps off a bridge or building should wear a light fall suit" (anon).

23. Hedda Hothead pressed a suit against her husband, burning him badly (anon).

24. Herkimer Jerkimer, brakeman for the railroad for 23 years, severed all ties and caused a 7-car derailment (anon).

25. Court Jester Ricardo III contracted the Bubonic plague in the year 1230 and became the world's first "sick comedian" (anon).

26. Archimedes assured his students that "geometry is easy as pi" (anon).

27. Tillie Tartt reported her boy friend to the postal inspectors, calling him an obscene male (anon).

ESSAYS

The following is excerpted from an essay by H.L. Mencken in the *Baltimore Evening Sun* on April 7, 1924:

28. It is almost as safe to assume that an artist of any dignity is against his country, i.e., against the environment in which God hath placed him, as it is to assume that his country is against the artist. The special quality which makes an artist of him might almost be defined, indeed, as an extraordinary capacity for irritation, a pathological sensitiveness to environmental pricks and stings. He differs from the rest of us mainly because he reacts sharply and in an uncommon manner to phenomena which leave the rest of us unmoved or at most merely annoy us vaguely. He is, in brief, a more delicate fellow than we are. . .(and) takes to artistic endeavor which is at once a criticism of life and an attempt to escape from it. . .

Dante put all of the patriotic Italians of his day into Hell and showed them boiling, roasting and writhing on hooks. Cervantes drew such a devastating picture of the Spain that he lived in that it ruined the Spaniards. Shakespeare made his heroes foreigners and his clowns Englishmen. Goethe was in favor of Napoleon. Rabelais, a citizen of Christendom is still trying in vain to suppress. Swift, having finished the Irish and then the English, proceeded to finish the whole human race. The exceptions are few and far between and not many of them bear examination. . .

Art Hope wrote this *Fable With a Happy Ending* in the *San Francisco Chronicle:*

29. Once upon a time, there were two tribes named the Goodguys and the Badguys who lived in a beautiful green valley where wildflowers grew. They both loved the beautiful green valley and the wildflowers very much. It was a common bond.

But the Goodguys had a system called Wonderfulism. Which each said he'd be happy to die for. And the Badguys had a system called Awfulism. Which each said he'd be happy to die for. So they hated each other.

Moreover, each Goodguy said he'd be happy to die to save the Badguys from Awfulism. And each Badguy said he'd be happy to die to save Goodguys from Wonderfulism. Whenever the Goodguys and the Badguys met, they naturally threw rocks at each other to save each other's systems. Occasionally, somebody would get hit by a rock. But rock-throwing relieved everybody's frustrations and wasn't so bad.

Then one day, the Wizards invented a new animal called the Psnxtl. Which only the Wizards could understand. It was awesome. It was so awesome that everybody stopped talking about how happy they would be to die. And each side even stopped throwing rocks at the other side for fear the other side would unleash its dread Psnxtl.

So the valley lay in peace. No rockthrowers trampled on the wildflowers and they bloomed more profusely than before. Everybody said how delightful peace was and how much they loved the wildflowers.

But the Wizards naturally wished to test their Psnxtls. To see how awesome they were. In order to ensure peace. And then they wanted to see if they could invent even more awesome Psnxtls to ensure peace even more. All the Wizards conceded the Psnxtls would poison the air in the valley, but most Wizards said they would only poison the air a little bit. And everybody agreed peace was worth it.

After many years, both the Goodguys and the Badguys got used to having the Psnxtls around. And pretty soon they beagn saying that being killed by a Psnxtl was no worse than being killed by a rock. This made everybody feel better. And they began saying, once again, that they'd be happy to die for Wonderfulism (or Awfulism, as the case might be). And that they'd be happier dead than Awful (or Wonderful). And the Psnxtl thus became the symbol of happiness and security.

So, to be happy and secure, the Goodguys and the Badguys both naturally raised more Psnxtls and bigger Psnxtls and more and bigger and more and bigger and. . .Eventually, of course the Psnxtls ate everybody up. They ate up the Goodguys and the Badguys and Wonderfulism and Awfulism. And all the wildflowers.

But, actually, this is a happy ending. Because the Goodguys happily saved everybody from Awfulism. And the Badguys happily saved everybody from Wonderfulism. So everybody died happy. Except maybe the wildflowers. Moral: People don't love wildflowers as much as they say they do (Peterson, 1963, pp. 111-112).

ETHNIC HUMOR

Ethnic humor is humor primarily based on racial, religious, national, regional, local, social, sex or sexist, age characteristics or other differences. Ethnic jokes almost always involve simplistic and stereotyped thinking, bias and prejudice, usually condescending. While there can be some sympathy and support, if the joke teller shares the same ethnic background, most ethnic humor is disparaging and derisive. Any group can be the victim of the ethnic put-down. Most groups named in the samples which follow could be changed and the humor content would likely not change significantly.

Arieti (1976) cited Jewish and Italian ethnic humor as examples of self-deprecation when used from within and anti-Semitism and anti-Italian when imposed from without. "Jewish jokes by Jews and non-Jews differ," he wrote (p. 124). Freud's view was that when Jews joke about themselves they are "sincere admittances of one's real shortcomings." But Arieti maintained "this habit of the Jews is paradoxically an unconscious defense against anti-Semitism. Surrounded for centuries by a hostile environment the Jews have tried to make. . .the majority discharge their hostility by means of such relatively harmless jokes. It is better to be accused of stinginess and dirtiness than of deicide and ritual murder. . . better to be laughed at than to be massacred" (ibid).

Arieti, himself of Italian descent, saw the same basic dynamic in Italian ethnic humor, though the implication is the same for other minorities. He referred to "making fun of" the "poor pronunciation of English" as a common method of self-deprecation. Myron Cohen's Yiddish dialect and distinctive speech styles improve the effectiveness (power) and efficiency (process) of ethnic humor. Referring to the stereotypy of Italians eating spaghetti, Arieti observed "it is better to be accused of eating too much spaghetti than of being gangsters" (p. 126). He concluded that "social groups under environmental stress resort to the neurotic social defense of creating self-accusatory jokes. . .if one can manage to be a target for laughter one is not likely to be a target for hostility" (ibid).

"Laughter extinguishes anger, hostility and allied affects," Arieti claimed, "at least for the period during which the laughter continues. Many comedians use masochistic techniques to evoke laughter, particularly when an audience is being unresponsive" (ibid). In his 1978 *Complete Book of Ethnic Humor,* comedian-writer Larry Wilde stated "the most popular kind of ethnic joke is the put-down joke which ridicules specific 'character traits' of a particular group" (p. 3). Irish and drinking, Scots being tightwads, German stubbornness, French lovers, British stuffiness are all exaggerated traits but based on the overgeneralizations. Wilde offered a regional joke, from Southern California, as an example:

30. The best time to be on the Los Angeles freeways is Sunday morning because the Catholics are in church,
    > Protestants are still asleep,
    > Jews are in Palm Springs,
    > Indians are restricted to the reservation,
    > Chinese are stuffing fortune cookies,
    > Blacks are stealing hubcaps and
    > Mexicans can't get their cars started.
    > (Wilde, 1978, p. 3)

"If we were to take the eccentricities that are identifiable with specific nationalities and use their quirks and peculiarities to create a humorous situation," Wilde wrote, "we would have the following joke:"

31. A cruise ship, with passengers from all over the world, was caught in a severe storm and wrecked on a remote and unexplored island. Soon the island began to buzz with activity.
    > The Germans drilled the natives into an army,
    > Jews opened a department store,
    > Italians began organizing some hookers, the
    > French started a restaurant,
    > Scots were financing the whole thing and
    > A couple of Englishmen were still standing around
    >   waiting to be introduced (p. 4).

32. A patient seeks a brain transplant and is offered a Jewish brain for $5,000 or a Polish brain for $10,000. Asked why the difference in price, the patient is told: "The Polish brains have never been used" (Raskin, 1984, p. 187).

33. This one's Canadian, heard in Winnipeg, Manitoba in 1974. A man consults a brain surgeon: "I insist on being a Ukrainian. I want a Ukrainian brain transplant." The surgeon explains this requires that half his brain be removed. He agrees, the surgery is performed by special com-

118 *Humor*

puterized laser—which malfunctions. In the recovery room the surgeon tells the patient: "The surgery was successful but because of computer error we removed 90% of your brain, not 50%. How do you feel about that?" The patient exclaims wide-eyed: "Mon Dieu!" (anon).

34. Two Canadians are driving down a country road and see a man in a rowboat in the middle of a plowed field nowhere near any water. "Look at that dumb Uke," the first Canadian says, "somebody should tell him you can't row a boat in a plowed field." "Yes," the second Canadian comments, "I'd go over and tell'im but I can't swim" (anon).

35. A public health worker sees four Polish men in an alley shooting drugs with the same needle. "Don't you know you can get AIDS by using the same needle?" she asks. "No problem," they reply, "we're all wearing condoms" (anon).

36. How many mental health workers does it take to change a light bulb? One, but the bulb has really got to want to be changed (anon).

37. An Asian immigrant goes to a Greek restaurant for lunch. "I want the *flied lice,*" he tells the Greek proprietor. "I don't serve anybody who can't speak plain English. I got *fried rice* but no *flied lice.*" The Asian leaves, angry and frustrated. Three weeks later he returns, angrily eyeballs the Greek and says: "I'll have *fried rice, you Gleek plick*" (anon).

38. Hispanic driver at a gas station: "feel'er up." The attendant looks at the driver, then at his wife seated next to him: "What, now, with you here?" (Raskin, 1984, p. 184).

39. Two Irish manual laborers were digging in a street in front of a brothel. A rabbi drove up and went into the brothel. "And what do you think of that, Pat? What a bold heathen!" says one Irishman to the other. The rabbi left and a Protestant minister drove up and went in. "Sure'n the world's goin' to hell, Pat, just look at that. Black Protestant, what can you expect?" The minister left and a Catholic priest drove up and went in. The Irishmen take off their hats, and holding them over their hearts, one says: "Faith and Begorrah, Pat, there must be someone awful sick in there" (anon).

40. Members of the congregation reported a bitterly anti-English Irish priest to the bishop for mercilessly attacking the English in his Sunday sermons. The bishop reprimanded him and told him that he himself would be sitting in the congregation the next week: "And I don't want to hear any attacks on the English." That Sunday, the Irish priest spoke on the Last Supper. The bishop was pleased until the priest described when "Jesus said 'someone here will betray me.' And Judas asked: 'Blimey, Guvnuh, you wouldn't mean me now, would you?' " (anon).

41. "I was made by a Dago and presented to the American people on behalf of the French government for the purposes of welcomin' Irish immigrants into the Dutch City of New York" (O. Henry, *The lady higher up* (1911), in Bartlett, 1968, p. 864).

42. Two viciously anti-Black white racists die and find themselves in the waiting room just outside the Gates of Heaven. Saint Peter enters and says to one of them: "God will see you now." After a few minutes the redneck returns red-faced and perspiring and says to his buddy: "No sense you goin' in there. She's colored" (anon).

FREUDIAN SLIPS (SLIP OF THE TONGUE)

It seems a valid generalization that we've all experienced the phenomenon of a "slip of the tongue." Freud claimed that such slips can be momentary bursts of repressed material that bubble up in "normal" conversation. For example:

43. Willard Warthogg, the boss, really irritated about his secretary's cluttered up desk and disorganized work says: "Miss Jones, fix this **litter**—I mean, letter" (anon).

Freud would likely say he meant both: correct the letter and clean up the litter. In this way, "Freudian slips" are like double meaning or double entendre humor, they have a dual meaning, the manifest content being the apparent error and the latent meaning being what lurks behind the "mistake."

44. A sales executive in a tightly competitive industry meets her counterpart in a competitive firm with: "So pleased to **beat** you—er, uh, **meet** you" (adapted from Motley, 1987, p. 27).

45. A student approaches a teacher and asks to be excused from taking a scheduled final exam: "Last night," the student says, "my grandmother **lied**—I mean, **died**" (Motley, 1987, p. 25).

Some slips are just that, a momentary laziness of the tongue and inability to articulate a word. One can overanalyze, like the two psychiatrists who meet on the street: "How are you?" one says to the other. "What do you mean by that?" the second asks. Much conversation is ritualistic and without deep meaning. When we say "how are you?" we really don't expect nor do we have time to hear a detailed description of one's present life situation, physical and mental health status. Likewise, Motley, commenting on the student's request to be excused from the final exam offered several explanations: "One possibility is that she fabricated the excuse and. . .awareness of the lie prompted the error" (a classic Freudian slip). She could be telling the truth but apprehensive she might be perceived as lying. In a deeper Freudian sense she could be experiencing "repressed guilt about a lie she once told her grandmother." And it could be a lazy tongue "innocent slip" (1987, p. 25). Humans have such an enormous vocabulary that some "misfiring" of word associations is probable and predictable.

Mechanical, automatic, really accidental slips can be "the result of competition between similar verbal choices. These aren't conscious and deliberate. . .but automatic, instantaneous choices of casual speech." It is "competition between these choices, or indecisions about them (that) lapse in the mental attention normally devoted to resolving competition" (ibid, p. 26). Motley (1987) explains slips of the tongue by **spreading activation theory.** A person's "mental dictionary is organized with other words associated by meaning, sound or grammar somewhat like the interconnections of points in a complex spider web" (p. 26). Stimulated by environmental cues, what's happening in the sensory world, and by the content of conversation, "activation spreads first to the most closely related word then to words associated with them and so on. Each word activates an alternate path through the web" (ibid). According to Motley, slips of the tongue could result from "competing choices that have equal or nearly equal activation levels" (ibid). A better analogy might be electrical circuits such as in radio and TV, "tuning" to various frequencies or channels based on current flow. What happens to us verbally and nonverbally alters the current of our mental circuits and elicits a selective variety of responses: related ideas, memories and words that emerge spontaneously from them.

Motley and his colleagues conducted research where men read aloud and at the same time completed fill-in-the-blank sentences. The group was divided in half, one performing this task while "mildly sexually aroused" by "an attractive and provocatively attired woman" administering the task, the other completing the identical task given by a man. Word choices relating to sex were "almost twice as frequent" in the sexually "aroused" group as compared to the unstimulated group. For example, one of the sentences was: "The old hillbilly kept his moonshine in big _____." The "overwhelming answer of the aroused group" was "jugs." Most men in the other group answered "vats" or "barrels" or "jars." For the sentence "Tension mounted at the end when the symphony reached its _____" the arousal group answered "climax" more frequently than the non-aroused group which preferred "finale" or "conclusion" or "peak" (ibid, p. 27). Motley suggests this research confirms an associative network and it is likely this can and does influence spontaneous verbalizations among which are slips of the tongue.

Motley provides other examples of verbal slips such as the receptive male who meets an attractive woman and says: "I don't think we've been properly **seduced**—uh, **introduced**" (ibid, p. 28). Readers: why not fake a slip as a little verbal weather balloon or test of the other person's involvement? Gotta seem natural. Motley's other examples: **Fraud's** theory for **Freud, garish cheapsake** or **cheapskate** for **cherished keepsake** (like the proverbial gold retirement watch, a token given without feeling), **chilled grease sandwich** for **grilled cheese sandwich** (ibid).

Based on Motley's research but also on your own readily observed slips of the tongue, the basic motivation can be an unconscious bubbling through of **real** opinions and feelings or simply a verbal accident, a misfiring or short circuit of the mind-brain memory bank and associative network. Motley opts for verbal competition" but concedes "hidden thoughts" can be the source of competition "in some cases." He adds that there are some verbal slips not explainable by either the Freudian or the semantic-brain-mind approaches (ibid).

IMPERSONATION

"The impersonator," Koestler wrote, "is two different people at one time" (1964, p. 68). Koestler held that the audience will laugh "if the result is degrading," and if led to "sympathize or identify" with the impersonated "hero" the audience "will experience that state of split-mindedness known as **dramatic illusion** or the magic of the stage" (ibid). Achieving this "magic" is a complex function of the impersonator's skill but mostly as Shakespeare described it "in the ear of him that hears it" rather than "the tongue of him that makes it" (*Love's labor lost,* Act III, Bartlett, 1968, p. 222).

Koestler pointed out that impersonation is an ancient dramatic form, dating back through the masks of Greek tragedy, Japanese No to the earliest primitive tribal dancing worldwide. The goal can be tragedy, comedy or both, as in Romeo and Juliet who were "victims of absurd coincidences, Oedipus' marriage to his mother due to mistaken identity, Rosamund in *As You Like It* and Leonora in *Fidelio* are both disguised as men . . .in one case the result is drama, in another comedy. The technique of creating character-types is also shared by both: in the classical form of tragedy whether Greek, Indian or Japanese, characterization is often achieved by standardized mask; in the comedy, down to Moliere, by the creation of types: the miser, the glutton, the hypocrite, the cuckold. . . the classification of character types has been the aim of incessant efforts from the 'four temperaments' of the Greeks, to Kretschmer, Jung, Sheldon and so on" (ibid).

JOBS, PROFESSIONS

The popularity of the movie and TV series *Nine to Five* and many standup comedy routines involving occupations are evidence of humorous aspects of the work world.

When computers were introduced there was talk of **computer phobia,** a fear, a morbid dread of computers replacing people. Much of that fear was based on myth and fantasy; much of it based on Bergson's **man-automaton** conflict. Early auto workers had the same apprehension about the "assembly line" Henry Ford introduced. Then it was robotization. If computer phobia could speak, it'd say something like: "The computer is the enemy. It is always ready. It never makes mistakes. It works faster than most workers can think. It has unlimited capacity. Like *Ole Man River* 'it just keeps rollin' along.' " Well, it isn't quite like that. We know now that it's GIGO (garbage in, garbage out). They are wonderful machines but that's all they are. And when the computer system is "down" or "out" so are we.

Over the past few years, computer operators have found ways to "humanize" the otherwise dull routines of balance sheets and standard reports. *Open Systems* (1987) of Stamford, Connecticut reported the use of standard computer-typed figures to apply some good-natured humor to everyday computer operation. It helps to more easily appreciate the humorous content if you turn the page sideways clockwise.

46. :) says "I'm happy"
    :(says "I'm sad"
    :s means "I'm all mixed up"
    8) means "I'm wide-eyed awake"
    :o says "I'm surprised"
    (:o says "I'm VERY surprised!"

47. Moliere wrote this ditty about writing as a profession which he entitled *Writing is Like Prostitution:*
    First you do it for the love of it,
    Then you do it for a few friends,
    And finally you do it for money.

48. A new patient bursts into a psychiatrist's office making frantic gestures as if brushing something off his clothes.

Patient: Doctor, doctor, help me! Look, I'm full of bugs.

Psychiatrist (jumping back up from his desk and standing back): Be careful! Don't get'em on me!

(Arieti, 1976, p. 114)

Arieti (1976) felt this joke was funny because "the psychiatrist accepts the patient's way of thinking, whereas he is expected to reject it." He maintained that the delusions and bizarre ideation of the mentally ill can be humorous because of its reversed logic:

49. ". . .a patient examined many years ago had the habit of oiling her body. Asked why she did so she replied: 'The human body is a machine and has to be lubricated.' The word 'machine'. . .had led her to her identification with man-made machines. . . She did not know that what she was saying was witty; she meant what she said quite literally. Her delusional remark is witty only for us; we, not the patient, create the joke because we recognize the illogicality in her apparent logicality (1976, p. 114).

50. An auditor was convicted and sentenced to death by the guillotine, the third person to be executed that day. Each was asked whether he wanted to face downward or upward in the chopping block. The first preferred face downward and was placed in that position. The guillotine was released but jammed a few inches from his neck. As was the custom after a failed execution he was given freedom. The second preferred face upward, was placed in that position, the guillotine released, but again it jammed. He was freed. The auditor asked to face upward, was placed in that position, and just before the guillotine was released, exclaimed: "Oh, I see the problem. There's a knot up there in the rope" (anon).

MOVIES-TV

With the convenience of video rental outlets and the availability of less expensive videotape players, the world of comedy is within easy access. For your own personal humor, research, for groups and classes, here are but a few representative samples of the variety of comedy for further study:

Disney and other cartoon features, to compare child to adult humor and evaluate the idea of regression to "the eternal child" and Berne's "OK Kid."

Peter Sellers in the *Pink Panther* series presents a slapstick detective role which can be contrasted to Peter Falk's style as *Columbo*. The *TV Bloopers* series provides a good study of spontaneous, unexpected humor. Old back-and-white comedies of Harold Lloyd, Buster Keaton, Charlie Chaplin, The Three Stooges, Our Gang, Marx Brothers, Ritz Brothers, W.C. Fields and Mae West can be compared to the more recent full color movies by Monty Python and Mel Brooks; TV series such as *Saturday Night Live,* Johnny Carson, David Letterman and made-for-TV HBO specials of Buddy Hackett, Richard Pryor, Billy Crystal and Robin Williams. There are a limited number of TV and audiotapes of Jack Benny, Fred Allen, Fibber McGee and Molly which provide an excellent opportunity to compare comedy style and content.

MUSIC

Opera such as Leoncavallo's *I Pagliacchi,* comic opera such as those of Gilbert and Sullivan, and symphonic music by a variety of composers worldwide, reflect in microcosm the great variety and versatility of humor.

Ruggiero Leoncavallo (1838-1919) first produced *Pagliacchi* in Milan on May 21, 1892. Like Shakespeare's *Hamlet* it is a "play within a play." For classroom study, Zeffirelli produced a film version of this classic done at La Scala in 1982. Leoncavallo was part of the **verissimo** "realism" movement which also produced *Carmen* and *Madam Butterfly.* Leoncavallo was the son of a judge, and he personally witnessed a murder during a play. As is true of most writers, he wove this real-life experience into his music.

Pagliacchi is a clown in a travelling troupe of performers. His real-life name is Canio, leader of the clown troup and husband of Nedda who participates in clown skits. He is easily moved to anger but basically good-hearted. Tonio, a hunchback in the troupe loves Nedda but she rejects his advances. Silvio is a young peasant having an affair with Nedda. Beppo is a member of the troup who plays Harlequin in the clown skits. The opera is in two acts, the first a real-life segment providing the background and dramatic buildup for the second act, the clown skit which turns from comedy to tragedy.

In Act I, the hunchback Tonio, seeing Silvio and Nedda together, informs Canio of this. Canio arrives in time to see Silvio kissing Nedda, but Silvio quickly exits. Canio tries to stab Nedda but Beppo snatches the dagger from his hand. It is performance time and Canio sadly sings that he must now "jest with my heart maddened with sorrow" (Mendelsohn, 1913).

Act II begins with the clown skit beginning. Pantaloon (Tonio), declares his love for Columbine (Nedda). She rejects him, as in real-life. Harlequin (Beppo) sings outside her window, then invites him in and his advances are accepted. Pantaloon rushes in to warn that Pagliacchi, Columbine's husband, is coming. He arrives enraged in a dual role of fantasy and real-life, for the play becomes total reality for him. She denies everything. In his comic clown role and also in tragic, awful reality Pagliacchi stabs her. Silvio rushes on stage to intervene, and Pagliacchi stabs him as well. Up to this point the audience has been reacting to what they saw as tragicomic entertainment. The full realization comes when Pagliacchi shouts bloody knife in hand: "No Punchinello am I— but a man." The audience leaves in panic and horror as Pagliacchi slumps, dazed, crying: "The comedy is ended."

Federico Fellini's movie *La Strada* (1954) won an Oscar for best foreign film. While not an opera or musical it is also the story of a headstrong, circus-type performer played by Anthony Quinn. He wants to love but he can't "let go," let his true feelings flow. Like *Pagliacchi*, the action builds. If it were a Greek tragedy, the chorus would be chanting to him to "go for it." The itinerant circus performer (Anthony Quinn) allows a shy, passive woman (Giuletta Masina) to travel with him and help with the act. She becomes attached to him but he avoids her, is indifferent to her, mistreats and insults her. Scheuer (1984) described this film as "basically a simple story" but "one of the most memorable films available" (p. 387).

For twenty golden years, 1870 to 1890, W.S. Gilbert and Arthur Sullivan teamed together to produce musical comedies which have continued consistently to evoke laughter throughout the world. There is derision in the sprightly, cutting satire yet warm sympathy in their multiple story lines, an 1870s version of today's soap operas. There are videotapes available of *HMS Pinafore*, *Mikado*, and *Pirates of Penzance* and they are excellent study aids. The following excerpts are taken from the undated Modern Library edition of *The complete plays of Gilbert and Sullivan* (Random House):

51. I am the very model of a modern Major General,
    I've information, vegetable, animal and mineral,
    I know the kings of England and I quote the fights historical,
    From Marathon to Waterloo, in order categorical;

I'm very well acquainted too with matters mathematical,
I understand equations, both the simple and quadratical,
About binomial theorem I'm teeming with a lot o'news—
With many cheerful facts about the square of the hypotenuse. . .

I'm very good at integral and differential calculus,
I know the scientific names of being animalculous;
In short, in matters vegetable, animal and mineral,
I am the very model of a modern Major General. . .

I know our mythic history, King Arthurs's and Sir Caradoc's,
I answer hard acrostics, I've a pretty taste for paradox,
I quote in elegiacs all the crimes of Heliogabalus,
I conics I can floor peculiarities parabolous. . .

Then I can write a washing bill in Babylonic cuneiform,
And tell you every detail of Caractacus's uniform;
In short, in matters vegetable, animal and mineral,
I am the very model of a modern Major General. . .

For my military knowledge though I'm plucky and advertury,
Has only been brought down to the beginning of the century;
But still in matters vegetable, animal and mineral,
I am the very model of a modern Major General.
                        (*Pirates of Penzance,* 1880, pp. 156-157)

52. A more humane Mikado never did in Japan exist,
To nobody second I'm certainly reckoned a true philanthropist.
It is my very humane endeavor to make to some extent,
Each evil liver a running river of harmless merriment.

My object all sublime I shall achieve in time,
To let the punishment fit the crime,
The punishment fit the crime;
And make each prisoner pent unwillingly represent
A source of innocent merriment!
Of innocent merriment!

All prosy dull society sinners
Who chatter and bleat and bore,
Are sent to hear sermons from Mystical Germans
Who preach from ten till four.
The amateur tenor whose vocal villainies
All desire to shirk, shall during off-hours
Exhibit his powers to Madame Tussaud's waxworks. . .
The advertising quack who wearies
With tales of countless cures,
His teeth, I've enacted, shall all be extracted
By terrified amateurs. . .

The billiard sharp whom anyone catches,
His doom's extremely hard—
He's made to dwell in a dungeon cell
On a spot that's always barred
And there he plays extravagant matches
In fitless finger-stalls
On a cloth untrue, with a twisted cue
And elliptical billard balls!

(The Mikado, 1885, pp. 383-384)

"Mood music" is now a standard component of movies and TV shows. You may remember how music escalated the emotions in horror movies when you were a child. Remember the unreal musical score in *Spellbound?* The sharp, shriek of the background music in the shower murder scene in *Psycho?* There is **humorous** music, too. For courses on humor a "musical montage" of audiotaped excerpts played on good equipment after a brief description of the composer's idea and purpose is an effective demonstration of humor applied to music. Feel free to read from the following descriptions if you do not have time to develop your own. Playing excerpts for and to yourself can help lighten your mood, a musical prescription when needed. The following is a sampler of composers who have applied humor to their music:

Leroy Anderson (1908-1975) wrote light, melodic, spirited music such as *The Syncopated Clock, Bugler's Holiday, Blue Tango, Belle of the Ball, Fiddle Faddle, Trumpeter's Lullaby, The Typewriter, Sleigh Ride, The Waltzing Cat* and others which have been audience favorites for many years. Anderson was able to express a playful, positive mood in his music.

Hector Berlioz (1803-1869). His *Symphonie Fantastique* is a macabre, unreal "altered state" kind of music of the fuzzy overlapping worlds of dreams, death, witches and wizards, ghosts and goblins. It is "fantastic" as the name implies, in the mood of Jung's *Trickster* and the Tarot *Magician.* Turn the lights down (or off!), light a candle (dare you!), turn up the volume (and the bass!) for a trip into the Jungian unconscious.

Paul Dukas (1865-1935). A change of pace from the dungeon heaviness of Berlioz is Dukas' *Sorceror's Apprentice.* Walt Disney used this music in his animated color cartoon feature *Fantasia.* The story line is 2000 years old, described by the German philosopher Goethe as an "impish tonal anecdote." It has a "motor" of incessant rhythm that puts to music **syzygy** theory's **power** construct.

Claude DeBussy (1862-1918). Popular for his beautiful, soft, lilting melodies, DeBussy also composed music with a humorous flavor such as the *Children's Corner Suite* and *Golligwog's Cake Walk* which he wrote in

1908 for his 4-year-old daughter. They are a musical secret passage to childhood simplicity and joy, to the Eternal Child, the OK Kid.

George Gershwin (1898-1937), died at age 39, a tragic loss for all of us. He was able to put free, natural, spontaneous emotion into music, a nostalgic mental-emotional trip back, down and into the playful mood of childhood. Try *Of Thee I Sing, Clap Yo' Hands, Strike Up the Bank, Fascinatin' Rhythm, I Got Rhythm* (see if you can keep your feet — and heart still). *It Ain't Necessarily So* appeals to the Zorba-like directness and impulsivity, simplicity and sensuality of childhood and provides a glimpse at the pre-civilized, asocial pagan we were eons ago.

Franz Josef Haydn (1732-1809), referred to affectionately as "Papa Haydn" was a prolific composer of hundreds of works, among which are 80 marches, 62 string quartets and 12 masses. His music has an earthy, joyous love of nature and of life. Of special interest to a study of humor is his *Toy Symphony*. Haydn put laughter to music, that of the carefree, uninhibited peasant, reminiscences of his own modest upbringing as one of 12 children.

Engelbert Humperdinck (1854-1921). His only real "big hit" — and it's spectacular — was (and is) *Hansel and Gretel* (1893). Second only to Tchaikowsky's *Nutcracker Suite,* it contains positive and negative polarities, Jungian archetypes and a great deal of power. Two selections especially relevant to the study of humor are the *Witch's Song* ("Mousy, mousy eat my housy") and the deeply moving *Children's Prayer.*

Dimitri Kabalevsky (1904-   ) composed the 10-part orchestral suite *The Comedians* for a children's play in Moscow in 1938. It is a series of quickly changing (like a kid's mind) carefree, impulsive musical pictures well in motion from the playful mood of the first bars of *The Epilogue* through the *Gallop, March,* and *Waltz* of prancing circus clowns.

Aram Khatchaturian (1903-1978) composed the *Masquerade Suite* in 1939 as musical accompaniment to a Mikhail Lermontov tragedy written a hundred years before. It is a musical satire of the Russian aristocracy stripped of pretensions in the reckless abandon of a masquerade ball. You can feel it draw you away from reality and dance you into fantasy, ending in the *Galop,* a wild frenzy of conflicting rhythms and a kaleidoscope of tonal colors. This powerful music deals almost exclusively with a humor theme and transcends language, culture and time in the universal language of music.

Felix Mendelssohn (1809-1847) died at age 38, another great loss. His *Midsummer Night's Dream* was completed in 1826 when he was but 17. I've always associated it with the magical mood of Shakespeare's *Tempest.*

Grabbe (1940) described it as "airy, youthful, permeated with a feeling of mischievous hobgoblins and dancing elfs" (p. 120). Listen and compare it to Berlioz's *Fantastique* or Strauss' *Till Eulenspiegel*. There **is** magic in it!

Modeste Moussorgsky (1839-1881) died at 42. It is the third and fifth movements of his *Pictures at an Exhibition* of special interest to us. Grabbe characterized the third movement as "joyous confusion of chattering children and scolding music" (p. 126). Of the fifth movement, *The Ballet of Unhatched Chickens*, with flute, strings, oboe and bells, Grabbe wrote: "A whimsical piece and great favorite with concert audiences" (ibid).

Wolfgang Amadeus Mozart (1725-1791) died at age 35 and was buried in a pauper's grave. His good humor, capricious nature and his ingenuity characterized his music. His style was brisk and with a characteristic childlike impulsivity.

Serge Prokofieff (1891-1953). A strongly impetuous child is unleashed in Prokofieff's music: *Lieutenant Kije Suite, Peter and the Wolf, Love of Three Oranges,* and *Chout* (means buffoon), a pantomime ballet for two clowns composed for Diaghilev at the *Ballet Russe*. Grabbe described his style as a "bold humor which can be impish, teasing or acrid in its bite" (p. 134).

Maurice Ravel (1875-1936) composed music of sophisticated restraint or lilting melody, of "delicate finesse, luminosity and sophisticated precision" with "overtones of irony (and) acrid humor" (Grabbe, pp. 145-146). His music especially relevant to humor: *Mother Goose Suite; La Valse; Le Tombeau de Couperin.*

Gioacchino Rossini (1792-1868). Older readers will remember Rossini's *William Tell Overture*, the background music for *The Lone Ranger* radio series (did you know they also used Liszt's *Les Prelude?*). He wrote the *Barber of Seville* overture in thirteen days. Grabbe described Rossini's music as "combining an elegant and sparkling melodiousness with clarity and both of these with laughter. Its wit, however, is not always playful for it is often slyly devastating, even steely, in its thrust."

Charles Camille Saint-Saens (1835-1921) died at age 86. He composed the orchestral suite *Carnival of the Animals* when he was 56 years old but did not release it except in his will after his death. It waited 35 years after its composition to be played.

Friedrich Smetana (1824-1884) died in a mental hospital. His music had the "boisterous ring of peasant humor, often poetic and extremely moving" (Grabbe, p. 184). His *Bartered Bride* was composed for a 3-act comedy and is typical of his quickly moving melodic style. *The Moldau* is a flowing river put to music.

Johann Strauss (1804-1849) has become know as "the father of the waltz" and he was the biological father of Johann Strauss, Jr. who became known as "the waltz king." Both composed music which became very popular for dancing. Yes, the *Blue Danube* is the name of the waltz; the river is brown, not blue.

Richard Strauss (1864-1949). Nothing at all like the Johanns! His music is audacious, impulsive. He liked to "rattle your chain"—couldn't just let you sit there. He tried to get "into" you, to get you involved. *Till Eulenspiegel's Merry Pranks* is the musical story of "a legendary rogue whose clever wit and inexhaustible bag of tricks personify the triumph of nimble wit over the more sedate virtues of the day-to-day world" (p. 195). Claude Debussy wrote his impression of this music: "Hearing it all, you burst out laughing or howled in agony and when it was all over you were amazed to find things in their normal place" (Grabbe, ibid). *Das Heldenleben* (a hero's life) and *Don Quixote* are relatively serious musicalized personality profiles (especially *Heldenleben*), with less humorous content.

Igor Stravinsky (1882-1971). His is "salty music with a street-song quality and a robust freshness that have so far successfully withstood the test of time" (Grabbe, p. 199). *Petrouchka* is the musical story of a puppet in a marionette show, a "symbolic figure always struggling pathetically and comically against a fate he cannot master" (ibid). The theme suggests Bergson's man-automaton conflict. The music has a primitive surrealistic, sometimes festive sing-song carnival quality, gaudy, bold and impulsive. Let yourself go with the music and you'll feel yourself becoming a puppet, the strings being pulled!

Deems Taylor (1885-1966) composed *Through the Looking Glass,* the "wistfully tender fairy tale journey" of *Alice in Wonderland* (Grabbe, p. 206).

Peter Ilich Tchaikowsky (1840-1893). Perhaps the most popular and the greatest popularizer of children's fantasies, as well as beautiful ballet music. It is interesting that he wrote *Nutcracker Suite* and the very sombre, heavy *Symphony No. 6,* known as *Pathetique* ("pathetic") at the same time. *Nutcracker,* based on the fairy ballet *Casse Noisette* of Hoffman, was played in 1882. It's ALL child without a wasted note, a true classic. *Pathetique* was played October 16, 1893. Tchaikowsky died a week later of cholera.

Richard Wagner (1813-1883) was, like Richard Strauss, a "heavyweight." You also don't doze off during Wagner—the fire of the gods will be under your seat! His music is turbulent, dark, deep and brooding. On the other hand, the *Spinning Song* and *Sailor's Song* in his opera *Flying Dutchman* are of a much lighter mood.

POETRY, LIMERICKS

53. There was a young belle of old Natchez
    Whose garments were always in patchez.
    When comment arose
    On the state of her clothes,
    She drawled, When Ah itchez, ah scratchez!
    Ogden Nash (1941, p. 502)

54. SONG OF THE OPEN ROAD
    I think that I shall never see
    A billboard lovely as a tree.
    Indeed, unless the billboards fall
    I'll never see a tree at all.
    Ogden Nash (ibid, p. 21)

55. THE TURTLE
    The turtle lives 'twixt plated decks
    Which practically conceal its sex.
    I think it clever of the turtle
    In such a fix to be so fertile
    Ogden Nash (ibid, p. 40)

56. WHAT'S THE USE
    Sure, deck your lower limbs with pants;
    Yours are the limbs, my sweeting.
    You look divine as you advance—
    Have you seen yourself retreating?
    Ogden Nash (ibid, p. 91)

57. ARTHUR
    There was an old man of Calcutta,
    Who coated his tonsils with butta,
    Thus converting his snore
    From a thunderous roar
    To a soft, oleaginous mutta.
    Ogden Nash (ibid, p. 95)

58. THE COW
    The cow is of the bovine ilk;
    One end is moo, the other, milk.
    Ogden Nash (ibid, p. 210)

59. We asked the cyclone
    To go around our barn
    But it didn't hear us.
    Carl Sandburg (1936, p. 260)

60. 'Twas brillig, and the slithy toves
    Did gyre and gimble in the wabe;
    All mimsy were the borogroves,
    And the mome raths outgrube.
    Lewis Carroll (*Through the looking glass*, 1872, p. 745)

61. "In my youth," said his father,
    "I took to the law and argued each case with my wife;
    And the muscular strength which it gave my jaw
    Has lasted the rest of my life."
    Lewis Carroll (ibid)

PROVERBS, EPIGRAMS AND SAYINGS

In this section we will discuss and consider examples of brief funny sayings and two new sources: bumper stickers and individualized auto license tags. Bumper stickers are short messages or slogans which are, technically, puns based on literalization in the form of catch phrases and a play-on-words.

62. These "do it" bumper stickers are direct associations with sexual function:

    • Radio hams do it with more frequency.
    • Musicians do it with more rhythm.
    • Scholars do it studiously.
    • Doctors/nurses do it with more care.
    • Engineers do it with precision (Raskin, 1984, p. 150).
    • Snakes do it in cold blood (ibid).
    • Tigers do it with ferocity (ibid).

Literalization can evoke humor. A common example easily observed in everyday life is the figure of speech. Steve Allen (1987) frequently used this device. To "I don't give a hoot" he added: "If you were an owl you might wanna" (p. 34), **Euthaniasia** as "youth in Asia" and **to bear fruit** as "bare fruit" (p. 33). He often split words, such as to "I was hornswoggled" adding "if you've ever had your horn swoggled you know how painful that can be" (ibid). This reminds me of another example, from a Western movie with Burl Ives as the father of a son continually getting into trouble. Rebelling against his father's badgering, the son says: "You know, Paw, I naver asked to be born." Ives stared icily and retorted: "And if you hadda, maybe the answer wouldda been NO."

Marsh and Collett (1987) observed that automobiles can be "a powerful means of self-expression," extensions of the owner's personality, identity or values. Some car owners use first or last names on their license tags. For example, Ernest Borgnine license tags BORG 9. Pet names or contractions of husband and wife names are fairly common, much like boat names (MAR-JO, ADA-BOB, MEL-MAR). Marsh and Collett maintain that for some "license plates are an important matter, a piece of automotive jewelry as essential as the car itself." They pay extra for these "vanity plates" which "say something about them or their car." The license tags become "mobile billboards," personal calling cards or personal messages to others (p. 22).

63. License tags seen in California (Marsh & Collett, 1987, p. 22):
      EYE EYE (ophthalmologist)
      STORKS (obstetrician)
      CLUESO (private detective)
      MESUE4U (lawyer)
      2P C ME (urologist)
      EIEIO (farmer)
      AQUANUT (surfer)
    Observed in Virginia (author):
      SHRINK (psychiatrist)
      HOLY JO (priest)
      ATTRNY (attorney)

64. California auto license tags with a message (Marsh & Collett, 1987, p. 22):
      IMOKRU
      4 MY EGO
      IMNXNYR
      XCYTE ME
      I LUST 2
      IM SOFT
      BCALM
      ENJOY

65. I KNEW statements:
      I knew Rip Torn before he went to pieces.
          Gregory Peck when he was just a half-pint.
          Desi Arnaz before he lost the Ball.
          Gloria Graham when she was still a cute cookie.
          Jack Lemmon when he was just a little squirt.

Walter Abel when he was ready and willing.
Hugh Downs before things began looking up.
Barbara Nichols before she made any cents.
Tarzan before he became a monkey's uncle.
Julie London when she was still in a fog.
Johnny Cash when he didn't have any. (anon)

66. Mottos or slogans are yet another "set" of funny sayings:
Nuclear physicists motto: "Don't put too many ions in the fire."
Texas landowners: "Oil wells that end well."
Hillbilly rednecks: "A Mrs. good as a mule."
Femlibbers: "Return him stamped fourth class male."
Boxers: "Better to have gloved and lost than never to have gloved at
all."
Marital therapists: "A man's house is his hassle."
Garbage collectors: "Look before you heap."
Coal miners: "There's no fuel like an old fuel."
Surgeons: "Fried goeth before the gall."
Airport restaurants: "Out of the frying pan into the fliers."

Acronymns, words resulting from abbreviations read aloud, can be funny: "Boopers" for BuPers (Bureau of Personnel), "Fanny May" FMHA (Federal Mortgage and Housing Administration) and historically "OK" for correspondence ending "oblige kindly" or "Order of the King" and the most nefarious of all four-letter words which may have evolved from Felony Under the Crown of the King or Fornication Unlawful, Under the Crown of the King. During World War II, SNAFU was commonly used to describe "Situation Normal: All Fouled Up." The verb-form actually used was not "fouled" but something "stronger." Admiral Byrd is credited with coining the term FUBAR after he visited a base that was a step beyond SNAFU. FUBAR is "Fouled Up Beyond All Recognition."

I use CATWOT to describe boring, meaningless meetings that are a Complete And Total Waste of Time. The computer age has brought us GIGO for Garbage In, Garbage Out. Communications experts gave us KISS for Keep It Simple, Stupid. MOM, as any nurse can tell you, is Milk of Magnesia and a TV commercial soothingly tells you "when you're not feeling well you need your MOM." Some acronymns can be quite crude, such as BAM, another World War II term for a member of WAM, Women's Auxiliary Marines: a "Broad Ass Marine." It was a term of endearment. BS, MS and PhD have been defined as "Bull Shit, More of the Same and Piled Higher and Deeper." I refer to my PhD as a "Fud." There are some humorous applications of higher degrees, such as a man with a Master of Arts degree who's a MA! or a woman with a Master of Arts in Nursing who's a MAN!

Dialects, regionalisms, slang and idiomatic expressions can become funny sayings:

67. Define these words:
    CAUDAL   COD   HEP   MOMEBACK   HO
    CAUDAL is what the Southern gas station attendant tells you your engine needs: "Yew need uh caudal." When in Boston, if you don't have cash you must carry a fish with you which is legal tender. They will ask you for your COD. If you are in distress or in need deep in the heart of Texas, someone may approach you to HEP you. MOMEBACK is what Southerners will tell you to help you back your car out of a tight spot. HO is the term Eddie Murphy has used to get laughs, for a lady of the evening, a hooker or whore.

Slang and figures of speech can be quite humorous. **Hell** is a word used (and misused) frequently. "It was hot as hell" is an appropriate though crude figure of speech to describe an uncomfortably warm place or situation. I've also heard "It was colder'n hell." How can that be? Does the Devil have air conditioning? Someone "ran like hell." Does hell **run**? You can have a "**helluva** time" which means an enjoyable experience or that you had a miserable time. It can be used positively or negatively. The same is true for many of so-called "four-letter" words. Some say defecating ("doing Number Two" or "a big job") is to **take** a shit but if you say you **don't give a shit** you are frustrated about something — and not constipated. Boring politicians have been described as **full of shit**. They're not constipated, either. If someone misleads or deceives you they're **shitting you.** That person is **being shitty** or **acting shitty**. So the same word is also used to describe relative significance. Thus, in their usage these words have **polarity** and **power**.

Proverbs and epigrams are much higher level forms of humor than those thus far described. They offer advice or an opinion with a dash of wit to spice it up, to drive the point home. If the intent is against a person or group, government, nation or religion, it would more appropriately be classified as ridicule or satire and these are described later in this chapter.

68. Stretch the truth and make a hit;
    Tell the truth and get hit.
                              Norman Vincent Peale

69. Love your enemies;
    It'll drive'em crazy! (anon)

70. When the gods wish to punish us, they answer our prayers.
    Oscar Wilde (Bartlett, 1968, p. 76)
71. I must get out of these wet clothes and into a dry martini.
    Alexander Woollcott (ibid, p. 999)
72. A little **incompatibility** is the spice of life,
    particularly if he has income and she's pattable.
    Ogden Nash (ibid, p. 1052)

PUNS, PLAY-ON-WORDS

Max Eastman (1922) defined a pun simply as "a verbal absurdity" (p. 68). Arthur Koestler (1964) considered the pun "a single phonetic form with two meanings, two strings of thought tied together by an acoustic knot" (pp. 64-65). Steve Allen (1987) described puns as formed from rhymed words, **alliteration** (recurring sound), nonsense prefixes, suffixes or syllables or splitting of words. His analysis of the underlying dynamics is similar to Koestler's: "receiving mechanisms having quickly heard and interpreted a common phrase in the customary way have in the next instant been forced to recognize an alternative interpretation. This comes as a surprise of a playful sort to which the usual response is laughter" (p. 30).

According to Koestler, the pun's "immense popularity with children, its prevalence in certain forms of mental disorder ('punning mania') and its frequent occurrence in the dream" are evidence of "the profound unconscious appeal of association based on pure sound" (1964, p. 65). He saw puns as the simplest form of humor which proceeds through "play of words" to "play of ideas" in its highest form. In addition to **alliteration**, word splitting and nonsense prefixes, suffixes and syllables (Allen, 1987), Eastman (1922) cited these **figures of speech** as sources of humor:

synechdoche (substituting a part for the whole),
metonymy (using the name of one for another),
simile (comparing two unlike things) and
metaphor (figuratively attributing characteristics of one thing on
    another).

73. "I got a quarter that says you can't" (insert any difficult achievement).
    "Whaddya know, a talking quarter"
    Allen (1987, p. 53)

In this pun there is a **bisociation** of two incompatible **matrices** (Koestler, 1964) which are suddenly transcended by **joke logic.**

74. "Parlez-vous Francaise?"
    "Nein"

Allen (1987, p. 54)

This pun is based on **reversal** or **paradox.** Both statements are quite proper of and by themselves—of neutral polarity—but in two different languages. When placed together they become absurd and humorous. Attempting to apply the usual word meanings from one language to another can also cause humor. An American woman travelling in Germany commented to her fellow (German) passengers on a trolley "Ich bin heiz" ("I am hot"). Her attempt at friendly chatter was met with icy stares. To the Germans it meant she was sexually aroused! The same lady told me that German express elevators are termed "fast fahrt" (meaning "quick journey"). American women dating British or Australian men should know that when he says: "When I get my screw I'll knock you up" he's being quite gentlemanly and means he'll phone you for a date when he gets his paycheck. In Canadian restaurants, especially in Quebec, you ask for a **serviette** and NOT a "napkin," the latter being a feminine hygiene product!

The following involves reversal of logic and association rather than word usage and meaning:

75. Steve Allen reported that he simply read aloud the following newspaper headline, unemotionally and "straight": *Nixon Stoned in South America* (ibid, p. 30). That was enough to evoke considerable laughter. There was no need to embellish the pun with figures of speech, timing, emphasis, gestures or play on words. The conflicting, dichotomous meaning from the same word **(stoned)** in separate contexts produced a ready-made pun.

Koestler (1964) also offered examples of puns and he analyzed them for us:

76. "A sadist is a person who is kind to a masochist"
    Koestler (1964, p. 65)

This is quite similar in its dynamics to Allen's reading of the newspaper headline. It contains two messages: a sadist is kind by acceding to the desire to the masochist to be tortured; just by showing kindness the sadist tortures the masochist. Either way, Koestler observed, "the sadist must go againt his own nature." He analyzed the dynamics: ". . .in either interpretation 'kind' should be understood both literally and metaphorically at the same time; in other words, by playing simultaneously two games governed by opposite rules" (ibid).

77. "The superego is that part of the personality which is soluble in alco-
    hol"

Koestler (1964, p. 65)

"Soluble as used here is split into two meanings in "the context of the chemical laboratory and. . .the metaphorical dissolution of one's high principles" by drinking. "The first few words. . .arouse perhaps a mild irritation with the Freudian jargon, or apprehension as the case may be, which is tittered away through the now familiar mechanism" (ibid). Try analyzing these puns and word play:

78. "My prize bull wandered onto the tracks and the train come and hit him square in the ass," the farmer testified in court. "No, no" the judge interrupted, "you mustn't say that. You should say **rectum.**" The farmer glared at the judge and said: "Wrecked'm hell, it killed'm" (anon).

79. There was once a statistician who drowned in a lake the Mean depth of which was two inches (anon).

80. Angry truck driver to pregnant woman who stepped in front of his rig: "Lady, you can get knocked **down,** too" (anon).

81. "How many people work in Vatican City?"
    "About half" (attributed to Pope John I)

Coffee mugs, wall posters, placemats, billboards, TV commercials and MTV rock video selections are all rich in puns, verbal and visual. One of the oldest commercial puns, long before TV, was the line drawing of *Morton Salt Girl,* walking in the rain, umbrella in one hand, leaky salt package in the other, with the caption: "When it rains, it pours." *RCA Victor* used the dog sitting attentively in front of the old wind-up "Victrola" and the caption: "His master's voice." Years ago, *Exxon* successfullly used an animated cartoon tiger character and the slogan "put a tiger in your tank." *Coppertone* sun tan lotion used the market appeal of children, pets, sun and fresh air with billboards picturing a little girl with a dog pulling the back of her pants down exposing untanned skin.

There are products more difficult to sell. How would **you** market men's underwear on nationwide TV? How do you get and keep attention, impact the senses and imprint consumer memories of your product? The trend is toward funny gimmicks. *Fruit of the Loom* used human-sized fruit characters, silly and clownlike, proudly pushing the brand's undies. *Hanes* countered with picky drill-sergeant-like Supermom "Inspector 12." The "battle of the beers" is another example of applying humor to commercials. *Bud Light* used "Spuds MacKenzie," a black-spotted white pit bull terrier, behaving like a playboy, surrounded by pretty girls. It inspired a nationwide T-shirt and wall poster craze. *Bud Lite* used the pun "Gimme a Lite" **(light)** to create bizarre situations and special effects in bars where this product is ordered.

We are daily surrounded by high-pun-potential verbal and nonverbal cues. Here's a limited sampling: **Papal bull** and **titular head** (contradictory?), lawyers' **briefs** (their papers not their panties), **therapist** (the/rapist), **peer review** (inspecting piers and docks?) and **nun** and none. A **pink slip** can be lingerie, or being laid off, fired! A review of job want ads in your own daily newspaper will show **systems anal** and **prog anal** (sounds even more painful!). Hypnosis is practiced in all public buildings: The signs say **entrance**. Highway signs tell you to **keep off the median** (avoid mediocrity), **yield ahead** (violators will be beheaded) or **gas — food** (burp!).

RIDDLES AND CONUNDRUMS

Technically, a riddle is "a mystifying, misleading, or puzzling question posed as a problem to be solved or guessed" (Mish, 1983, p. 1014). Its root is from the Old English **raedelse,** opinion, conjecture or riddle, closely related to **raedan,** to render meaning from. It has been used for more serious enigmas, such as "the riddle of the Sphinx" or in detective stories. When a riddle's answer or solution is a pun it is a **conundrum** and not a riddle (ibid, p. 286). You can use conundrums and still get AIDS! (That sentence **is** a conundrum.) Some conundrums have been included earlier in this book and in this chapter because their content was pertinent to the subject matter there. Here are more for your analysis of their polarity, power on you, and comparison of content and dynamics with others listed here and with other forms and theories of humor.

82. Why do cannibals like people who've been drinking?
    They're stewed

    (Anon, *Love is a riddle*, 1964, p. 5).

83. What did the lady of King Arthur's court say as she sneaked back to her chambers in the morning?
    "What a knight!"

    (ibid, p. 23)

84. What was the unethical lawyer doing last night with pretty Widow Brown?
    Trying to break her will

    (ibid, p. 24)

85. In what way was Lady Godiva a gambler?
   She put everything she had on a horse
            (ibid, p. 28)

86. Name two ancient sports.
   Anthony and Cleopatra
            (ibid, p. 36)

87. How could you survive locked alone in a room with only a bed and a calendar?
   Drink water from the bed springs and eat dates from the calendar
            (ibid, p. 57)

88. Mrs. Bigger had a baby. Which was bigger?
   The baby. It was a little Bigger
            (ibid, p. 29)

89. Exactly where was Solomon's Temple?
   On the side of his head
            (ibid, p. 41)

90. Translate: Y y u r y y u b
           I c u r y y 4 me.
   Too wise you are, too wise you be,
   I see you are too wise for me
            (ibid, p. 54)

91. What character in *Hamlet* killed the most ducks and chickens?
   Hamlet's uncle: "He did murder most foul"
            (ibid, p. 60)

92. What animal can jump higher than a house?
   Any kind – since houses can't jump at all (anon).

Riddles are popular with children and this easily observed fact further suggests the essential nature of humor is basically regressive. As "all roads lead to Rome" so all forms of humor lead inward and backward to the uninhibited, playful mood and spontaneous joy of early childhood.

RIDICULE, SATIRE

Ridicule and satire fit Plato's derision theory more than the others. The derision can be soft or hard, gentle or caustic, cutting or gently corrective. "Ridicule is not the original or characteristic kind of comedy or wit," Eastman wrote, "it is merely the easiest kind to create" (Eastman, 1922, p. 34).

93. Aristophanes was asked whether in his opinion Aeschylus or Euripides should sit with the gods as The Master of Tragedy. "Euripides," he replied, "because he had his tragedies right on hand, they all having died with him."

Eastman (1922, p. 35)

We have seen a great variety of forms of humor and also a considerable variety within each form. Such is also true of ridicule and satire:

Caricature is a "ludicrous exaggeration of the characteristic features of a subject" (Mish, 1983, p. 208). Political cartoons, line drawings that exaggerate facial features which imply personality or character traits is the most common example. **Burlesque** (mockery as well as exaggeration), **parody** (exaggerated imitation to destroy an illusion) and **travesty** (subject contrasted as unchanged but still absurd) are related terms and concepts. Koestler described these forms of humor as functioning like "the distorting mirrors at fun-fairs. . .our familiar shapes being transformed as if the body were merely an elastic surface that can be stretched in all directions" (1964, p. 70).

Carnival mirrors, Koestler observed, distort "in one spatial direction" and "the caricaturist distorts by exaggerating features which he considers characteristic of his victim's appearance or personality." This is accomplished by **oversimplification** and **exaggeration.** Oversimplification "minimizes or leaves out features which are not relevant for the purpose." Exaggeration is a form of distortion. Koestler wrote: "The product of the clever caricaturist's distortions is something physiologically impossible yet at the same time visually convincing—he has superimposed his frame of perception on our own" (ibid). "The humorist thrives on deformity," he concluded, "the artist deforms the world to recreate it in his own image." He maintained that "the humorist's motives are aggressive, the artist's participatory, the scientist's exploratory." Each applies a "selective emphasis on the relevant factors and omission of the rest" (ibid, p. 72). Will Rogers agreed: "Give me the truth. I'll exaggerate it and make it funny" (Fadiman, 1955, p. 227).

Satire is a "verbal caricature which distorts characteristic features of an individual or society by exaggeration and simplicity (Koestler, 1964, p. 72). Existence itself can be a caricature, as the philosopher George Santayana (1863-1952) observed in his 1922 *Soliloquies in England*: "The world is a perpetual caricature of itself; at every moment it is the mockery and the contradiction of what it is pretending to be" (Bartlett, 1968, p. 867). Frank Moore Colby (1865-1925) agreed: "Were it not for the presence of the unwashed and the half-educated. . .the unreasonable and absurd, the infinite shapes of the delightful human tadpole, the horizon would not wear so wide a grin" (Bartlett, 1968, p. 870).

Socrates said to his jurors before his execution: "No evil can befall a good man." Some maintain ridicule and satire should be encouraged as a test of truth. In his *Essay on the freedom of wit and humor,* the Earl of Shaftesbury (1671-1713) wrote:

> How comes it to pass, then, that we appear such cowards in reasoning and are so afraid to stand the test of ridicule? Truth 'tis supposed may bear all lights and one of the principal lights or natural mediums by which things are to be viewed. . .is ridicule itself.
>
> Bartlett (1968, p. 483)

Allegory is a form of satire projecting personalities, social customs or traditions against a different or contrasting background or backdrop such as *Goldilocks* in the bear's home, *Snow White* amid the dwarfs, Gulliver among the Lilliputians, Charlton Heston on the *Planet of the Apes,* the Enterprise among *Star Trek's* distant galaxies, or little *ET* lost among earthlings. Koestler (1964) offered the writings of Aristophanes, Swift and Orwell as examples. He analyzed the dynamics of satire and allegory:

> . . .we are made suddenly conscious of conventions and prejudices which we have unquestionably accepted, which were tacitly implied in the codes of control of our thinking and behavior. The confrontation with an alien matrix reveals in a sharp, pitiless light what we failed to see in following our dim routines; the tacit assumptions hidden in the rules of the game are dragged into the open (p. 73).

The satirist need not be a radical or reactionary at heart, though he or she seeks to change society's attitude. Jonathan Swift (1667-1745), one of Koestler's exemplar satirists, wrote this self-analysis:

> Yet malice never was his aim;
> He lashed the vice but spared the name. . .
> His satire points at no defeat
> But what all mortals may correct;
> For he abhors that senseless tribe
> Who call it humor when they gibe.
>
> *Verses on the death of Dr. Swift* (1731)
> (Bartlett, 1968, p. 390)

Classic satire lives beyond its contemporary application. A good example is Gilbert and Sullivan's characterization or perhaps caricaturization of the Lord of the Admirality in *HMS Pinafore.* Audiences knew and laughed more heartily knowing that the target of the satire was the current Lord of the Admiralty or "ruler of the Queen's navy" who had no nautical experience at all:

94. When I was a lad I served a term
    As office boy to an attorney's firm.
    I cleaned the windows and I swept the floor,
    And I polished up the handle of the big front door.
    I polished up that handle so carefullee
    That now I am the ruler of the Queen's Navee. . .

    Of legal knowledge I acquired such a grip
    That they took me into the partnership.
    And that junior partnership I ween,
    Was the only ship that I ever had seen.
    But that kind of ship so suited me,
    That now I am the ruler of the Queen's Navee!

    I grew so rich that I was sent
    By a pocket borough into Parliament.
    I always voted at my party's call,
    And I never thought of thinking for myself at all.
    I thought so little they rewarded me
    By making me the ruler of the Queen's Navee!

    Now landsmen all, whoever you may be,
    If you want to rise to the top of the tree,
    If your soul isn't fettered to an office stool,
    Be careful to be guided by this golden rule—
    Stick close to your desks and never go to sea,
    And you all may be rulers of the Queen's Navee!

    H.M.S. Pinafore (1878)
    (Gilbert & Sullivan, undated, p. 111)

The old black-and-white monster movies shocked and frightened us, but if you screen them again you will find much humorous content with a satirical flavor. The effect of this aspect of the films and their story lines was intended to awaken us to some of our follies and foibles. Plato's cave, Kafka's confused and wandering hero, Gilbert and Sullivan's singing, prancing characters, *Gulliver's Travels, Alice in Wonderland, Wizard of Oz,* and more recent films such as *ET* and *Brazil* also contain varying degrees of "shock value," seasoned and softened with humor. There is much satire in them and sometimes direct questioning of many of our basic assumptions about "truth" and what is "right."

The following samples were selected for their more purely satiric content and for their variety of target subject matter.

95. "Comrade, what is **capitalism?**"
    "It is the exploitation of man by man."
    "And what is **communism?**"
    "It is the reverse"
                                  Raskin (1984, p. 90)

This satiric joke "cuts" both West and East. Most satire is more narrowly focussed, proceeding in only one direction, with clear polarity (negative), aimed at a single target.

"It looks like rain" when everything's flooded, "it's a little cool" during a blizzard or "it's a bit moist" in a monsoon are examples of **understatement** as well as oversimplification. Eastman (1922) gave examples of Fred Astaire who, when asked what he considered his occupation, replied: "I do a little dancing," and Michelangelo who stated simply: "I am a painter." W.C. Fields preferred that his epitaph be: "On the whole I'd rather be in Philadelphia." What makes this understatement more humorous is that Fields often expressed disfavor for that city.

Another form of satiric **understatement** are self-disparaging statements, "self put downs." Abraham Lincoln used this technique often:

96. In one of the Lincoln-Douglas debates, when Senator Douglas called Lincoln "two-faced," Lincoln replied: "I leave it to my audience—if I had another face to wear, do you think I would wear this one?"
    (ibid, p. 43)

97. "Does God have a sense of humor? He must have if He made us."
    Jackie Gleason (*60 Minutes* TV interview, 1987).

98. On certain levels of the American race, indeed, there seems to be a positive libido for the ugly, as on other and less Christian levels there is a libido for the beautiful. It is impossible to put down the wallpaper that defaces the average American home of the lower middle class to mere inadvertence, or to the obscene humor of the manufacturers. Such ghastly designs, it must be obvious give a genuine delight to a certain type of mind.
    H.L. Menken (1927)

99. All the sincerity in Hollywood can be put into a gnat's navel and still have room for three caraway seeds and an agent's heart.
    Fred Allen (In *Zolotow*, 1987, p. 56)

100. I respect the institution of marriage. I have always thought that every woman should marry, and no man.
    Benjamin Disraeli (1804-1881)

101. Great minds discuss ideas.
     Average minds discuss events.
     Small minds discuss people.
     Petersen (1963, p. 141)

102. **Gabriel:** How 'bout cleanin' up de whole mess of'em and startin' all over agin wid some new kind of animal?
     God: And admit I'm licked?
> Marc Connelly (*Green Pastures,* 1930, in *Fadiman,* 1955, p. 229)

103. I've had a wonderful evening—but this wasn't it.
> Groucho Marx to a Hollywood hostess (In *Fadiman,* 1955, p. 258)

104. You can always tell a Harvard man, but you can't tell him much.
> James Barnes (ibid, p. 288)

105. Radio brings information at the speed of light but has not increased the speed of thought by a single mph. . .wisdom still plods in the dust far to the rear.
> John Crosby (*New York Herald Tribune,* July 3, 1946, ibid, p. 244).

106. Mr. Creston Clarke played the King (Lear) as though under momentary apprehension someone else was about to play the ace.
> Eugene Field (*Denver Tribune,* 1880, ibid, p. 226)

107. I always said I'd like Barrymore's acting till the cows came home. Last night the cows came home.
> George Jean Nathan (His review of *My Dear Children,* ibid, p. 225)

108. To stop smoking is the easiest thing I ever did. I've done it a thousand times.
> Mark Twain (ibid, p. 250)

109. Smells like gangrene in a mildewed silo, tastes like the wrath to come and when you absorb a deep swig of it you have all the sensations of having swallowed a lighted kerosene lamp. A sudden, violent jolt of it has been known to stop the victim's watch, snap his suspenders and crack his glass eye right across.
> Irvin S. Cobb (definition of "corn likker," ibid, p. 254)

110. When I was a boy I was told anyone could become President; I'm beginning to believe it.
> Clarence Darrow (ibid, p. 330)

111. Once there were two brothers. One ran away to sea, the other was elected Vice President. Nothing was ever heard of them again.
> Thomas Reilly Marshall (ibid, p. 334)

In 1987, political writers, cartoonists, humorists and comedians from eleven nations met in Philadelphia to "explore the role and state of political humor around the globe" (William Stevens, *New York Times,* June 28,

1987, p. 26). Most of those attending agreed that political humor vents frustration. In open societies it reduces pomposity and exposes "political shenanigans." In closed societies it provides an occasional breath of fresh air in a stagnant bureaucracy, a way to relax under rigid controls. Art Buchwald commented that "this is not an easy time for humorists because the Government is far funnier than we are."

There was concern expressed that "American television, by establishing a low common denominator, discourages developing a sustained, more elevated brand of political humor." Some felt that there should be limits and controls placed on political humor, especially with respect to ethnic and minority groups. Dave Broadfoot of the *Royal Canadian Air Farce* supported controls: "Malice has no place in what we do; we want to send people up, not put them down" (ibid). Emil Draitser, formerly a writer for *Krokodil,* a Soviet humor magazine now teaching humor at Hunter College, pointed out that similar jokes are perceived as funny despite language and cultural differences. Aging leaders such as Ronald Reagan and Leonid Bezhnev are easy targets. Canadian Don Ferguson quoted President Reagan: "I may be 76 but I have the mind of a 12-year-old." Draitser told of Bezhnev's failing mental and physical health. When someone knocked on his bedroom door, the Premier put on his glasses, fumbled for a note on the night table and read: "Who is it?"

Arthur Koestler (1964) described how "the princes of the Renaissance collected midgets, hunchbacks, monsters and Blackamoors for their merriment" (p. 74). Deviations from the norm both physical and mental are more noticeable and attract attention. Language and cultural differences, or of sex, religion, occupation, region or neighborhood can also set people apart. Any of these if an easily differentiated minority group can become the target of derisive humor. "Bodily and functional deformities," Koestler wrote, "are laughable to the uncouth mind for the same reasons as impersonation and caricature" (p. 75).

Many of the samples of humor listed previously throughout this chapter contain satiric content, evidence of the great diversity of humor.

SEX AND LOVE
(The dirty joke)

These are jokes and other forms of verbal or graphic humor with sexual function or romance as its central theme or intent. If the content is derisive, its polarity is negative. If it is sexually stimulating, facilitates pleasurable imaginal experiencing or is disinhibiting, contributing to a playful accepting attitude the polarity is positive. This is not a value judgment but based on whether or not the humor is conducive to psychophysiologic function ("positive") or derision ("negative"). Humor involving sex and romance can provide socially appropriate venting and partial substitution for suppressed or repressed sexual desire (what Freudian theorists call **sublimation**).

Love and romance. Forms of humor on this theme are not as widespread in usage as "dirty jokes." Here's a sampling:

112. **Daughter:** What do you give a man who has everything?
Mother: Encouragement.
Greenman (1967, p. 8)

113. **Nancy Nougat:** Do you know why I won't marry you?
Ned Nerd: I can't think.
Nancy Nougat: Right on!
(ibid, p. 27)

114. **Kitty Kat to her blind date:** "I'd like another drink. It makes you so witty."
(ibid, p. 18).

115. Senator Fogbound presented his wife with a necklace and medallion he obtained on a tour of Asia. She wore it proudly to a formal diplomatic reception. Chatting with the Chinese ambassador, she asked him to translate the message inscribed on it. "Licensed Prostitute, City of Shanghai," he replied.
(ibid, p. 19)

116. The young lovers, seized with passion, sought a secluded spot to hug and kiss. They decided on the train station where they stood by each departing train as though bidding each other a very fond and warm farewell. A sympathetic porter approached them and said: "Why don't you go to the bus station. Buses leave there every three minutes."
(ibid, p. 22)

117. An Indian brave was sending his girl friend smoke signals in Nevada just as there was a nuclear test. Gazing at the enormous mushroom cloud, he commented: "Gosh, I wish I'd said that."
(ibid)

118. **Pretty Penny:** You shouldn't have kissed me like that when the lights went out. There were so many people there.
Shy Guy: But I didn't kiss you—I wish I knew who did, I'd teach him a thing or two.
Pretty Penny (wisftully): You couldn't teach him a thing!
(ibid, p. 34)

119. **Boston Betty:** Men are all alike.
   Virginia Vickie: Ah yes! Men are all ah like, too.
            (ibid)

Sex jokes. Sex jokes differentiate from those with a romantic theme by explicit sexual content or direct association with sexual function. There are common themes: physical endowment; sexual performance; embarrassment about sex; and problems involving sexual function. Interestingly, these themes are worldwide and endure well over time. In addition to polarity, power and process, "dirty jokes" exhibit what might be termed an **R-scale** for sheer **raunchiness.** Some are quite crude and usually aggressively derisive. Arieti (1976) maintained that sex jokes make possible "frank admission of sexual drives" even to the point of "sexual exposure and consummation" (p. 119). He added that the fact they are "extremely numerous" is evidence of "the repression to which sexual drives are subjected by society" (ibid).

120. Two macho Texas males have need to urinate. They stand side by side on a bridge over a river. "Oh, this water's cold," one Texan says. "Yep," the other adds, "and deep" (anon).

121. An elephant lumbers past a man lying nude on his back sunbathing. As he passes, the elephant says: "You mean you eat through that little thing" (anon).

122. A man in a whorehouse is told: "We have girls working here part-time. You can choose a quality control clerk, a telephone operator or a school teacher." He chooses the teacher. "Fine," the madam says, "but for our future marketing plans could you tell me why you chose her?" The man replies: "I figured the quality control clerk might ask me if that's the best I can do, the phone operator might tap me on the shoulder before I was finished and tell me my time's up, but I hoped the teacher would tell me I gotta do it over and over till I get it right" (anon).

123. Macho Mike, boasted he could have sex with 50 women in one night. A meeting hall was rented and 50 hookers in 50 beds awaited him. The meeting hall was crowded. Macho Mike arrives and began. At the 11th hooker, he broke out in a sweat. At number 13 he gasped for air. At number 17 he passed out and rolled off the bed onto the floor. Revived by a bucket of water, Mike commented: "I can't figure it out. Everything went so well at rehearsal this afternoon" (anon).

124. A 100-car freight train came upon a couple having sex on the railroad tracks. The engineer slammed on the brakes. The train stopped just inches from the couple who continued their passionate action without the slightest hesitation. The train engineer rushed up to them: "What

the hell's wrong with you? Didn't you see me coming?'' The man, now finished, stood up and said calmly: ''Yup. You were comin' and we were comin' and you were the only one with brakes'' (anon).

125. **Police Officer** (shining light into parked car on lover's lane: What're you doing'?
     Young man: Uh—just neckin'.
     Police Officer: Well put your neck back in your pants and get out of here (anon).

126. **Mother:** Masturbating is not good for you. You can go blind doing it.
     Little Gwendolyn: Can we do it just till we need glasses? (anon).

127. Once upon a time there was an old woman who bought an ancient lamp at an auction. She rubbed it and a Genii appeared. ''I will grant you one wish,'' the Genii said. She reflected on this, then said: ''I wish that my cat Felix would be transformed into a handsome prince.'' It was done. She ran into the handsome prince's arms. Embracing her, he said: ''And now you will probably wish you hadn't had me neutered'' (anon).

128. An oversexed very wealthy woman needed sex 50 times a night. She advertised nationwide, offering half her fortune to any man who could pass a 1-night test of sex whenever she wanted it. There were many applicants but none passed the 1-night test. One day a frail man applied and said weakly: ''I am Cosmo and I can satisfy your every need but I am shy and can only perform in the dark.'' She agreed and all through the night her every craving was satisfied. Amazed and curious she switched on the light to behold a stranger in bed with her. ''Where's Cosmo?'' she asked. The stranger replied: ''You mean that little guy downstairs selling tickets?'' (anon).

129. Macho Mike dated Savvy Sally. Noticing his amorous intent she took him to her favorite bar and when Mike wasn't looking signalled the bartender to put something in his drink to cool his passion. They left and Mike took her to his favorite bar and when she was not looking signalled the bartender to put a sexual stimulant in her drink. Several nights later Mike returned to his favorite bar and the bartender asked how he made out. ''Let me put it this way,'' Mike said, ''did you ever try to put a wet noodle up a wildcat's ass?'' (anon).

130. Two Russians walk into a woman's hut in Siberia, followed by a huge bear. Later, one man leaves the hut, then the second man, and finally the bear. ''You no-goodniks,'' the woman shouts, ''you call yourselves men. Hah! Get out of here and never come back. But you, the one with the fur coat, come back in here.''
     Raskin (1984)

131. During World War II, Eleanor Roosevelt visited a detachment of Marines on a Pacific Island. Walking through the galley, she saw bare-

chested perspiring Marines rolling dough on their chests. "My, my," she said, "isn't that a bit unsanitary?" The chief cook replied: "Hell, lady, if you think this is bad, you should see how we make doughnuts" (anon).

132. Dialogue on a wedding night. **He** (placing her hand on his penis): Do you know what this is? **She:** Yes, it's a wee-wee. **He:** No, it's a penis. **She:** I know what a penis is and this one's a wee-wee (anon).

133. The young farmer said to his bride: "Never look in the trunk of my car." She did not do so until their 40th wedding anniversary when curiosity got the better of her. There she found three ears of corn and $10,000 in cash. She confessed what she had done and asked him about the trunk's strange contents. He said that every time he was unfaithful he would put one ear of corn in the trunk. She reflected that three times in 40 years was not too awfully bad. "But what is the $10,000 for?" she asked. He replied: "Every time I get a bushel of corn I sell it."
Dear Abby (Richmond Times-Dispatch, 1987)

It is hoped the foregoing examples were mild to moderate on the "R-scale" of raunchiness. It is difficult to anticipate readership of a book such as this and to establish an optimal level of good taste. This leads to the question of what constitutes **obscenity.** Hartogs (1967) observed: "The process that separates "smart" from smut is part of a great perennial puzzle. It leads from the physical to the metaphysical and along the way touches the profoundest of philosophic mysteries: the relation of word to reality" (p. 18). Certainly, media standards for movies and TV have become more liberal as a sampling of dialogue easily demonstrates. Clark Gable's "Frankly, my dear, I don't give a damn" to Scarlett O'Hara in *Gone With the Wind* hardly raises an eyebrow today.

Hartogs saw obscenity as "the language of anti-value. . .the obverse of the acknowledged good. . .the counter-code to whatever orthodoxy prevails. . .unspeakable in the usual language which is precisely why a special language be coined for it." (p. 20). Some call this the "language of the street" or "gutter language." High **R-index** humor (raunchiness, remember?) is referred to by such terms as "bathroom humor" or "locker room humor" or "barracks humor." The movie and TV comedy of Mel Brooks, Buddy Hackett, Richard Pryor's earlier comedy specials and Eddie Murphy have been characterized as such. They are "high R."

Like it or not, obscenity is universal, international, cross-cultural, and "sexuality is a predominant theme" according to Hartogs. "Only in America," he observed, "are objects invested at least linguistically with a lively and rather rambunctious sexuality." He attributed this to the typical American rebellion against Puritan rigidity, an "intensified sexual imagination characteristic of many Americans" (p. 26). Viewing TV commercials during any given week confirms Hartogs' hypothesis:

> The sexualization of inanimate objects has, of course, been widely exploited in advertising. Marketplace psychologists use their persuasive wiles to make cars the country's predominant sex symbols and designers are obliged to equip our basic means of transportation with mammary and phallic appendanges, often to the detriment of their efficiency and safety (p. 28).

Hartogs claimed "many men depend on obscenity for adequate sexual performance." It has been my clinical experience that this is so for a certain number of both men and women. This is the "talk dirty to me" group and it is my impression that the use of sexually explicit language is for them disinhibiting, as if "talking dirty" is a kind of joke magic to make the illicit permissible. "Dirty jokes" can be used in the same way, to gradually move toward a playful and permissive mood. They also function to overcome self-consciousness. Sex therapists use several explicit movies shown side by side to desensitize couples to sexual language and behavior. They have found people converse more easily after experiencing this audiovisual flooding.

When we utter obscenity we violate taboo. When we violate taboo we "stir the mysterious powers behind the forbidden. It's getting at the gods through the back door" (ibid, p. 105). This is suggestive of Jung's **Trickster,** archetypal imagery and alchemical transmutation and also the Tarot **Magician** we will examine more closely in the next chapter. "Emotionally," Hartogs wrote, "this adds up to a double payoff." We have "symbolic security" in ritual and taboo; we "cash in an extra emotional dividend" by violating them. There is a positive and a negative phase or polarity here just as in humor.

The role of the Tarot **Magician,** Jung's **Trickster,** "a shaman, a 'sinful' priest or medicine man" is a useful and practical way for us to rebel against what is forbidden "without our getting ourselves dirty. In western cultures, the role of the shaman has often been assumed by alienated entertainers—the court fool of the middle ages and today's 'black humorist' " (ibid, p. 106). Hartogs described Lenny Bruce as a "shaman for the American middle class" in his "nortorious use of obscenity" and "relentless attacks on fashionable sacred cows." Hartogs quoted Albert Goldman who in 1963 described Bruce as taking on "the role of exorcising the private fears and submerged fantasies of the public by articulating in comic form the rage and nihilistic savagery hidden beneath the lid of social inhibition" (ibid, p. 107).

THE THEATRE

Theatre as used here applies only to "live" onstage performances such as drama, comedy and musicals and not movies and TV which are described earlier in this chapter. Many Broadway comedies, musicals and night club stand-up comedy routines have been made into movies. These are now readily available in videocassette for individual or class study. In this format they have the added advantage of excerpting a sample humorous section to study it in depth, stopping the tape at intervals to discuss and further analyze the humor involved and repeating specially relevant selections. Excerpting saves time and focusses attention only on the humorous situation. In these ways the tapes serve as a ready reference for self and group study. Use good equipment with sound fidelity and picture and color quality, in a comfortable dim or dark room. You will need elapsed time or footage readout to locate excerpts and later review them if needed.

Musicals. Humor occurs frequently in musicals, spoken, sung or danced. The following listings are popular Broadway musicals available in videotape cassette to excerpt or show in their entirety.

American in Paris (1951, 113 minutes). An Oscar winner with George and Ira Gershwin music, written by Alan Jay Lerner, directed by Vincent Minelli and starring Gene Kelly as the American in Paris and who choreographed this production, Leslie Caron and Oscar Levant who plays *Rhapsody in Blue*. Colorful, spirited, good special effects. Scheuer (1985) described it as "one of the finest American musicals ever made" (p. 20). Without doubt a delightful piece of cake! Show it in its entirety!

Camelot (1967, 179 minutes). Lerner and Lowe's hit Broadway musical of King Arthur's court starring Richard Harris, Vanessa Redgrave, David Hemmings and Franco Nero. The humor is best shown excerpted since the entire production runs three hours.

Can-Can (1960, 131 minutes). The story of a cafe owner accused of performing the can-can, a lewd dance, with Frank Sinatra, Shirley Mac-Laine, Maurice Chevalier and Louis Jourdan and Cole Porter's music. Best excerpted.

Carousel (1956, 128 minutes). A Rodgers and Hammerstein production with Gordon MacRae and Shirley Jones in the lead roles. A blend of tragedy and comedy, the story of an unlucky carnival barker and a trusting, innocent women.

Funny Thing Happened on the Way to the Forum (1966, 99 minutes). Originally a hit Broadway musical of a slave seeking his freedom, this film version has deleted much of the music and regrettably too much of the original comedy. It is a good example of loose, fast burlesque style humor by experienced comics such as Buster Keaton, Zero Mostel, Phil Silvers and Jack Gilford. This one should be viewed in its entirety. Note quick delivery of jokes, gesture, staging, time and timing and the humorous adaptation of Roman names!

Guys and Dolls (1955, 138 minutes). Frank Loesser's songs, Damon Runyon's characters, the story of a gambler who falls in love with a Salvation Army "Sally Ann." Stars Frank Sinatra, Marlon Brando, Jean Simmons and Vivian Blaine. Best excerpted.

The Mikado (1939, 90 minutes). British version, 50 years old, of the Gilbert and Sullivan operetta but is aging well because it was so well done. Stars with Kenny Baker, Jean Colin and the unsurpassed Martyn Green. Especially recommended. At 1½ hours, ideal for classroom use. You may want to show this twice (analyzed the second time) and supply the text of funnier selections so you or the class can follow along.

Oklahoma (1955, 145 minutes). Rodgers and Hammerstein hit choreographed by Agnes DeMille and starring Gordon MacRae, Shirley Jones, and young Rod Steiger, Gloria Grahame and spirited dancing by Gene Nelson. Best excerpted.

Paint Your Wagon (1969, 151 minutes). Touching, warmly humorous story of the movement West, with macho Clint Eastwood and devilish Lee Marvin both in love with Jean Seberg. Best excerpted.

Show Boat (1951, 107 minutes). Musical about Mississippi River paddlewheeler showboat with music by Jerome Kern, dance by Marge and Gower Champion, and starring Kathryn Grayson, Howard Keel, Ava Gardner, Joe E. Brown and Agnes Moorehead. One of the first big production musicals. Of historical value to compare to recent productions.

South Pacific (1958, 167 minutes). Rodgers and Hammerstein Broadway hit, the story of a Navy nurse who falls in love with a French planter on a South Pacific island in World War II. Stars Mitzi Gaynor, Rossano Brazzi, Ray Walston and France Nuyen. Best excerpted.

West Side Story (1961, 155 minutes). Heavy, tragic story line of Romeo and Juliet set in a New York ghetto but with several humorous selections. Music by Leonard Bernstein, choreography by Jerome Robbins and stars Richard Beymer and Natalie Wood as the lovers, Rita Moreno, Russ Tamblyn, and George Chakiris. Excerpt the humorous dance, gestures and selections so the powerful tragic content does not overwhelm the humor.

Tales of Hoffman with Robert Rounseville is not listed in Scheuer's *Movies on TV* but should be available in videocassette and is well worth the search. It is a musical, heavily symbolic and mystical (Jung would love it — so would Freud!), with good music, costuming and special effects. I call it a mystical musical. See what you think. Best shown in its entirety and without stops except for perhaps one intermission. Use good equipment for sound and sharp focus. *Red Shoes and Wizard of Oz* make a splended trio to study for archetypal and unconscious symbolism.

Pirates of Penzance, the 1980s version of the Gilbert and Sullivan operetta with Linda Ronstedt, is also not listed in Scheuer but should be available in videocassette. It can be compared to *Mikado* and *Pinafore.* Requires attention since the lines flow so quickly so use good equipment.

Plays. Movies have been made of Neil Simon plays and other comedies originally produced live on stage and later made into movies. Of special interest are *Mister Roberts* (Henry Fonda, Ray Walston) for humor applied to military life, *Teahouse of the August Moon* (Marlon Brando, Glenn Ford, Eddie Albert) for cross-cultural Asian-Caucasian humor (as also the musical *South Pacific*) and *No Time for Sergeants* (Andy Griffith, Nick Adams, Myron McCormick) another spoof of military life with added cross-cultural content of country boy vs. society's stuffy regulations and boring routine. Shakespeare's *MacBeth, Hamlet, Midsummer Night's Dream* and *Tempest* are available in videocassette and are best excerpted, though *Dream* and *Tempest* have value shown in their entirety.

In his 1978 book *Comedy High and Low,* Charney described six kinds of theatre comedy:

1. **Farce.** This is comedy with "an extravagant plot in which anything can happen." The characters develop by "quirks" and "eccentricities" rather than by "believable psychological truth" (p. 97).
2. **Tragic Farce.** Here "themes and techniques of tragedy are absorbed and comically transformed" (p. 105).
3. **Burlesque Comedy.** This comedy form "mocks the moral and stylistic pretensions of tragedy and romance" (p. 115). Colorful, garish "funny" costumes of the old burlesque theatre (Ed Wynn, Soupy Sales), circus clowns, Keystone Kops and slapstick are examples of this "funny costumed" comedy.
4. **Comedy of Manners** is comedy in which "wits are arbiters of good taste while the butts are awkward, stiff, pretentious and social misfits" (p. 121). This is the kind of comedy Bergson and Meredith also described, mechanical and by puppetlike characters.

5. **Satiric Comedy** is that which "seeks to display and control its villain-heroes" (p. 127).

6. **Festive Comedy** "vanquishes all obstructions and asserts a hedonistic, holiday, carnival spirit" (p. 135). New Orleans *Mardi Gras*!

Charney cautioned that all comedies do not fit neatly into these six categories. Leoncavallo's *Pagliacchi* is a clown and this role and behavior fits **burlesque** and **festive** comedy. The intricate story line of play-within-a-play and Columbine being loved by three men suggests **farce**. Victimized by murderous passion and jealousy moves into **tragic farce**. The automaton, puppetlike supporting characters fit **Comedy of Manners**. If you had to place *Pagliacchi* in but one category which would it be?

According to Charney there is a **metaphysics of comedy** which consists of six also overlapping factors:

1. **It is discontinuous.** Comedy is a break from reality and from rational order and causality. This is achieved by sudden, unexpected shifts in perspective, joining of seemingly incompatible ideas or parts, changes in timing or sequence, or of subject and object. This results in a feeling of bewilderment or bemused uneasiness. Freud linked laughter to the irrational, illogical component of the unconscious which he saw as instinctive.

2. **It is accidental.** It flows of and by itself, by its own "accidental" nature, spontaneously, serendipitously, especially from and through everyday things and situations. This is a "grand creativity" where the most trivial can be rich in comic potential.

3. **It is autonomous,** in Bergson's sense of automaton-like, lending itself to being or becoming animated.

4. **It is self-conscious.** It has its own clear awareness of itself, of its own nature and what it is about.

5. **It is histrionic,** clownish, magician-trickster-fool-telesphoros, dramatic and in motion.

6. **It is ironic** in the sense that it is oppositional, different, nonconforming.

CHAPTER 7

HUMOR IN HISTORY

The comic. . .means village revelry or
merrymaking and has relics in its
aroma of winedrinking in the evening
and of ribald song and organized
conviviality after the day's work is done

Max Eastman (1922)
The sense of humor

MAKEUP, MASKS AND COSTUMES

IN HER BOOK *An Outline of Humor* (1932), Wells wrote that "when our archaeologists hold the mirror up to prehistoric nature we see among the earliest reflected pictures a procession or group. . .about to sacrifice human victims. . .showing a certain festive cheerfulness." The figures are "fantastically dressed and wear horns and painted masks. . . the first glimmerings of a horrid mirth. . .the adjunct of such celebrations." She commented that while prehistoric evidence is limited, being pictorial not verbal, we "know a few things about the late Paleolithic people. . .they had a leaning toward paint. They buried their dead after painting the body and they also painted the weapons and ornaments that were interred with them. . .the pigments of black, brown, red, yellow and white still endure in the caves of France and Spain" (pp. 23-24). So—makeup is prehistoric and was used before we learned to write!

THE WORLD'S FIRST LAUGH

Wells suggested we probably "mimicked" before we could talk as observing babies confirms, and these "earliest mimicries" were amusing,

157

reinforced by grunts or applause which "stimulated fresh effort." Thus, she concluded, "the ball was set rolling and the fun began" (1932, p. 23). Humorous evolution continued, from mirth through exaggeration, evidenced by the "painted masks, grotesque and mirth-provoking" or "to inculcate fear.   .sorrow and woe." As emotions became more directly stimulated, complex reactions themselves, the whole process of humor also became more complicated: "Emotions at first were rather inextricably intermingled nor are they yet entirely untangled and straightened out" (Wells, ibid). From Shakespeare to Broadway musicals, Gilbert and Sullivan to today's most popular TV sitcom, there is a mixture and layering of comedy and tragedy, of varying power and polarity and usually several processes operating at the same time. The clown seems a simple figure, immediately recognized, direct, eliciting smiles and laughter even without speaking or doing anything, yet, in terms of the unconscious, the clown also exists in the deepest, darkest reaches of the mind.

Paleolithic people were Cro-Magnom stone age people, nomadic hunters and gatherers who lived in caves and used fire, flint blades and bone tools. "We are told," Wells wrote, "his mentality was similar to that of a bright little contemporary boy of five" which "would give him the power of laughter at simple things and it seems only fair to assume that he possessed it" (p. 24). This coincides with Eric Berne's idea that "OK kid" and "not OK kid" gaming functions at a 4-year-old level. Wells' hypothesis is easily tested by observing and chatting with a 5-year-old. They do indeed have a sense of humor. You can also catch a glimpse of Cro-Magnons by talking to a 5-year-old!

CARICATURE AND RIDICULE

The oldest Paleolithic cave drawings were of the bison, horse, ibex, cave bear and reindeer, according to Wells, "at first primitive but later. . . astonishingly clever and lifelike." There was also "some attempt at sculpture in the way of little stone or ivory statuettes." She concluded that these "incline to caricature and are probably the first dawning of that tendency. . ." She conceded there is little direct evidence "that can be definitely styled humorous. . .they left scant traces of it" but she quoted from Thomas Wright:

> A tendency to burlesque and caricature appears indeed to be a feeling deeply implanted in human nature, and it is one of the earliest talents displayed by people in a rude state of society. An appreciation of

and sensitiveness to ridicule, and a love of that which is humorous are found even among savages and enter largely into their relations with their fellow man (p. 25).

Based on archaeological and anthropological research, Wells maintained that ridicule also had deep historical roots "before people cultivated either literature or art." When the chief "sat in his rude hall surrounded by his warriors, they amused themselves by turning their enemies and opponents into mockery, by laughing at their weaknesses. . . and giving them nicknames" (p. 25).

FOOLS AND BUFFOONS

Wells dated the emergence of the role and function of a fool and buffoon at "between 10,000 BC and 12,000 BC." They were associated with merrymaking, eating and drinking at feasts: "The fool, who was not yet a wit, won the laughter of the guests by his idiocy or often by his deformity. The wise fool is a later development." Bards or rhapsodists were also at the feasts, entertaining by chanting and reciting stories, many of which were humorous. Before books and newspapers, they were "living books" of myth and legend and they "kept alive folktales and jests that remain to this day" (ibid, p. 26).

HUMOR IN HISTORY

This chapter provides additional samples of the versatility and variety of humor, none less than 100 years old and some 3500 years old, the oldest source yet known. For convenience, humor samples are divided into three groups by their historical context:

Oldest sources, prehistoric to 500 BC
Ancient sources, 500 BC to 500 AD
Medieval, Renaissance, Modern sources, 1000 AD to 1850 AD

The 5000 years separating the oldest from contemporary samples demonstrate the universality of humor and its cross-cultural appeal. The fact that humor survives time, the catastrophes of history, and the most dramatic differences in culture and language, suggests great power in and of itself and more complexity than simple learning theory or experiential conditioning. Are we born with a sense of humor or do we learn it solely from experience? It's Locke vs. Leibnitz, Darwin, Watson, Freud and Maslow onstage again!

OLDEST SOURCES (PREHISTORIC TO 500 BC)

Sumer. The archaeologist Samuel Noah Kramer excavated, catalogued and translated proverbs and sayings from fragments of ancient Sumerian cuneiform. In his book *From the Tablets of Sumer* (1956), he reported that the Hebrew book of *Proverbs* was "long believed to be the oldest collection of maxims and sayings in man's recorded history" but "in the past century and a half collections of Egyptian proverbs and precepts were uncovered which antedate the Biblical book of *Proverbs* by many years." He then added that even "these are by no means the oldest of man's recorded aphorisms and adages. . .the Sumerian proverb collections antedate most, if not all, of the known Egyptian compilations by several centuries" (p. 152).

Sumer was an ancient civilization in southern Mesopotamia eventually overrun by the Babylonians. Several ancient Sumerian cities have been excavated, most notably Ur, and their contents studied. The facial expression on statuary of human figures unearthed there is wide-eyed and smiling. Sumerians routinely used irrigation, their pottery and metalwork as distinctive and of high quality in construction and as art. They had a jury system of peers and fines instead of imprisonment. Most important for our study of humor, **they wrote** in a form of cuneiform Dr. Kramer has been able to translate for us. Especially significant are the **Nippur Tablets** conservatively dated to the 18th century BC. Their content reflects the universal concerns and frustrations of everyday life then and now. In Kramer's words:

> One of the significant characteristics of proverbs in general is the universal relevance of their content. If you ever begin to doubt the brotherhood of man and the common humanity of all peoples and races, turn to their sayings and maxims, their precepts and adages. More than any other literary product, they pierce the crust of cultural contrasts and environmental differences and lay bare the fundamental nature of all men, no matter where and when they live. The Sumerian proverbs were compiled and written down more than 3500 years ago and many had no doubt been repeated by word of mouth for centuries before they were put in written form. They concern a people that differs from us in language and physical environment, in manners and customs, in politics, economics and religion, and yet the basic character revealed by the Sumerian proverbs is remarkably like our own. We have little difficulty in recognizing in them reflections of our own drives and attributes, foibles and weaknesses, confusions and dilemmas (p. 153).

Here's a sampling of 3500-year-old Sumerian riddles, proverbs and sayings. The titles are mine, to facilitate comparison with other samples in this book.

134. *World's oldest dirty joke?*
Can one conceive without sexual intercourse?
Can one get fat without eating?
Kramer (1957, p. 154)

135. *Ridicule*
If you were put in water the water would stagnate;
If you were put in a garden the garden would rot.
(ibid)

136. *Living among turkeys!*
I am a thoroughbred steed
But I am hitched to a mule
And must draw a cart
And carry reeds and stubble.
(ibid, p. 155)

137. *Love and marriage*
(Sumerian Archie Bunker!)
Who has supported wife and child
His nose has borne a leash?
(ibid, p. 156)

138. *The IRS was there, too!*
You can tolerate a lord or a king
But the man to fear is the tax collector
(ibid, p. 159)

Egypt. Wells (1932) paraphrased the Egyptologist, Sir Gardner Wilkinson, that "Egyptian artists cannot always conceal their natural tendency to the humorous which creeps out in a variety of little incidents." Heiroglyphs on one of the great monuments at Thebes describe a "wine party" attended by men and women: "Among the females, evidently of rank. . .some call the servants to support them as they sit, others with difficulty prevent themselves from falling on those behind them and the faded flower ready to drop from their heated hands is intended to be characteristic of their own sensations" (ibid, p. 27).

Wells also reported that "more than a thousand years B.C. there was drawn on an Egyptian papyrus a cat carrying a shepherd's crook and driving a flock of geese," part of a longer scroll showing animals "treating their human tyrants in the manner they are usually treated by them" (ibid, p. 27). She described another papyrus in the British Museum of a unicorn playing chess with a lion, a common figure on ancient monuments, and a 3000-year-old limestone stela in the Egyptian collection of the New York Historical Society of a lion sitting on a king's throne with a fox as High Priest offering him a goose and a fan (ibid, p. 28). Animal-human symbolization very likely developed from belief in metempsychosis, transmigration of the human soul at the moment of death into animals. It may also be the origin of animal-human comic characters with human traits. If you think we moderns are too sophisticated for this imagery, what about "puppy love, foxey or catty woman or bitch, bull in a China shop or pigging out"?

Babylonian and Assyrian. Wells reported that "eminent authorities state that there is not a single element of the amusing in the art or literature of the Babylonians and Assyrians." But, she pointed out, it may be "the eminent authorities hadn't a nose for nonsense or the statement may be true. We shall never know." She concluded that "there are no existing records of any sort" to substantiate her opinion and so "the ancient Babylonians and Assyrians must go down in history as serious-minded folk" (ibid, p. 29).

Hebrew. "The Hebrews show up much better," Wells reported, and the most frequent forms of humor used was parody and satire. "Parody," Wells maintained, "is the direct outcome of the primeval passion for mimicry. The first laugh-provoker was no doubt an exaggerated imitation of some defect or peculiarity of another." According to Wells, "Hebrew literature is renowned for its parodies of serious matters both of church and state." As for satire, Wells claimed it developed and grew rapidly from parody. She quoted from Chotzner:

> Since the birth of Hebrew literature many centuries ago, satire has been one of its many characteristics. It is directed against the foibles and follies of the miser, the hypocrite, the profligate, the snob. The dull sermonizer who puts his congregation to sleep fares badly and even the pretty wickness of the fair sex do not escape the hawk-eye of the Hebrew satirist (p. 30).

Examples of satire from the *Old Testament* reported by Wells: Isaiah, ridiculing the luxury and extravagance of the "daughters of Zion," Bileam satirized by his ass (in this case, an animal!), and Haman who had to pay homage to Mordecai, his arch enemy; book of *Isaiah* (chapter 14) where a Babylonian king is derided; book of *First Kings* (chapter 18) where Elijah ridicules the false prophets of Baal; two fables of *Jothan* and *Nathan;* Josephus reported that Solomon and Hiram of Tyre frequently exchanged riddles. Ben Sira (c. 180 B.C.) wrote a book containing satirical criticism of "vain women" and the "arrogant rich." More sharply honed satire came from "some of the ancient Rabbis" who produced the "vast and interesting Talmudical literature" (Wells, 1932, p. 31).

Arabian and Turkish thought and speech, Wells observed, "seem to be tinged with the sense of the bizarre and strange." She cited the example of the *Arabian Nights* which developed from ancient folk tales passed down from one generation to the next. Evidence of the power of this story is the poetry, music, art and film it has inspired. Here are two ancient Arabic riddles:

139.   *The riddle of the Sphinx*
       What animal goes on four legs in the morning, two at noon and on three at night?
       Man. He goes on all fours in infancy, walks upright in midlife and on a cane or staff in old age.
                              (ibid, p. 35)

140.   The loftiest cedars I can eat,
       Yet neither paunch nor mouth have I.
       I storm when'er you give me meat,
       When'er you give me drink I die.
       What am I?
       Fire

                        (ibid)

India produced much folklore quite similar in style and content to that of Arabia but low in directly humorous content. Eastman (1922) wrote that "Hindu sages were of the opinion that unrestrained laughter is not characteristic of the wise and strong" (p. 6). Even so, there is evidence of wit and humor in ancient India. Stories, usually long and elaborate to occupy much of an evening in the telling were widespread and popular in ancient times. Here is an ancient Hindu tale entitled *The Good Wife and the Bad Husband*, from Wells (1932):

141.   Once there lived in a secluded village a rich man who was very miserly and his wife who was kind and charitable but who believed everything she heard. One day the miser rode away on business, a clever rogue went to the house and lied to the woman that he had just come from visiting her husband's parents. She invited him into the house asking him many questions about the old people. He told her at length how hungry they were and in rags because the miser sent nothing to them. Moved, she packed her best clothes, jewels and the miser's best clothes and all the cash in the house and gave it to the rogue who promised to take it at once to the old people.

       When the miser returned, his wife proudly informed him of what she had done and rebuked him for ignoring his parents needs. Controlling his anger he asked which road the man took that he might give him a message for his parents. The miser rode hard and fast and found the man walking along the trail. Unable to escape, he ran to a tree and climbed to the highest branch. Now enraged even more, the miser tied his horse to the tree and began to climb up to the rogue. When he was nearly to the top, the rogue jumped from branch to branch, reached the ground, untied and mounted the miser's horse and rode off with his booty. The miser walked home. His wife greeted him happily: "I knew it! You have even given your horse to your aging parents. How wonderful!" Vexed as he was, he forced a smile and replied in the affirmative to conceal his own folly (pp. 37-39).

Greece. When Homer lived is conjectured anywhere between 1200 B.C. to 850 B.C. Like works attributed to Shakespeare it is debated whether Homer alone wrote *Iliad* and *Odyssey*. An ancient riddle about Homer:

142. Homer came upon some boys returning from a fishing trip. He asked them if they had any luck fishing. They laughed and replied: "What we caught we threw away and what we didn't catch we have."
    They referred to fleas not fish and his inability to guess this so enraged Homer that he killed himself.
                              Wells (1932, p. 35)

China. There are two books from ancient China significant to a study of humor: the *I Ching* or *Book of Changes* (MacHovec, 1971) and *The Book of Tao* or *Tao Teh Ching* (MacHovec, 1962). The *I Ching* is the product of the "Classical Age of China" (1500 B.C. to 300 B.C.), the oldest of the five classics of China and possibly the oldest book in the world. Legend credits authorship to Emperor Fu Hsi (c. 2800 B.C.) who also invented writing and the calendar. There are eight trigrams and 64 hexagrams, inspired by Fu Hsi observing them on a tortoise shell. Another legend credits authorship to King Wen (1231-1135 B.C.) while imprisoned.

The *I Ching* was used for divination and advice for the future, the ancient Chinese version of counseling or therapy. Nowhere does it advise levity and lightheartedness. Like most ancient philosophic and religious works it fosters serious reflection. Some of its content is relevant to what we now know about the nature of humor. Hexagram 58 urges a sympathy-empathy approach rather than derision: "It is always better to seek higher pleasures, those which lead to the fully enlightened mind" (MacHovec, 1971, p. 47). Hexagram 25 recommends the playful innocence of childhood: "A childlike simplicity is a virture which should be developed" (ibid, p. 29). Hexagram 30 cautions us it can be depressing to "see that life is very fragile," when we "see human nature as vain. . .

causes cynicism." We should "not be misled by the myriad parts of a problem but rather seek out its central theme, its source, its seed idea, and avoid extremes and excess" (ibid, p. 34).

The *Book of Tao* (English) or *Tao Teh Ching* (Chinese) is at least 2500 years old and may have been written by Huang Tsi, the "Great Civilizer of China" about 2697 B.C.. A more popular legend credits authorship to the mystical LaoTse (or Lao Tzu). **Lao** means ancient or venerable; **Tse** or **Tzu** means master or teacher. Legend has it he was born in 604 B.C. in Honan Province. Like Jesus, details of his early life are unknown. He was Keeper of the Imperial Archives of the court of Chou and was known as the wisest man in all of China (MacHovec, 1962).

It is said that when he was very old (90 by one account), he approached Kwan Yin, Commander of the Guard, seeking to ride a donkey into the mountains and die there. Kwan Yin refused unless he left his wisdom for the world. He sat and wrote the 5000 words which have become the *Book of Tao*. It was declared a classic in 150 B.C. by Emperor Ching-Ti. Emperor Chan Ch'ien-ming said that "with Tao a corpse could govern the empire." Zen Buddhism is the intermixture of Taoism and Buddhism. A childlike simplicity, in language and idea, is a major element of Taoism as these samples demonstrate:

143.　From *Sutra 8*
　　The highest motive is to be like water:
　　Essential to all life
　　Yet it does not demand a fee
　　Or proclaim its importance.
　　Rather, it flows humbly
　　To the lowest level
　　And in so doing
　　Is much like Tao

　　　　　　　　(ibid, p. 16)

144.　From *Sutra 23*
　　Nature is sparing in its talk.
　　Unusually strong winds
　　Seldom last the whole morning;
　　Unusually heavy rains
　　Seldom last the whole day.
　　And where do these originate?
　　Within nature.
　　And if nature so spares it talk
　　How much more, then, should you?

　　　　　　　　(ibid, p. 17)

The *Book of Tao* uses some typical elements of humor. *Sutra 64* uses dramatic contrast: "A tree with an arm-girth of trunk grows from a tiny sprout; a nine-storied terrace arises from a heap of dirt; a 1000-mile journey begins with the first step" (ibid, p. 39). *Sutra 15* is rich in metaphor, describing "ancient followers of Tao" as "cautious, like crossing a stream in midwinter; observant, like moving through a hostile land; modest as ice retiring beginning to melt; dignified as an honored guest; genuine, like natural, uncarved wood; receptive as an open valley; friendly as muddy water freely mixing (ibid, p. 48). *Sutra 60* is a pun and a proverb: "Rule a great state as you cook a small fish: do not overdo it!" (ibid, p. 55). *Sutra 48* is a proverb based on reversal: "The scholar needs to know more and more each day; the follower of Tao needs to know less and less each day" (ibid, p. 42).

ANCIENT SOURCES (500 BC to 500 AD)

This segment of time in the history of humor marks the awakening of interest in humor and the entrance of Plato's **derision theory** and Aristotle's **disappointment** or **frustrated expectation** theory.

Sypher (1956) traced the origin of comedy to ancient feasts and orgies:

> Comic action is a Saturnalia, an orgy, an assertion of the unruliness of the flesh and its vitality. . .triumph over mortality by some absurd faith in rebirth, restoration and salvation. Originally, of course, these carnival rites were red with the blood of victims. The archaic seasonal revel brought together the incompatibilities of death and life. No logic can explain this magic victory over winter, sin and the devil. But the comedian can perform the rites of Dionysus and his frenzied gestures initiate us into the secrets of the savage and the mystic power of life. Comedy is sacred and secular (p. 220).

It may be helpful to readers not familiar with mythology to know that Saturnalia (from Saturn, god of the harvest, father of Jupiter, Juno, Ceres, Pluto and Neptune) was an ancient Roman ritual feast to celebrate the harvest. In ancient cultures that also meant fertility, human and vegetable! So it was a wild Mardi Gras spectacular. The ancient Greek counterpart to Saturn was Cronus, titan son of Uranus, god of heaven and Gaea, goddess of earth. The ancient Greeks also had the **satyr** as a symbolization of fertility, revelry and mischief. He was a lesser deity, hence without a "proper" god-name, believed to live in forests and mountains. He was a hairy little man with a tail and goatlike ears. Irish leprechauns, gremlins, and Mr. Spock's pointed ears on *Star Trek* share some of the satyr's imagery.

By 500 BC the more primitive feasts with human sacrifice and madly reckless abandon gave way to more structured and less permissive annual and seasonal celebrations. Comedies of Aristophanes and Menander in Greece and of Plautus and Terence in Rome and the tragedies of Sophocles were staged in theatres built for the purpose, with music, chorus but with masks, a vestige of the dark past. These are referred to as "Greek new comedy." Sypher considered comedy superior to tragedy in certain of its aspects such as freedom "to yield its action to surprise, chance and all the changes of fortune that fall outside the necessities of tragic myth," freedom to present characters for their own sake even above plot considerations and comedy "keeps more of the primitive aspect of play than does tragedy" (ibid).

Aristophanes (c. 448-380 BC) was an Athenian comedy playwright who produced more than 40 satiric comedies only eleven of which survived. Eastman (1922) wrote: "His plays are good-natured great farcical exploits of imaginative tomfoolery. Plato said of him: 'He is always in the company of Dionysus and Aphrodite' " (p. 126). *Lysistrata* (411 BC) is the story of women joining together to refuse sex to men until they stop waging war. Not a bad idea but would men consider it a comedy? *Plutus* (388 BC), while humorous, gives us a glimpse inside the Asklipian temple of sleep, a subject with scarcity of reference material.

Menander (c. 343-291 BC) was a prolific Greek comedy playwright. He wrote more than 100 comedies, most of which have regrettably been lost. His style was fresh, with sharp wit and the content ingenious and innovative. On a surviving fragment of his comedy *Those Offered for Sale* he wrote: "At time, discretion should be thrown aside and with the foolish we should play the fool" (Bartlett, 1968, p. 102).

In their 1968 book *Comedy,* Brown and Kimmey described how Greek new comedy survived through the Roman playwrights Plautus (c. 254-184 BC) and Terence (c. 190-159 BC) who were inspired by the Greek model and continued to use it. They considered the emphasis on intricate plot development as the major contribution of Greek comedy. Evidence of its power is its effect on the Romans and the fact that it became a standard feature of comedy theater. The Greeks also diminished the religious and ritualistic character of the plays as well as the function and importance of the chorus. "Comedy has become wholly preoccupied with human foibles and illusions," Brown and Kimmey observed, "it has cut loose from its religious associations" (p. 4).

Roman comedy, compared to the brilliance and prolificity of the Greeks Aristophanes and Menander, was weaker in quality, quantity and duration and "almost ceased to be written by the 1st Century BC." Sypher (1956) reported that four of the six comedies of Terence were derived from Menander and the other two from Apollodorus. Since so much of Menander's comedies were lost, we owe Plautus and Terence a debt of gratitude for continuing his ideas. Their plays were in Latin and they enjoyed fairly wide readership through the Middle Ages when Greek plays were "virtually forgotten," according to Brown and Kimmey (ibid). Their major contribution was to continue the Greek tradition of the "neatly intricate plot" now a standard feature of comedy writing. Later writers improved on this ancient model, most notably Moliere, Shakespeare's *Comedy of Errors* after Plautus, and Wycherly's *Eunuchus* after Terence. The English poet and novelist George Meredith (1828-1909) considered Menander's *Misogynes* "the most celebrated of his works" and Menander and Terence, Shakespeare and Moliere had a "beautiful transparency of language. . .comic poets of the feelings and ideas. . .who idealized upon life" (Sypher, 1956, pp. 25-28). "The great comic dramatists of the Renaissance were attracted to the structure of these Roman plays," Brown and Kimmey concluded, "its stereotyped plot became the essence of their dramaturgy" (ibid).

Previous chapters have included material generated during this time period and what follows is a sampling of additional sources.

Aesop (c. 620-560 BC) was, according to legend, an ugly and deformed Greek slave and a skilled storyteller. His stories taught commonsense logic and have survived 2000 years, evidence of great power. Here is one paraphased to save space:

145.   *The lion, the bear, the monkey and the fox*
The Lion, King of the Forest, commanded all his subjects to come to his royal den. The Bear pretended to be offended by the steam in the King's home and held his nose. This so angered the Lion that he killed the Bear with one blow. The Monkey, seeing this, trembled in fear and praised and flattered the Lion so as not to offend him. He said that in his opinion the Lion's home smelled like it was perfumed with Arabian spices. He condemned the Bear for his rudeness to the Lion King. He admired the rare beauty of the Lion's paws, designed so well to correct the insolence of lesser animals. Instead of being received as expected this proved no less offensive to the Lion and the Monkey was struck dead to lie by the side of Sir Bear. And now the Lion, King of the Forest, cast his eye upon the Fox. "And what scent do you discover here, Sir Fox?" the Lion asked. "Great

Sire," the Fox cautiously replied, "I have never esteemed my nose to be my most distinguishing sense and since I also unfortunately have a terrible cold I would by no means venture to give an opinion."
Reflection: It is often more prudent to suppress your sentiments than to either criticize or to flatter.

Wells (1932, pp. 44-45)

Aeschylus (525-456 BC) was a Greek tragedian born in Eleusis. He wrote 90 plays only seven of which have survived, and was awarded thirteen national prizes for tragedy. He was an Athenian army combat veteran and participated in many major battles. The following is from *Fragment 135* of his works:

146. There was once an eagle
Struck by an arrow
Who said when he saw
The fashion of the shaft
"With our own feathers
Not with others' hands
Am I now smitten"

Fragment 135
(Bartlett, 1968, p. 76)

Cicero (106-43 BC) is remembered in history as a great orator, persuasive and forceful, a statesman and a philosopher. Roman, he lived after the great Greek playwrights and no doubt sat in the audience and saw firsthand many of the comedies and tragedies we have discussed here. In his *De Oratore* he made direct reference to the use of humor: "It is part of the nation's business to raise a laugh because it lessens, confounds, hampers, frightens and confuses the opponent" (Eastman, 1922, p. 130). He also had an ear for jokes:

147. A man did not want to see the visitor outside the door and he instructed the maid to tell the visitor that he was not at home. She did so but the visitor complained in a loud voice, pointing to the upstairs window: "I know he's in. I can see him looking out the window." The man upstairs then stuck his head out the window and shouted: "I'm not in!" The visitor shouted back: "What? You **are** in. I can see you!" The man yelled from the window: "You rascal! You didn't believe my maid and now you don't believe **me** when I tell you myself!"

Eastman (1922, p. 63)

Martial (c. 1st century AD) was a Roman writer of epigrams, fourteen books of which have survived. He was a friend of Juvenal and the Emperors Titus and Domitian. Here are two samples of his epigrams.

148.   *To Linus*
    You ask what I grow
    On my Sabine estate.
    A reliable answer is due.
    I grow on that soil
    Far from urban turmoil
    Very happy at not seeing you!
                 Wells (1932, p. 109)

149.   *Numbers sweet*
    Two of your teeth
      you blew out by a cough
    And a subsequent cough
      blew out two.
    You can now cough away,
      Delia, all night and day
    There's nothing
      a third cough can do.
              (ibid)

From Charles Kao's book *Chinese Wit and Humor* (1974) are these two samples of 4th century BC Chinese humor. The first is an oft-quoted piece from ChuangTse, follower of LaoTse. The second is a sample of ancient Chinese folk humor or "laugh talk" which has been handed down orally from generation to generation.

150.   *The butterfly dream*
I once dreamed I was a butterfly, fluttering here and there, to all intents and purposes a butterfly. I was conscious only of following my fancies as a butterfly and unconscious of my individuality as a man. Suddenly I woke. There I lay, myself again. I do not know whether I was then dreaming I was a butterfly or whether I am now a butterfly dreaming that it is a man (p. 17).

151. A man's shrewish wife died. The henpecked husband, gazing at her portrait, thought of all the wrongs he had suffered at her hands and made a fist as if to strike her. A sudden breeze came and the picture ruffled on the wall. The man quickly withdrew his fist and said fearfully: "Oh, I was just kidding" (p. 241).

MEDIEVAL, RENAISSANCE TO MODERN SOURCES
(1000 AD to 1850 AD)

It is important to an accurate understanding of the development of humor to realize that the word **humor** for what's "laughable" or "funny" did not come into widespread use until the 17th century. Eastman (1922) cited Murray's *New English Dictionary* as dating the first use of humor as we know it in 1682 AD (p. 252). *Webster's Ninth New Collegiate Dictionary* (Mish, 1983) traced its origin through the Middle English **humour** and the Middle French **humeur.** In Shakespeare's *As You Like It,* the Duke is described as being "humorous," meaning that he was **angry** (Eastman, 1922). In modern French **humeur** "when not modified by an adjective still implies anger" (ibid).

Relating humor directly to experiencing emotions was the oldest association, evident in the word usage that can be dated such as the Latin **humere** (moisture) and the Greek **hygros** (wet), relating to body fluids or secretions which, it was believed, caused emotions. Hippocrates' **humoral theory** of personality is based on that interpretation. As late as the 16th century, Ben Jonson described people as "dominated by humors or fixed traits such as jealousy or greed. That is, they become human machines" (Brown & Kimmey, 1968, p. 3). If you think we're more objective today why do we still say we love "with all our heart" and use heart symbols on Valentine's Day?

Humor as "funny" emerged slowly, from the plays of the ancient Greeks and Romans through the works of inspired individuals who facilitated its flow: "Very likely the habit of comedy is as old as civilization and much of the time it stays at a sub-literary level till some artist or genius at the right moment knows how to exploit it" (ibid, pp. 3-4). In other words, humor evolved through "funny" writers and comedians who were the right people at the right time with just the right materials. The comedies of Menander and Aristophanes seem to confirm this hypothesis. Yet another factor which slowed the development of humor was the fact that people were relatively unaware of its power and separate identity. In his *Poetics,* Aristotle keenly observed: "Comedy has had no history because it was not at first treated seriously" (ibid, p. 1). Read that sentence again, it's a bisociated pun!

While we in the West may have been "slow learners" with respect to understanding and appreciating humor for its own sake, other civilizations awakened to it earlier. More than 600 years before western Europeans associated humor with levity and laughter there were Sanskrit references to these aspects of it. In the 10th century AD, *Dasarupa* described certain humorous elements of drama: "Mirth, *hasa,* is caused by one's own or another's strange actions, words or attire; developing this is the comic sentiment, *hasyn*" (Eastman, 1922, p. 163). In a section entitled *Mirror of Composition* the *Sahitya Darpana* described how "the comic spirit. . .(in) the attendants of Shiva. . .may arise from distorted shapes, words, dress, gestures, etc." (ibid).

Antoine Galland (1646-1715), the French scholar of Oriental literature, translated *Arabian Nights*, a legendary collection of 1000 tales told to an ancient king who was in the habit of killing his wives after one night with them. By leaving each tale unfinished, the storyteller's life was spared — one night at a time. That's the legend. The truth appears to be that these tales are not by a single author and represent three distinctively difference sources: Persia, India and Arabia. Their content, style and form suggest an origin at about the 10th century AD, though some authorities place *Sinbad* (originally *Sindibad*) as early as the 8th century AD. Most scholars agree the stories as we now know them were probably compiled in the 13th century.

Galland (1909) titled his translation *The Thousand and One Nights* and in them are the stories of *Ali Baba and the Forty Thieves* (interestingly, not in Oriental versions), *Sinbad, Alladin's Lamp* (originally *Ala-ed-din and the Wonderful Map*), and *Scheherazade* (originally *Shahrazad*). These are powerful stories which inspired Rimsky-Korsakoff to compose enduring, moving music about them (*Scheherazade*), Tennyson to write numerous poems which also live on, and Douglas Fairbanks Sr. who produced and directed a classic silent movie (*Sinbad the Sailor* — NOT the 1947 movie by Douglas Jr.!). Here's a sample paraphrased from the Lane-Poole version (1909):

152.   *The Story of the Husband and the Parrot*

There once was a wealthy merchant who was very jealous of his attractive wife. Business required that he make a long journey and he bought a parrot that would watch over his wife and report to him whatever happened in his absence. He made the journey and when he returned he took the parrot aside and asked it to report. "Thy wife has a lover," the parrot squawked, "he was here every night." Enraged, the husband beat his wife who steadfastly denied any wrongdoing.

Once again, the merchant had to go on an overnight trip. This time the wife, aware of the parrot spy, arranged for water to drip into the cage from above, ran a grinding mill under it, and set a moving mirror off to one side of it. When the husband returned he asked the parrot what had happened in his absence. "O Master," the parrot replied, "I could neither see nor hear anything because of the terrible storm, the thunder, rain and flashing lightning." The merchant knew the weather was fair and there was no storm and became enraged. He drew his sword. The parrot swore that what he said was true but the merchant struck him dead.

Some time later, returning from a business trip, the merchant actually saw his wife's lover sneaking out of the house. He drew his sword and killed the man on the spot, then did the same to his wife. He discovered that the parrot had told the truth and he mourned grievously for the loss (pp. 37-38).

Medieval period. There are three authors cited by most literary scholars as major sources of humor in the Middle Ages: Dante Alighieri (1265-1321); Giovanni Boccaccio (1313-1375); and Geoffrey Chaucer (c. 1343-1400). They reflect the quality of humor during the time they lived: situational (Medieval sitcoms!), childishly crude, irreverent and impetuous. Dante's satirical method was to send people to hell, in levels according to their deeds. He called it, significantly, *The Divine Comedy*. Bocaccio wrote more of the sensual and of sexual improprieties by the most respectable members of society. Chaucer used these themes, too, but he described people as warmly and weakly human. He wrote of feminists and chauvinists, vanity and infidelity, using irony in overstatement and reversal. The major contribution of these and other writers in the Middle Ages was to take the cares and concerns of people, the high and the low, and transform them into humor and the humor into literary art.

Lest you think this was a simple task, try this excerpt from Chaucer's 39-page *Merchant's Tale* from *Canterbury Tales* in the English as it was spoken at the time:

153. Thus laboureth he till the day gan dawe,
And thanne he taketh a sop in fin clarree,
And upright in his bed thanne sitteth he;
And after that he soong ful loude and clere,
And kiste his wife and made wantoune cheere:
He was al coltissh, ful of ragerye,
And ful of jargon as a flekked pie.
The slakke skin aboute his nekke shaketh
While that he soong, so chaunteth he and craketh.
But God woot what that May thoughte in hir herte
Whan she him saw up sitting in his sherte,
In his night-cappe and with his nekke lene—
She praiseth nat his playing worth a bene.
Donaldson (1958, p. 255)

Dante Alighieri (1265-1321) entitled what we refer to today as *The Divine Comedy* simply *Commedia* which meant a form of poetry between elegy and tragedy. Technically, it's also an allegory of the journey of the soul in life. This journey is through Limbo, where the unbaptized dwell, into various circles or levels of Hell, of carnal sinners, the gluttonous, prodigals and avaricious, wrathful and gloomy, heretics and the violent, up the mountain of Purgatory and into Heaven where the beautiful Beatrice awaits. It is Dante's own search for meaning, and so it is autobiographical. In the introduction to his translation, Cary commented that "Dante summarizes the literature, the philosophy, the science and religion of the Middle Ages. . .he at once sums up and transcends a whole era of human history" (p. 4).

Dante's humor is subtle, symbolic, indirect. In *Canto XX* Dante described persons in Hell who are human in every respect except that their heads are on backwards!

154. Earnest I looked into the depth that opened to my view, moistened with tears of anguish, and beheld a tribe that came along the hollow vale, in silence weeping: such their step as walk quires, chanting solemn litanies on earth. As on them more direct mine eye descends, each wonderously seem'd to be reversed at the neckbone so that the countenance was from the reins averted; and because none might before him look, they were compell'd to advance with backward gait.
                    Cary (1909, p. 83)

Renaissance period. Humor blossomed along with all the arts and sciences during the Renaissance, roughly that time interval between the 14th and 16th centuries. For comedy and humor, the Renaissance was a bridge between ancient Greek and Roman comedies and a newly awakened comic spirit. "Aristophanes, Rabelais, Voltaire, Cervantes, Fielding, Moliere," Sypher wrote, "the very invocation of them act on you like renovating air" (1956, p. 38). Brown and Kimmey (1968) observed that Ben Jonson (c. 1573-1637) "carried Chaucer's work forward. English stage history from Jonson to Shaw has been in fact largely a history of comedy" (p. 6).

During these centuries there was an awakening interest in humor for its own sake. Baldassare Castiglione (1478-1529) wrote: "Whatsoever causes laughter, the same makes the mind jocund and gives pleasure, and softens a man in that instant to mind the troublesome griefs our life is full of" (Eastman, 1922, p. 128). To Greek and Roman comedic ideas, Maggi (c. 1548) added **surprise,** Robetelli humor as "a mild corrective," and Hobbes in his *Leviathan* (1651) as "sudden glory. . .the passion which maketh these grievances called laughter" (ibid, p. 139).

The intellectualism and inquiry of the Renaissance increased coarse satire, consistent with derision theory as well as sympathy-empathy. According to Sypher (1956): "When Machiavelli laughs it is a sneer like the Brigias. Erasmus's style was quiet satire, Rabelais of 'monstrous glee,' Shakespeare's Falstaff a blend of coarseness, love and wisdom, his Hamlet the same but tinged with a 'brooding melancholy,' Don Quixite gentle and thoughtful" (p. 203) "but in sharp outline, as of skeletons in quick movement as marionettes" (p. 29). Goethe's *Faust* was "unrefined, abstract fancy, grotesque or grim. . .spiritual laughter was not yet attained" (ibid, p. 30). The *Arabian Nights* was "worse than the Italians, much worse than the Germans. . .in the degree. . .of treating women worse" (ibid, p. 31).

Leonardo Da Vinci (1452-1519) was an "intellectual giant who dominated the High Renaissance and stood as a bridge between the medieval and the modern mind. . ." (Baskin, 1959, p. 1). A man of many talents, some of his works demonstrate an understanding and mastery of humor. The following is a sampling from Baskin's 1959 book *Leonardo Da Vinci: Philosophical Diary.*

155.   *Diverse riddles*
We beat mercilessly the thing that gives
us life: We thrash grain!
The bones of the dead in rapid motion decide
the fortune of their mover: Dice!
(ibid, p. 80)

156.   *Chanelling 1500 AD*
Calling on the authority of Pythagoras, a man tried to prove to another that he lived previously: "I remember you were then a miller." The other man confirmed that this was true and that he now remembered that the first man had been the ass that used to carry flour for him.
(ibid, p. 85)

157. A priest went through his parish on Good Friday sprinkling holy water in the house as was the custom. Coming into the studio of a painter he sprinkled holy water on some paintings. The painter, somewhat angered, asked why he had done so. The priest explained the custom and that it was his duty, that he was doing good and whoever does good can expect good and better in return since God promised that every good deed is returned a hundredfold from above. The painter waited until the priest had gone outside then poured a pail of water on his head saying: "You are receiving a hundredfold from above for the good you did with your holy water that ruined half my paintings."
(ibid, p. 87)

158.   *Anonymous* (c. 1600 AD)
"A bed, a bed," Clerk Saunders said,
"A bed for you and me!"

"Fye nay, fye nay," said Maid Margaret,
"Until we married be!"

Bartlett (1968, p. 1088)

159. From *Laughter,* in *Human Nature* by Thomas Hobbes (1588-1679):

Men laugh often—especially such as are greedy of applause from everything they do well. . .at the infirmities of others. . .in the elegant discovering and conveying to our minds of some absurdity of another and in this case also the passion of laughter proceedeth from the sudden imagination of our own odds and eminency. . .

I may therefore conclude that the passion of laughter is nothing else but **sudden glory** arising from a sudden conception of some eminency in ourselves by comparison with the infirmities of others, or with our own formerly, for men laugh at the follies of themselves past, when they come suddenly to remembrance except they bring with them any present dishonour. It is no wonder, therefore that men take heinously to be laughed at or derided—that is, triumphed over. Laughing without offence must be at absurdities and infirmities abstracted from persons, and when all the company may laugh together; for laughing to one's self putteth all the rest into jealousy and examination of themselves.

Wells (1932, pp. 366-367)

160. Dialogue between Polonius and Hamlet from Act II, Scene 2 of *Hamlet* by William Shakespeare (1564-1616):

Polonius: Do you know me, lord?

Hamlet: Excellent well; you are a fishmonger.

Polonius: Not I, my lord.

Hamlet: Then I would you were so honest a man. . .

Polonius: What do you read, my lord?

Hamlet: Words, words, words.

Polonius: What is the matter, my lord?

Hamlet: Between who?

Polonius: I mean the matter that you read, my lord.

Hamlet: Slanders, sir. For the satirical rogue says here that old men have grey beards, that their faces are wrinkled, their eyes purging thick amber and plum-tree gum and that they have a plentiful lack of wit, together with the most weak hams: all of which, sir, though I most powerfully and potently believe, yet I hold it not honestly to have it thus set down; for you yourself, sir, should be as old as I am if, like a crab, you go backward.

Polonius (Aside, to himself): Though this be madness, yet there is method in't. (To Hamlet, aloud): Will you walk out of the air, my lord?

Hamlet: Into my grave?

Polonius: Indeed, that is out o' the air. (Aside): How pregnant sometimes his replies are! A happiness that often madness hits
on, which reason and sanity could not so prosperously be
delivered of...

Craig (1947, pp. 881-882).

161. Dialogue between Hamlet and Ophelia from Act III, Scene 2 of Shakespeare's *Hamlet:*

Hamlet (lying down at Ophelia's feet): Lady, shall I lie in your lap?
Ophelia: No, my lord.
Hamlet: I mean, may I lay my head upon your lap?
Ophelia: Ay, my lord.
Hamlet: Do you think I meant country matters?
Ophelia: I think nothing, my lord.

(ibid, p. 888)

From about 1650, Japanese **haiku** poetry emerged, enjoyed widely
in Japan but not discovered in the West for at least another century.
Haiku is a short poem of seventeen syllables in three lines of five, seven
and five syllables respectively. Its themes are of life and the unique life
experience of the poet. The following samples were selected for their humorous content. Japanese **haiku** (Beilenson, 1958, 1960, 1962, 1970):

162. Tremendous forces
stone-piled fence all
tumbled down
by two cats in love.

Shiki

163. If things were better
for me, flies, I'd invite you
to share my supper.

Issa

164. Holy noon duet:
basso-snoring priest; devout
contralto cukoo.

Shiki

165. Companion cuckoo
keep your eye peeled on my hut
until I come back.

Issa

166. Take the round flat moon
snap this twig for handle.
What a pretty fan!

Sokan

167. I must turn over.
     Beware of local earthquakes,
     bedfellow cricket.

                                        Issa

Rabbi Israel (1700-1760) is credited with writing the *Baal Shem Tov* ("master of the wondrous name") and a major source of Hassidic fables and miraculous deeds and a standard reference in a study of the Cabbala. Reference is made to it here because its origins are much earlier than 1700, told by storytellers for generations before Rabbi Israel set them down in writing. The following is an excerpt from Levin's 1985 book *Classic Hassidic Tales*, a reprint of an earlier 1931 edition.

168. Once Rabbi Israel passed through a house of prayer. An old Jew sat there huddled over a book, reading in a hasty mumble, reading faster and faster, hour after hour. Rabbi Israel said: "He is so absorbed in his learning that he has forgotten there is a God over the world" (p. 114).

Francois Marie Arouet (1694-1778) became one of the world's best known satirists under the pen name *Voltaire*. The following sample is from *Voltaire's Alphabet of Wit* edited by Paul McPharlin (1955):

169. *Optimism*
      According to Plato, divinity chose the best of all possible worlds. . . but many think it is the worst of worlds instead of the best. . .

      To be driven out of a delightful garden where we might have lived forever if only an apple hadn't been eaten, to bring forth poor children into misery that they may bring forth more to be sick with so many diseases, vexed with so many disappointments, to die amidst grief and in recompense to burn throughout eternity—is this the best of all possible lots?. . .

      The origin of evil has always been a knotty problem. Thus, many ancient philosophers resorted to a belief in two equal powers of good and evil. . .

      The Syrians had a pretty story about man and woman who were created in the fourth heaven; they tried eating a cake, though ambrosia was their usual food; ambrosia was exhaled through the pores but the cake made a new problem. They asked an angel to direct them to the W.C. (toilet). "See that little globe down there?" the angel said. "That's the earth, the toilet of the universe." Man and woman hastened down and have been there, with evil, ever since. . . (pp. 41-42).

The "classic period" of English stage comedy, according to Brown and Kimmey (1968) was the period between 1660 and 1700, historically known as The Restoration. During this time the **comedy of manners** flourished most notably through the works of William Congreve (1670-1729) and William Wycherly (c. 1640-1716). "These comedies hold up fops, boors, country people, older, middle-class or serious people for unfavorable comparison to witty lovers" (Brown & Kimmey, 1968, p. 6). It is interesting to note how the comic operas of Gilbert and Sulivan continued in this direction more than a century later. In Congreve's *The Way of the World* "we are amused by the elderly Lady Wishfort" and in Wycherly's *Eunuchus* (1675) it is Horner who is amusing when he "pretends to be a eunuch to gain the trust of wives and avoid their husband's suspicions." Brown and Kimmey concluded that "the essence of a comic situation, high or low, is incongruity" (ibid).

In his 1877 essay *The Idea of Comedy and the Uses of the Comic Spirit*, George Meredith (1828-1909) commented that the English comedy of manners "might be imaged in the person of a blowsy country girl. . . when at home never disobeyed her father except in the eating of green gooseberries, transforming into a varnished city madam with a loud laugh and mincing step" (Sypher, 1956, p. 6). Eastman (1922) considered Meredith's essay "a rare beautification of Hobbe's theory of the Comic Spirit" (p. 146). Here's Meredith's definition of The Comic Spirit from his essay:

170. It has the sage's brows and the sunny malice of a faun lurks at the corners of the half-closed lips drawn in an idle wariness of half tension. That slim feasting smile, shaped like the long-bow, was once a big round satyr's laugh that flung up the brows like a fortress lifted by gunpowder. The laugh will come again but it will be of the order of the smile, finely tempered, showing sunlight of the mind, mental richness rather than noisy enormity. Its common aspect is one of unsolicitous observation. . . Men's future on earth does not attract it; their honesty. . .does; and whenever they wax out of proportion, overblown, affected, pretentious, bombastical, hypocritical, pedantic. . .whenever it sees them self-deceived. . .drifting into vanities, congregating in absurdities, planning short-sightedly, plotting dementedly. . .whenever they are at variance with their professions and violate the unwritten but perceptible laws binding them in consideration one to another; whenever they offend sound reason, fair justice, are false in humility or mined with conceit, individually or in the bulk; the Spirit overhead will look humanely malign and cast an oblique light on them, followed by volleys of silvery laughter. That is the Comic Spirit.

Sypher (1956, pp. 47-48)

The following are samples of how humor's "comic spirit" casts Meredith's "oblique light" on aspects of everyday living:

171.   *To a Louse*
        Oh would some power the gift to give us
        To see ourselves as others see us!
        It would from many a blunder free us
        And many a foolish notion.
                                Robert Burns (1759-1796)
                                (ibid, p. 493)

172.   *Tobacco*
        Tobacco is a filthy weed
        That from the devil does proceed;
        It drains your purse
        It burns your clothes
        And makes a chimney of your nose.
                                Benjamin Waterhouse (1754-1846)
                                (ibid)

Arthur Schopenhauer (1788-1860) considered laughter as "simply the sudden perception of incongruity between our ideals and their actualities" (Sypher, 1956, p. 204). In his *La Nouvelle Monadologie*, Schopenhauer considered humor as "a form of play" and laughter as the result or effect of "the release of reason translating itself physiologically" (Eastman, 1922, p. 185). According to Sypher, he was the first to define irony as "the desolate laugh of the 'underground man' " (p. 204). Friedrich Nietzsche (1844-1900), the "scorpion philosopher" specialized in this irony-to-desolation theme. Sypher described Nietzsche's *Dionysian Self*, the "uncivilized but knowing self that feels archaic pleasure and pain. The substratum of the world of art, according to Nietzsche, is the 'terrible wisdom of Silenus,' the satyr-god of comedy" (p. 200).

Writers of the 19th and 20th century have had to improvise more, uncertain about audience values or deliberately defying audience values. Brown and Kimmey (1968) consider Byron (1788-1824) to be a "brilliant improviser" whose heroes are "obsessively melancholy," such as in *Childe Harold* or optimistic and self-confident as in *Don Juan* (p. 6). Nikolai Gogol (1809-1852), Franz Kafka (1883-1924) and Fedor Dostoevski (1821-1881) were masters of the ironic and absurd.

Gogol's *The Rose* offered the absurd circumstance of a person with a detachable nose. Sypher (1956) observed how Kafka transformed comedy of manners "into pathos by looking or feeling from the angle of an alien soul" (p. 194). His novels are "a ghastly comedy of manners showing how the awkward and hopelessly maladroit hero, K, is inexorably an 'outsider' struggling vainly somehow to 'belong' to an order that is impregnably closed by some inscrutable authority" (ibid). In his note-books, Kafka explained that "he wanted to exaggerate situations until everything becomes clear" (ibid, p. 197). Dostoevski placed his "underground man" and his heroes in the absurd position of being seen from below or from within. Like Kafka, he had a "comic clarity, a frightening clarity of the grotesque, reducing life as totally as tragedy by means of a perspective that foreshortens everything to absurdity" (ibid).

Soren Kierkegaard (1813-1855) theorized that the comic and the tragic meet "at the absolute point of infinity at the extremes of human experience" (Sypher, p. 196). He believed the comic exists in every stage of life because "wherever there is life there is contradiction. . .the more thoroughly and substantially a human being exists, the more he will discover the comical. . .existence itself. . .is a striving and is both pathetic and comic in the same degree" (ibid, p. 197).

More recent writers continue to improvise. James Joyce's *Dubliners* (1914) was written "almost entirely in cliches" (Brown & Kimmey, ibid, p. 7). Ring Lardner's *Some Like It Cold* was written in modern dialect and idiom. Aldous Huxley's *Nuns at Luncheon* takes place in a world where "people have far more wit and eloquence and love to exhibit them. But they can be equally maudlin and even more pretentious" (ibid).

Henri Bergson (1859-1941), as we have seen, likened humor to puppetlike behaviors whenever people are forced to behave like machines. "It is the clash of the mechanical with the living or natural, says Bergson, that is the basis of comedy. This is another way of saying that the small private habits of daily existence often turn the human being into a machine" (Brown & Kimmey, 1968, p. 1). Bergson considered the circus clown an example of a "human machine" by his or her "tumbling and colliding in calculated rhythms. For Bergson, comedy is a playful game done according to accepted rules" (ibid, p. 3).

One of the classics of American education was *McGuffey's Eclectic Reader* introduced in 1879 and reissued in 1896. Widely used in the primary grades, its contents reflect what was considered appropriate and humorous at the time. The following samples are excerpted from this source:

173.   *The quarrel*
Under a great tree in the woods two boys saw a fine, large nut and both ran to get it. James got to it first and picked it up. "It is mine," said John, "for I was the first to see it." "No, it is mine," said James, "for I was the first to pick it up." Thus, they at once began to quarrel about the nut. As they could not agree whose it should be they called an older boy and asked him. The older boy said, "I will settle this quarrel." He took the

nut and broke the shell. He then took out the kernel and divided the shell into two parts as nearly equal as he could. "This half of the shell," said he, "belongs to the boy who first saw the nut. And this half belongs to the boy who picked it up. The kernel of the nut I shall keep as my pay for settling the quarrel. This is the way," said he, laughing, "in which quarrels are very apt to end" (pp. 44-46).

174. *Grandfather's story*

"Come and sit by my knee, Jane, and grandfather will tell you a strange story. One bright summer day I was in a garden in a city with a friend. We rested underneath a fig tree. The broad leaves were green and fresh. We looked up at the ripe, purple figs. And what do you think came down through the branches over our heads?"

"Oh, a bird, grandfather, a bird!" said little Jane, clapping her hands.

"No, not a bird. It was a fish; a trout, my little girl."

"Not a fish, grandfather! A trout came through the branches of a tree in the city? I am sure you must be in fun."

"No, Jane, I tell you the truth. My friend and I were very much surprised to see a fish falling from a fig tree. But we ran from under the tree and saw a fishhawk flying and an eagle after him. The hawk had caught the fish and was carrying it home to his nest when the eagle saw it and wanted it. They fought for it. The fish was dropped and they both lost it. So much for fighting!"

(ibid, pp. 117-118)

Joel Chandler Harris wrote the *Uncle Remus* tales in the late 19th century. Their content is quite similar to Aesop's fables, a rich storehouse of practical wisdom and folksy humor. Here's a sample paraphrased from the 1907 book *American Wit and Humor*.

175. One afternoon while Uncle Remus was sitting in the sun he drifted across the dim and pleasant borderland that lies somewhere between sleeping and waking. . .it seemed he was not so fast asleep that he was unable to hear the sound of stealthy footsteps near him. He knew at once that the little boy was trying to surprise him. Just as the boy was about to jump at him, Uncle Remus uttered a blood-curdling yell that would have alarmed a much larger and older person than the lad.

"Wuz dat you comin' 'long dar, honey," was Uncle Remus. "Ef 'twuz you kin jes go up dar ter the big house an tell'em all dat you saved my life. Dey ain't tellin' what woulda happen ef you hadn't come creepin' along an' woke me up cuz whilst I wuz dozin' I wuz on a train look like it wuz runnin' away. The brakeman wuz made outta straw. The train run faster and faster an' just 'bout the time everythin' was gittin smashed up you come along an' mightly good thing cuz ef I'da stayed on that train dey wouldn'ta been 'nough of me left fer de congregation ter sing a song over. Ah'm mighty thankful dat dey's somebody got sense 'nough fer te come along an' skeer me out er mah troubles."

This statement was intended to change the course of the little boy's thoughts, to forget that he had been frightened, and it was quite successful, for he began to talk about dreams in general, telling some peculiar ones of his own such as children have (pp. 117-118).

CONCLUSION

"Comedy," Sypher concluded, "not tragedy, admits the disorderly into the realm of art; the grotesque depends upon an irrational focus" (1956, p. 201). Ours is a "century of disorder and irrationalism" and as Goethe's Mephisto explained to God, "one cannot understand man unless one is able to laugh, for man must strive and striving he must err." The human species is defined by some as social animals, speaking animals, thinking animals or religious animals, according to Sypher. He added that we are also "laughing animals" (ibid). Brown and Kimmey (1968) concluded that comedy "contains a variety of forms and moods. . .diverse, reflecting the whole spectacle of the world. If it does not touch us as deeply as tragedy it does present more comprehensively our human condition" (p. 8).

CHAPTER 8

HUMOR AND YOU

In the midst of winter
I finally learned
that there was in me
an invincible summer.
    Albert Camus (1913-1960)
    ***Actualles** (Bartlett, 1968, p. 1068)*

DEVELOPING YOUR OWN SENSE OF HUMOR

REFLECTING on why some of us are or want to be funny, Steve
Allen (1987) concluded: "Clark Gable and Gary Cooper were re-
markably handsome men whereas most of the human race more closely
resemble Woody Allen and Don Knotts. It is therefore generally the
'character actors' among us, rather than the 'leading men' who learn,
usually early in life, that their ability to interest girls is enhanced by the
gift and exercise of humor" (p. 40). The same is undoubtedly true of
women who may use humor in the same way to compensate for what
they perceive as some physical or mental weakness. Using humor as
compensation occurs across sex, age, nationality and culture, as we've
seen in earlier chapters. It is likely, therefore, that you are now using humor in some way to compensate for embarrassing moments or for some
real or imagined weakness. Why not examine this aspect of your behavior more closely and perfect it so as to help yourself and others as well?

Koestler (1964) viewed an appreciation of humor as the product of
increased security feelings and an evolutionary cultural achievement: "It
follows that two conditions had to be fulfilled before **homo ridens,** the
laughing animal, could emerge: first, a relative security of existence. . .

185

second and more important, a level of evolution. . .where reasoning gained a certain degree of autonomy from the 'blind' urges of emotion, where thought. . .enabled it to detach itself from feeling. . .confront its glandular humors with a sense of humor. Only at this stage of 'cortical emancipation' could man perceive his own emotions as redundant and make the smiling admission 'I have been fooled' " (p. 63). Why not continue this security feeling and evolutionary achievement?

There is, too, a social advantage to humor used in sympathy-empathy. This motive was eloquently described by Albert Schweitzer:

> Open your eyes and seek another human being in need of a little time, a little friendliness, a little company, a little work. It may be a lonely, an embittered, a sick, or an awkward person for whom you can do something, to whom you can mean something. Perhaps it will be an old person or a child. Or else a good cause that needs volunteer workers. Do not lose heart, even if you must wait a bit before finding the right thing even if you must make several attempts.

> None of us knows what he accomplishes and what he gives to humanity. That is hidden from us, and should remain so, although sometimes we are allowed to see just a little of it so we will not be discouraged.

Attributed to Grellet are these words which echo Schweitzer's advice to us:

> I expect to pass through
> This world but once.
> Any good therefore
> That I can do
> Or any kindness
> That I can show
> To any fellow creature,
> Let me do it now.
> Let me not defer
> Or neglect it,
> For I shall not
> Pass this way again.

Humor is also an effective way to study human nature. In his *Essay on Man*, Alexander Pope (1688-1744) considered "the proper study of mankind" an inductive analysis beginning with the most basic human traits:

> All nature is but art, unknown to thee;
> All chance, direction, which thou canst not see;
> All discord, harmony not understood;
> All partial evil, universal good;

One truth is clear, whatever is, is right.
Know then thyself, presume not God to scan;
The proper study of mankind is man.

DISCOVERING WHAT'S FUNNY

One way to open yourself to more humor is to sharpen your observational skills, to be aware of everyday behaviors, yours and others, on the street, in supermarkets, restaurants, airports, on the job, at school, theatre, church or temple, everywhere. Tune in, listen unobtrusively to what's being said, how it is said—tone of voice, rate of speech, eye contact, gestures and mannerisms, eye contact. There's more live comedy out there than you realize! Even street and road signs have unintended humor such as "gas food. . .walk with light. . .entrance (hypnosis?). . . exit (X-it? Mark the spot?). . .ladies (not laddies). . .restrooms (who rests there?). . .Oedipus Rex (Edifice Wrecks, name of a wrecking company!)." Look around you, there are hilarious things going on!

In his 1987 book *How to Be Funny: Discovering the Comic You,* Steve Allen maintained "over 90% of us can be at least somewhat wittier and more amusing than we are" (p. 40). He recommended listening to jokes heard in person, on tapes and records, movies, TV and radio, even writing them down by subject, and reading humor in books, magazines, cartoons and comic strips, seeing live comedy in night clubs and theatre, watching funny people, animals at the zoo, children, and funny situations which can occur at any time. When's the last time you chose a book or theatre show just because it was funny, to use it to learn more about and further develop your own sense of humor? It can be a "fun learning" experience.

You should not suddenly envision yourself a standup comedian and overdo it. It's best to first be a videotape recorder and watch and listen to others, examine yourself as to what you think is funny, not necessarily what **is** funny to most others. There is an appropriate—and inappropriate—time and place for being funny. If the timing is bad there will be no laughter. If the time is right, the laughter is spontaneous and explosive. Funerals are serious but an Irish wake is more lighthearted and eases grief. A lady clown described how, while visiting a children's ward, she came upon a room in which a young child lay terminally ill. The clown walked into the room, handed the child a helium-filled balloon with the word **love** printed on it, smiled, touched the child's hand, then left. The family later reported that not only did it brighten the child's last moments but enabled them to show their love and support: "It was as if an angel came into the room," they said.

An example of poor taste and bad timing is given by Steve Allen (1987) and that is what he terms the "hideous mistake" of males who assume "talking dirty or telling stories about sex or toilet function is automatically appealing to the opposite sex. It is far more likely to have precisely the opposite effect." While this difference between male and female communications style may be learned and acculturated (I realize women also tell dirty jokes), the relish with which men do so suggests there **is** some significant difference in sex drive over and above sex role behaviors and social constraints. This is consistent, too, with animal behavior where males are almost exclusively more aggressive.

The same reservations should be applied to humor applied to racial, religious, cultural, political, national and other areas where there is more than usual sensitivity. Some humor helps, but if overdone becomes or is perceived to be ridicule. The ancient Chinese LaoTse in what has become known as *The Book of Tao* (MacHovec, 1962) wrote it is best to proceed "as you would cook a small fish: do not overdo it" (p. 55). Some Oriental word economy is also a good skill to develop, the KISS and 3-B techniques: KISS: Keep It Simple, Stupid! and the 3-Bs of BE prompt, BE brief and BEgone!

Some childish regression can help you avoid remarks you intend to be funny but which are perceived as crass or derisive. I've substituted all the "bad" 4-letter words with more childish ones. I say "poop"—which coming from a tall ex-Marine sounds funny. The other words would very likely sound rude and in poor taste. Witty expressions at a time of achievement humanize the recipient and lessen the pain of failure. Eastman described this aspect of humor as "giving a deeper poetic endorsement to them both" (1922, p. 22). Abe Lincoln and Mark Twain used humor effectively in this way. You can, too!

HUMOR AND HEALTH

In his 1979 book *Anatomy of an Illness As Perceived By the Patient,* Norman Cousins attributed his recovery from a very serious illness to his use of humor. The diagnosis was deterioration of collagen-connective tissue typical of that from heavy metal poisoning and with an accompanying streptoccocal infection. "I was coming unstuck," Cousins wrote, "I had considerable difficulty in moving my limbs and even in turning over in bed. Nodules appeared on my body, gravel-like substances under the skin, indicating the systemwide nature of the disease. At the low point of my illness my jaws were almost locked" (p. 30).

Physicians told him he was in a state of "adrenal exhaustion." He wrote that he felt he had to increase his adrenal functioning by "putting positive emotions to work. A good place to begin," he wrote, "was with amusing movies" (p. 35). He started with Allen Funt's *Candid Camera* series and the Marx Brothers' feature films. His nurses were the projectionists. "It worked," Cousins reported. "I made the joyous discovery that ten minutes of genuine belly laughing had an anesthetic effect and would give me at least two hours of pain-free sleep. When the pain killing effect of the laughter wore off, we would switch on the motion-picture projector again, and not infrequently, it would lead to another pain-free sleep interval" (p. 39).

He laughed at the humor E.G. and Katherine White's 1941 *A Subtreasury of American Humor* and Max Eastman's 1936 *The Enjoyment of Laughter*, two books I also found most helpful in writing this book. Cousins referred to Albert Schweitzer who "always believed that the best medicine for any illness he might have was the knowledge that he had a job to do, plus a good sense of humor. He once said that disease tended to leave him rather rapidly because it found so little hospitality inside his body" (p. 79). Cousins reflected on Schweitzer's experience with African witch doctors who would give herbs to some patients, incantations to others and with a third group "merely spoke in a subdued voice and pointed to Dr. Schweitzer" (p. 68). The herbs went to people the witch doctor was reasonably certain would be helped by them, the second group had psychogenic problems, the incantations being "African psychotherapy," and the third group had medical conditions which were likely to require surgery were referred directly to Dr. Schweitzer.

Cousins asked Schweitzer how anyone could be expected to be helped by a witch doctor. The kindly old doctor commented that Cousins was asking him to "divulge a secret that doctors have carried around inside them ever since Hippocrates. . .the witch doctor succeeds for the same reason all the rest of us succeed. Each patient carries his own doctor inside him. They come to us not knowing that truth. We are at our best when we give the doctor who resides within each patient a chance to go to work" (p. 69). This is a common element in Zen Buddhism and the ancient Greek cult of Asklipios (MacHovec, 1979).

Robert Burton, in his *Anatomy of Melancholy,* Cousins pointed out, "almost four hundred years ago cited authorities for his observation that 'humor purges the blood making the body young, lively and fit for any manner of employment. . .mirth is the principal engine for battering the walls of melancholy. . .a sufficient cure in itself' " (p. 84). Cousins then quoted from Immanuel Kant's *Critique of Pure Reason,* that laughter produces "a feeling of health through the furtherance of the vital bodily processes. . .that makes up the gratification felt by us so that we can thus teach the body through the soul and use the latter as the physician of the former." Cousins concluded: "It has always seemed to me that hearty laughter is a good way to jog internally without having to go outdoors" (p. 84).

Freud's "fascination with the human mind was not confined to its malfunctioning or its torments," Cousins wrote, "he believed that mirth was a highly useful way of counteracting nervous tension and that humor could be used as effective therapy." He quoted from Sir William Osler who regarded laughter as "the music of life" and that "there is the happy possibility" that one may keep "young with laughter" (p. 85). "Though its biochemical manifestations have yet to be explicitly charted and understood," Cousins wrote, "they are real enough." Long before his own "serious illness" Cousins described how he was convinced that "creativity, the will to live, hope, faith, and love have biochemical significance and contribute strongly to healing and to well-being. The positive emotions are life-giving experiences" (pp. 85-86).

Cousins believes that laughter and good humor may release endorphins, "the body's own anesthesia and a relaxant," that helps us tolerate pain. He conceded that we do not know "whether they might be activated by positive emotions. But enough research has been done to indicate that those individuals with determination to overcome an illness tend to have a greater tolerance to severe pain than those who are morbidly apprehensive." Thus "the human mind has a role to play in the control of pain. . .we need to look further than the phenomenon of the placebo to recognize that both on the conscious and subconscious levels the mind can order the body to react or respond in certain ways." Cousins concluded that "medical researchers may discover that the human brain has a natural drive to sustain the life process and to potentiate the entire body in the fight against pain and disease" (pp. 86-87).

Cousins justified his self-prescribed active use of humor with all of the foregoing and this additional commentary:

> How scientific was it to believe that laughter — as well as the positive emotions in general — was affecting my body chemistry for the better?

If laughter did in fact have a salutary effect on the body's chemistry, it seemed at least theoretically likely that it would enhance the system's ability to fight the inflammation. So we took sedimentation rate readings just before as well as several hours after the laughter episodes. Each time there was a drop of at least five points. The drop by itself was not substantial but it held and was cumulative. I was greatly elated by the discovery that there is a physiologic basis for the ancient theory that laughter is good medicine (p. 40).

It worked! Later, a report in the prestigious *New England Journal of Medicine* suggested that "just as the negative emotions produce negative chemical changes in the body, so the positive emotions are connected to positive chemical changes." Cousins wrote: "My attention was called to papers by Dr. O. Carl Simonton on emotional stress as a cause of cancer and by Dr. J.B. Imboden and Dr. A. Canter showing that moods of depression impair the body's immunological functions" (p. 143). Cousins' remarkable recovery stands as an example to all of us. Skeptics are dubious since it is but one case and we do need many more before we can reach any firm conclusions. But still, if humor worked for Cousins it can work for you and others.

In a 1987 article *Laugh and Be Well,* Patricia Long described how many hospitals and nursing homes nationwide are using **humor rooms, humor channels** of comedies on closed circuit TV in patient rooms, **humor carts** with assorted jokebooks, games, wind-up toys and false faces, and are taking a **humor history** of patients to include laughter in treatment plans—by doctor's written order. Babies Hospital in New York City has the **Big Apple Circus/Clown Care Unit** which provides clown visits to children hospitalized there. Long explained this attention to applied humor: "A good belly laugh could prompt the brain to block the manufacture of immune suppressors such as cortisone. Or it could speed up production of immune enhancers such as beta-endorphines." However, she conceded "it's a nice theory with few data so far to back it up" (p. 28).

Research is increasing to clarify and confirm the effect of humor on health. David McClelland at Boston University reduced saliva levels of immunoglobulin A for an hour in an experimental group by showing them a W.C. Fields movie. Lee Berk at California's Loma Linda University School of Medicine reported that laughter tends to reduce immune suppressors epinephrine and cortisol. A study at Paoli Memorial Hospital in Pennsylvania showed "patients whose rooms looked out on trees and green valleys experienced less pain, fewer complications and faster recovery than did patients who faced brick walls and rooftops." These data are consistent with findings at the Simonton Cancer Center at Pacific Palisades, California. Carl Simonton, a pioneer in the use of positive mental imagery which has significantly changed white cell counts in carefully controlled experiments, cautions that "being hopeful that you can get well doesn't mean that you will but it does mean there are still possibilities. . .this affects not only the quality of life but the quality of death" (ibid, p. 29).

DeKalb General Hospital in Decatur, Georgia has "a cheerful, brightly lit" **humor room** with no medical equipment but stocked with comedy videotapes, reruns of *Candid Camera* and audiocassettes of classic radio comedy series. Sandra Yates, head nurse on the medical-oncology unit, described the room as "an oasis. Some patients who previously had seemed to lose interest in life will revive. . .they'll say 'I want to get well and go home' " (AARP, 1987, p. 1). Special rooms for joketelling and laughter are in hospitals in Orlando, Schenectady, Houston, Phoenix and Los Angeles. "Humor breaks" for family members and others caring for the seriously or terminally ill are also on the increase (ibid).

The St. John of God Nursing Hospital in Los Angeles published *Humor: The Tonic You Can Afford,* a handbook of puns, 1-liners and skits resulting from their "humor project." Some samples: "It's better to have loved a short girl than never to have loved a tall" and "dieting is the triumph of mind over platter." Hokey, cornball? Maybe. But as Thomassine Young, then activities director at St. John's reported: "Through laughter many residents who hadn't been active in programs were coaxed out of their shells" (ibid, p. 10).

There is now some empirical validation to Norman Cousins' contention that laughing is "internal jogging." William Fry at Stanford Medical School found that hearty laughter increases the heart rate, blood pressure, breathing rate and blood oxygen, followed by reductions in these sometimes below normal levels. Fry suggested laughter may reduce the risk of heart disease, depression and other stress-related conditions (Long, 1987, p. 29). As for pain, laughter distracts attentions and reduces stress, a major component of the discomfort of pain, as well as facilitating the flow of endorphines which in view of research findings now seem likely.

Not only do happy, laughing patients fare better but there is empirical research which suggests that hospital staff happiness is another important element to therapeutic success. Knaus (1985) studied thirteen intensive care units in major medical centers and found that where hospital staff functioned as "a happy family" with good interpersonal relationships, open, sharing and supportive, with mutual trust and collaboration, the post-operative recovery rates were quicker and better. The study ranked thirteen units from most to least "happy" and outcome was significantly better for the "happier" units.

HUMOR AND PSYCHOTHERAPY

Schur (1972) reported that Freud used humor, in conversations with colleagues but "used this method in his treatment as well." He believed that if a patient could "recognize the humorous aspect of a situation, accept a joke or make one himself about it, this indicated a shift toward the dominance of the ego" (p. 425). Some patients have expressed their positive emotions during the psychotherapy process by writing touching, warmly humorous poetry, painting pictures or by drawings and other handicrafts. In his 1907 book *The Psychology of Humor*, L.W. Kline explained humor's potential as a therapeutic tool:

> Perhaps its largest function is to detach us from our world of good and evil, of loss and gain and enable us to see it in proper perspective. It frees us from vanity on the one hand and from pessimism on the other by keeping us larger than what we do and greater than what can happen to us.
> Eastman (1922, pp. 187-188).

Eastman (1922) described a smile as "a moving summary of the chief points of personality" and laughter as "but one addition of breath and voice and gesture to this already complicated act. It is a celebration of social pleasure, a blessing without which our lives would be but the spare outline of what they are" (pp. 3-4). Humor can facilitate psychotherapy by helping the individual laugh at the person they were and see the person they are becoming with the playful eagerness of a child.

In his book *Becoming* (1955), Gordon Allport wrote that "humor is a remarkable gift of perspective by which the knowing function of a mature person recognizes disproportions and absurdities. . .in the course of its encounters with the world" (p. 57).

Albert Ellis, founder of rational-emotive therapy, considers many mental disorders due to exaggerating the seriousness of things "and the ripping up of such exaggerations by humorous counter-exaggerating may well prove one of the main methods of therapeutic attack. . .what better vehicle for doing some of this ideological uprooting than humor and fun? . . .why not poke the blokes with jolly jokes? Or split their shit with wit?" Ellis uses "practically every kind of drollery ever invented,

such as taking things to the extreme, reducing ideas to absurdity, paradoxical intention, puns, witticisms, irony, whimsy, evocative language,
slang, deliberate use of sprightly obscenity and various other kinds of jo-
cularity" (Ellis, undated, pp. 1-2).

He lists ten advantages of using humor in psychotherapy:

1. Help clients laugh at themselves
2. Clarify self-defeating behavior in nonthreatening manner
3. Provide new data, better solutions
4. Relieve monotony and overseriousness of therapy
5. Help clients develop objective distancing
6. Dramatically, rudely interrupt old dysfunctional thinking
7. Help clients develop paradoxical thinking
8. Distraction to interrupt self-downing hostility
9. Show the absurdity, hilarity, enjoyability of life
10. Puncture grandiosity

HUMOR IN TEACHING AND TRAINING

Many teachers and trainers use humor, but regrettably most do not.
This is true in classrooms in schools and colleges, undergraduate and
graduate levels, and in the industrial setting. An example of the effective
use of humor in industrial training is Britain's Video Arts Limited which
has produced 70 films in 13 languages, used in 60 countries. John
Cleese, formerly with the Monty Python comedy team, stars in the
films. Anthony Jay, an executive in the firm, commented that "one can
never forget something learned by laughing at someone doing it wrong"
(Anon, 1984).

Cox, Read, Van Auken and Corwin (1986) studied job-related humor and found it to be a valuable asset to effective communication, that
it contributed to increased productivity, employee cohesion, and reduced stress, fatigue and anxiety. They reported that wit is one of the
best tools for managerial effectiveness, for influencing others, and as a
positive skill for interpersonal success. They recommend adding more
humor to speeches, reports, letters and newsletters and in training and
employee relations.

Computers are wonderful inventions. We really can't do without
them. Creative geniuses at one end of the intelligence curve design
them; those at the other end write the manuals! You and I are squeezed
in the middle. Computer courses can be dull and boring, their content

confusing and difficult. Fiderio (1986) found that a major factor in a student's decision to stick with a CBT (computer-based training) program was "the judicious use of humor." In a study of CAI (computer-assisted instruction), Roman (1985) found that humor as a teaching tool more quickly established rapport, overcame trainee resistance to change, maintained interest and effectively emphasized key points.

Kubis and McLaughlin (1967) studied the psychological aspects of extended space flight. A high level of intelligence, skills specific to space flight and a specialty relevant to space exploration are basic requirements. There is also a significant need to strengthen certain attitudes needed to cope with the unknown such as decisionmaking, self-confidence — and a sense of humor.

Humor has been found helpful in the training of mental health professionals. Nelson (1974) examined the stress and personal conflicts experienced by psychiatric residents in training. They learned terms and concepts, medications and treatment procedures and techniques relatively well because they could remain objective and scientific. However, to learn the "art" of medicine, the "human" touch, the residents had to allow themselves to become "selectively subjective" and this was considerably more difficult for them. Two major positive elements that helped: honesty and a sense of humor.

CONCLUSIONS

You have a sense of humor. Why not use it? Why not learn to use it more for your own enjoyment, to share with others, and help make this too-sad world happier? This chapter suggests doing so will make you, and those who laugh with you, healthier.

In 1970, *Medical World News* reported the oldest men and women in the world. The oldest living man was a 190-year-old Iranian and the oldest living woman was a 203-year-old Bolivian. The Soviet Republic of Daghestan had 47 times more people per million over a hundred years old than the United States, one 195 years old. *Medical World News* conceded the figures are difficult to verify and the ages equally difficult to validate. The factors relating to long life in Daghestan were: climate, diet, lifelong physical work (farming), good health services and family life — and a sense of humor.

Laugh, laugh, laugh, and meet me for a drink in 2100!

REFERENCES

AARP (1987). Ailing? Take two jokes and. . . *AARP News Bulletin, 28,* 1 and 10.

Anonymous (1907). *American wit and humor by one hundred of America's leading humorists.* New York: Review of Reviews.

Anonymous (1984). How laughter reinforces training. *International Management (United Kingdom), 39,* 25-27.

Anonymous (1954). *The little riddle book.* Mount Vernon, NY: Peter Pauper Press.

Anonymous (1970). Longevity — over 65. *Medical World News, 11,* 48.

Anonymous (1965). *Love and marriage.* Mount Vernon, NY: Peter Pauper Press.

Anonymous (1964). *Love is a riddle.* Mount Vernon, NY: Peter Pauper Press.

Allen, S., & Wollman, J. (1987). *How to be funny: Discovering the comic you.* New York: McGraw-Hill.

Allport, G.W. (1955). *Becoming.* New Haven, CT: Yale University Press.

Arieti, S. (1976). *Creativity: The magic synthesis.* New York: Basic Books.

Bachelder, L. (Ed.) (1965). *Abraham Lincoln: Wisdom and wit.* Mount Vernon, NY: Peter Pauper Press.

Bartlett, J. (Ed.) (1968). *Familiar quotations: A collection of passages, phrases and proverbs traced to their sources in ancient and modern literature.* Boston, MA: Little Brown.

Baskin, W. (Trans.) (1959). *Leonardo Da Vinci: Philosophical diary.* New York: Philosophical Library.

Beecroft, J. (Ed.) (1932). *Kipling: A selection of his stories and poems.* New York: Doubleday.

Beilenson, P. (Trans.) (1958). *The four seasons: Japanese haiku, second series.* Mount Vernon, NY: Peter Pauper Press.

Beilenson, P. (Trans.) (1960). *Cherry blossoms: Japanese haiku, third series.* Mount Vernon, NY: Peter Pauper Press.

Beilenson, P. (Trans.) (1970). *Lotus blossoms.* Mount Vernon, NY: Peter Pauper Press.

Beilenson, P., & Behn, H. (1962). *Haiku harvest: Japanese haiku, fourth series.* Mount Vernon, NY: Peter Pauper Press.

Bergson, H. (1900). Laughter. In W. Sypher (Ed.) (1947), *Comedy,* Garden City, NY: Doubleday Anchor Books.

Bergson, H. (1907). The evolution of life. In S. Commins & R.N. Linscott (Eds.) (1947), *The philosophers of science.* New York: Random House, pp. 275-293.

Berne, E. (1964). *Games people play.* New York: Random House.

Braidwood, R. (1957). *Prehistoric men.* Chicago, IL: Chicago Natural History Museum.

Braude, J.M. (Ed.) (1961). *Pocket portfolio of jokes, definitions and toasts for numerous popular occasions.* Englewood Cliffs, NJ: Prentice-Hall.

Brown, A., & Kimmey, J.L. (1968). *Comedy.* Columbus, OH: Charles E. Merrill.

Buescher, W.J. (Eds.) (1984). *Walt Beuscher's library of humor.* Englewood Cliffs, NJ: Prentice-Hall.

Cary, H.F. (Trans.) (1909). *The divine comedy of Dante Alighieri.* Volume 20, Harvard Classics. New York: P.F. Collier.

Chaplin, J.P. (1968). *Dictionary of psychology.* New York: Dell.

Commins, S., & Linscott, R.N. (Eds.) (1947). *Man and the universe: The philosophers of science.* New York: Random House.

Cooke, A. (Ed.) (1956). *The vintage Mencken.* New York: Vintage.

Cousins, N. (1979). *Anatomy of an illness as perceived by the patient.* New York: Norton.

Cox, J.A., Read, R.L., Van Auken, P., & Corwin, J. (1986). Respond with humor to communicate with effect. *Baylor Business Review,* Winter, 19-22.

Craig, W.J. (Ed.) (1947). *The complete works of William Shakespeare.* New York: Oxford University Press.

Dillard, A. (1987). Mother told jokes. *Reader's Digest,* October, pp. 122-125.

Domjan, M. (1987). Animal learning comes of age. *American Psychologist, 42,* 556-564.

Donaldson, M.T. (Ed.) (1958). *Chaucer's poetry.* New York: Ronald.

Eastman, M. (1922). *The sense of humor.* New York: Charles Scribner's.

Eastman, M. (1936). *Enjoyment of laughter.* New York: Simon and Schuster.

Ellis, A. (undated). Fun as psychotherapy. Unpublished paper. Author.

Fadiman, C. (Ed.) (1955). *The American treasury 1455-1955.* New York: Harper.

Fiderio, J. (1986). Humor, interactivity enhance CBT training. *Computerworld,* May 5, 60-61.

Freud, S. (1938). Wit and its relation to the unconscious. In A.A. Brill (Ed.), *The basic writings of Sigmund Freud.* New York: Modern Library.

Freud, S. (1954). *The origins of psychoanalysis.* New York: Basic Books.

Gilbert, W.S., & Sullivan, A. (undated). *The complete plays of Gilbert and Sullivan.* New York: Modern Library.

Grabbe, P. (1940). *The story of orchestral music and its times.* New York: Grosset & Dunlap.

Grant, E. (1987). It only hurts when I don't laugh. *Psychology Today, 21,* 21.

Graves, R. (1974). *Mrs. Fisher or the future of humor.* New York: Haskell House.

Greenman, M. (Ed.) (1967). *Love is a laugh.* Mount Vernon, NY: Peter Pauper Press.

Harris, T.A. (1967). *I'm OK — you're OK.* New York: Harper & Row.

Hartogs, R. (1967). *Four-letter word games: The psychology of obscenity.* New York: M. Evans.

Hogarth, P., & Salomon, J. (1962). *Prehistory: Civilizations before writing.* New York: Dell.

Isen, A.M., Daubman, K.A., & Nowicki, G.P. (1987). Positive affect facilitates creative problem solving. *Journal of Personality and Social Psychology, 52,* 1122-1131.

Jung, C.G. (1965). *Memories, dreams, reflections.* New York: Vintage Books.

Jung, C.G. (1969). *The archetypes and the collective unconscious.* Princeton, NJ: Princeton University Press.

Kao, G. (1974). *Chinese wit and humor.* New York: Sterling.

Kaplan, S.R. (1970). Tarot Cards instructions. New York: U.S. Games Systems, Inc.

Kipling, R. (1913). *departmental ditties, ballads and barrack room ballads*. New York: Review of Reviews.

Knaus, W.A. (1985). An evaluation of outcome from intensive care in major medical centers. *Annals of Internal Medicine*.

Koestler, A. (1964). *The act of creation*. New York: Macmillan.

Kramer, S.N. (1956). *From the tablets of Sumer*. Indian Hills, CO: Falcon's Wing Press.

Kubis, J.F. & McLaughlin, E.J. (1967). Psychological effects of space flight. *Transactions of the New York Academy of Sciences, 11*, 320-330.

Lane-Poole, S. (Trans.) (1909). *Stories from the thousand and one nights*. Volume 16, Harvard Classics. New York: P.F. Collier.

Lathem, E.C. (Eds.) (1967). *The poetry of Robert Frost*. New York: Holt, Rinehart and Winston.

Leavens. R.F., & Leavens, M.A. (Eds.) (1962). *Great Companions, Volume II*. Fifth edition. Boston, MA: Beacon Press.

Leclerq, J. (Ed.) (1959). *Honore de Balzac: Epigrams on men, women and love*. Mount Vernon, NY: Peter Pauper Press.

Levin, M. (1985). *Classic Hassidic tales* (1931). New York: Dorset.

Long, P. (1987). Laugh and be well? *Psychology Today, 21*, 28-29.

MacHovec, F.J. (1962). *Book of Tao* (Tao Teh Ching). Mount Vernon: NY: Peter Pauper Press.

MacHovec, F.J. (1971). *I Ching: Book of changes*. Mount Vernon, NY: Peter Pauper Press.

MacHovec, F.J. (1973). *Dreams, their meaning and interpretation*. Mount Vernon, NY: Peter Pauper Press.

MacHovec, F.J. (1974). *Games we all play — and shouldn't*. Mount Vernon, NY: Peter Pauper Press.

MacHovec, F.J. (1979). The cult of Asklipios. *American Journal of Clinical Hypnosis, 22*, 85-90.

Marsh, P., & Collett (1987). Driving passion. *Psychology Today, 21*, 16-24.

Maslow, A.H. (1968). *Toward a psychology of being*. Second edition. New York: Van Nostrand, Reinhold.

Maslow, A.H. (1970). *Motivation and personality*. Second edition. New York: Harper and Row.

McGuffey's Second Eclectic Reader (1896). New York: American Book Company.

McPharlin, P. (Ed.) (1958). *Voltaire's alphabet of wit*. Mount Vernon, NY: Peter Pauper Press.

Mencken, H.L. (1927). *A mencken chrestomanthy*. New York: Alfred A. Knopf.

Mendelssohn, F. (1913). *The story of a hundred operas*. New York: Grosset and Dunlap.

Mish, F.C. (Ed.) (1983). *Webster's ninth collegiate dictionary*. Springfield, MA: Merriem-Webster.

Motley, M.T. (1987). What I meant to say. *Psychology Today, 21*, 24-28.

Nash, O. (1941). *The face is familiar*. Garden City, NY: Garden City Publishing Company.

Nelson, S. (1974). Learning to become "selectively subjective." *Psychiatric Annals, 41,* 51-53.

Nichols, S. (1980). *Jung and tarot: An archetypal journey.* New York: Samuel Weiser.

Opie, I., & Opie, P. (Eds.) (1955). *The Oxford nursery rhyme book.* London, England: Oxford University Press.

Petersen, G.A.M. (Ed.) (1963). *Pengopia II.* Santa Clara, CA: Petersen Engineering Company.

Pigott, S. (Ed.) (1961). *The dawn of civilization.* London, England: Thames and Hudson.

Raskin, V. (1984). *Semantic mechanisms of humor.* Boston, MA: D. Reidel.

Raskin, V. (1985). Jokes: A linguist explains his new semantic theory of humor. *Psychology Today, 19,* 34-39.

Rimler, G.W., & Ballard, R.E. (1975). Humor in management: Sad commentary on training efforts. *Michigan Business Review,* May, 19-23.

Roman, D. (1985). Laughter leavens learning. *Computer Decisions, 70,* 72.

Sandburg, C. (1936). *The people, yes.* New York: Harcourt, Brace.

Scheuer, S.H. (Ed.) (1984). *Movies on TV.* Third printing. New York: Bantam.

Schur, M. (1972). *Freud: Living and dying.* New York: International Universities Press.

Shenderova, V.L. (1972). The personality traits encountered in parents of patients with adolescent schizophrenia. *Zhurnal Nevropatological i Psickhiatrii* (Moscow), *72,* 1195-1203.

Skinner, B.F. (1987). Whatever happened to psychology as the science of behavior? *American Psychologist, 42,* 780-786.

Sypher, W. (Ed.) (1956). *Comedy.* Garden City, NY: Doubleday Anchor Books.

Wells, C. (1932). *An outline of humor.* New York: G.P. Putnam's.

White, E.B., & White, K.S. (Eds.) (1941). *A subtreasury of American humor.* New York: Coward McCann.

Wilde, L. (1983). *The complete book of ethnic humor.* New York: Pinnacle.

Zimbardo, P.G. (1985). Allen Funt: Laugh where we must, be candid where we can. *Psychology Today, 19,* 43-47.

Zolotow, M. (1987). Unforgettable Fred Allen. *Reader's Digest,* October, pp. 55-62.

INDEX